STEPHEN
AND
MATILDA

THE CIVIL WAR OF 1139–53

Jim Bradbury

SUTTON PUBLISHING

First published in 1996 by Alan Sutton Publishing Limited,
an imprint of Sutton Publishing Limited
Phoenix Mill · Thrupp · Stroud · Gloucestershire GL5 2BU

This edition first published in 1998 by Sutton Publishing Limited

A catalogue record for this book is available from the British Library.

ISBN 0 7509 1872 1

Cover illustration: Outbreak of Knavery, *Chronicle of France or of St Denis
(14th century) British Library, London/ Bridgeman Art Library, London/ New
York*

To Stephen, Sue and Matthew

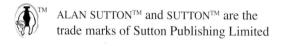
ALAN SUTTON™ and SUTTON™ are the
trade marks of Sutton Publishing Limited

Typeset in Erhardt 11/12 pt.
Typesetting and origination by
Sutton Publishing Limited.
Printed in Great Britain by
Butler and Tanner, Frome, Somerset.

Contents

Picture Credits

The author and publisher would like to acknowledge the following for their permission to reproduce photographs:

Bayeux Tapestry: 63, 64, 65; Bibliothèque Nationale de France: 67; British Library: 3, 5, 93, 108, 143, 166, 176, 181, 188, 189; Trustees of the British Museum: 7, 192; the Master and Fellows of Corpus Christi College, Cambridge: 8, 16, 56, 58, 89, 104, 109, 139, 158; the President and Fellows of Corpus Christi College, Oxford: 2, 14, 22; Exeter City Council: 28; Hulton Deutsch Picture Library: 17; the Master and Fellows of King's College, Cambridge: 46; the Mansell Collection: 9, 101; Musée des Arts et Traditions Populaires du Chinon Ais: 157; Musée de Tessé: 11; the National Museum of Wales: 105; the Pierpont Morgan Library: 85; the Master and Fellows of Trinity College, Cambridge: 132, 142; the Warburg Institute: 48.

The illustrations on pp. 122 and 123 are from Joseph Skelton, *Oxonia Antiqua Restauranta* (2nd edn, London, 1843).

With grateful thanks to Geoffrey Wheeler for his assistance with the illustrations.

All other photographs, maps, plans and diagrams remain the property of the author.

Preface

The beginnings of the idea of this book go back a long way. The reign of Stephen has appealed to me as a topic since at least 1976. In that year I studied for an MA at the University of London, and recall sitting with a group of like-minded, if mostly younger, students at the feet of Christopher Holdsworth and Allen Brown. In the case of Christopher it certainly felt like being at the feet of, as he loomed over us in his tower-like room at UC. It was in that room that I made up my mind to do some work on Stephen's reign, which became the topic for my MA thesis. Allen Brown's influence was soon brought to bear, and an interest in castles developed fast. I started on an M.Phil. thesis under his guidance, which developed into a Ph.D. thesis, before fading away after eight years of part-time work on it. It faded away because I had to make a choice between completing it or writing a book on the medieval archer, and I chose the latter. But the beginnings of the present book are in those fumbling efforts of the 1970s.

Many other things have diverted me in the meantime, but an interest in the reign never vanished. In the reorganized degree course at West London Institute of Higher Education, where I taught for over twenty years, with a larger medieval input to the syllabus than previously, I was able to introduce a third year special course on the reign. This meant that even when under the most severe pressure of marking and meetings, I was still able to keep up with new material and ideas.

The historians who inspired this interest by their writings are many. The first was undoubtedly John Horace Round, surely one of the oddest people ever to have lived, but also one of the most brilliant historians. I belong to a generation before Ralph Davis' *King Stephen* became the bible for the reign, and still find H.A. Cronne's book of great use. But there is no doubt that Davis gave the rather neglected reign a new lease of life, and has inspired many historians and students to look again at the period. A new dimension on the period was also opened by the work of Marjorie Chibnall on Matilda.

In recent times I have benefited from reading the works of, and listening to papers by, a new younger generation of historians, from David Crouch to Paul Dalton and Matthew Strickland, from Ed King (who I hope does not mind being classed as younger) to Richard Eales and Graeme White, to name only those who spring immediately to mind. Stephen and The Anarchy has become a growth industry. But on the whole, the actual warfare of the reign has not received the attention given to magnate agreements or the state of the administration – though the efforts of Richard Eales, Charles Coulson and Matthew Strickland are exceptions to this generalization in certain areas.

I am very grateful to Alan Sutton Publishing for giving me the opportunity to write this book, which I have enjoyed doing immensely. It has been finished more quickly than any of my previous books, indeed I have rather surprised myself by getting it finished so soon, even though it was still after the original deadline. But then I have never yet finished a book by the date originally agreed, so I hope Alan Sutton are duly impressed. I am particularly grateful to Roger Thorp and Jane Singleton who have been responsible for encouraging me to finish, and to Clare Bishop as editor. It is only fair to myself to explain that my previous book, on Philip Augustus, was interrupted by a heart attack in 1993, and the delay in finishing that book had a shuttle effect on the work on Stephen. The great advantage of all this was that I stopped working at West London and was able to concentrate on writing.

One of the reasons for being able to work quickly is that so many of the vital sources are available in print and can be worked on at home. There are also translations available of almost all the main chronicles, which certainly assists in speed, and should encourage undergraduates or others with an interest in getting into the reign to pursue their own studies. I have tried where possible to refer to translations as well as Latin versions in the footnotes.

When I worked at West London, I managed to obtain some assistance towards taking student groups on summer expeditions, generally staying in fairly modest accommodation such as the YMCA in York. Nowadays it is so much more difficult to arrange such trips; what a shame. Those who came with me were able to stay in Lincoln as well as York, and to tramp the battlefields of the Standard and of Lincoln, as well as visit a number of the castles involved in events of the reign. There have also been countless family trips to sites of interest in the reign, and my wife, Ann, has been particularly patient in trailing around muddy fields and mounds.

In order to collect some black and white photographs for use in this book, I have revisited many of the sites of importance in the reign, accompanied by my wife. I no longer have paid employment, but she keeps me in the style to which I am accustomed, and therefore these trips have been made during her rare and precious holiday periods. I hope she has enjoyed them as much as I have, staying in delightful guest houses and small hotels, such as Churchview Guest House in Winterbourne Abbas. We have also imposed upon various friends and relatives during these trips, such as Dr Hamish Little and his wife Françoise at Hazelbury Bryan in Dorset, or taking in Wallingford and Oxford en route to my nephew Simon's wedding. There is nothing I love more than standing on a site whose history has been much in my thoughts. I think now I have been to most of the main sites of battles and castles from the reign in both England and Normandy. But of them all, the trip to the mound of Castle Cary in Somerset particularly comes to mind, in its present quiet rural setting, which Ann and I examined in the spring of 1995, a beautiful day, with uninterrupted peace, and the enjoyment of finding a relatively unheralded site. In such places one has time to stand and muse over the past and its impact upon ourselves.

Some of the material in this book is based on work done for articles which have been published in various journals, and which demonstrate a continued interest in the reign over the years: on Greek fire in *History Today* in 1976, on Anglo-Norman battles at the Battle conference of 1983, on Geoffrey of Anjou at the Strawberry Hill conference in 1988, on the early reign and on the peace at Harlaxton in 1988 and 1995. All this material has been rewritten for the book, but obviously the opinions are often the same.

Jim Bradbury
Selsey, 1996

CHAPTER 1

The Causes of the Civil War

On 25 November 1120 a group consisting mainly of young nobility set sail from Barfleur for England. These young people were leaving behind a Normandy newly safe in the hands of King Henry I, who the year before, at Brémule, had defeated in battle and humiliated King Louis VI of France. There was a mood of celebration in the air. The master of the *White Ship*, Thomas fitz Stephen, had come to the king and offered his services. He said that his father had been employed by William the Conqueror for many years, and had actually been the one to take William over the Channel on the Hastings campaign of 1066. His own ship, he claimed, was well fitted out and would serve the present purpose. The king said he already had a good ship for himself, but that the *White Ship* would do excellently for his sons, William and Richard, along with their sister Matilda.[1]

The wind blew helpfully from the south; all seemed set fair for a good time. They brought on board with them a plentiful supply of wine. The leader of this group of some 300 passengers, which included heirs to many of the greatest estates in England and Normandy, was the king's only legitimate son, generally known as William the Atheling. His English title reminded everyone that he was the son of Edith-Matilda, descendant of the old line of West Saxon kings of England, as well as of the Conqueror's son Henry I. William, although only seventeen, was already married to Matilda of Anjou, and on them rested the hopes of the dynasty. Accompanying his half brother were two of Henry I's numerous illegitimate children: Richard, recently betrothed to the daughter of Ralph de Gael, and Matilda, wife of the Count of Perche. Other passengers included the young Earl of Chester and his wife, who was Stephen of Blois' sister Matilda, 140 knights, 18 noble women, virtually all the aristocracy of the county of Mortain, as well as a number of leading officials in the king's household. Henry of Huntingdon says that many in the party were homosexual, by which he seems to imply they deserved what they got.[2]

The royal sons led the partying on board. It was clear to some of the more level-headed passengers that danger threatened, and two monks, as well as the king's nephew, Stephen of Blois, William de Roumare, Edward of Salisbury and a few others, decided to get off and travel on another ship. Orderic says that in

Henry I crossing the Channel. (Corpus Christi College, Oxford, MS 157, ff. 382, 383)

Stephen's case he was also ill and suffering from diarrhoea. Before long the crew-members of the *White Ship*, as well as the passengers, were inebriated. There were fifty rowers on board, but also a number of young naval men who were already too drunk to know what was going on, and were shouting abuse at their social superiors. When a church party turned up to bless the voyage, these drunkards laughed at them, abused them and forced them to leave.

There is some difference in the chronicles about what happened next, not surprising since there were few survivors to pass on the news coherently. The preparations of the young people had delayed the ship's sailing, and the main fleet was already on its way. Like all such young bloods, they wanted to be in front of everyone else, and ordered the master to overtake the rest of the fleet. The master was by now himself drunk and promised to do as they wished. The ship cast off and raced through the waves, the oarsmen as drunk as the rest; so was the helmsman. According to the monk, Orderic Vitalis, the vessel then struck its port side against a rock with a great blow, cracking the timbers. The *White Ship* at once capsized and sank with virtually all on board. The master's head emerged from the water, shouting to find out what had happened to the prince. On being told that he must have drowned, the master despaired and let himself sink under the waves for good. The pathetic cries of those drowning could be heard from the shore, and from other ships in the fleet. A poet wrote: 'Those for whom dukes weep were devoured by sea monsters. . . . He whom a king begot became food for the fishes.'[3]

The sinking of the White Ship. *(BL MS Claudius DII, f. 45v)*

Orderic says only two people survived: a young noble, Geoffrey fitz Gilbert, who finally succumbed to the cold seas on a frosty night, and a Rouen butcher called Berold, who lived to tell the tragic tale. Fortunately for him he was clothed in warm ram skins rather than the fine but skimpy dress of most of the passengers. Wace says he was following the court to collect money owed to him by these careless young nobles. In the morning he was picked up by a fishing boat and brought to safety. The ship itself was later brought ashore, and the treasure on board rescued. A few bodies were eventually washed up some way along the coast, including that of Richard, Earl of Chester.

At first no one dared to tell Henry I. Finally, on the advice of Theobald, Count of Blois, a young boy cast himself before the king and revealed the dreadful news. The king was overcome and fell to the ground in distress, until he was helped up and taken to a private chamber, where he abandoned himself to grief. It is probably true to say that Henry never recovered from this blow, and that England suffered from it for decades to come. In essence the death of William the Atheling on the *White Ship* was the cause of the civil war which was to follow his father's death, a war which was at bottom a succession dispute over Henry I's throne.

Henry I had many illegitimate children, perhaps twenty-one altogether, by various mistresses known and unknown. His intercourse with such a large

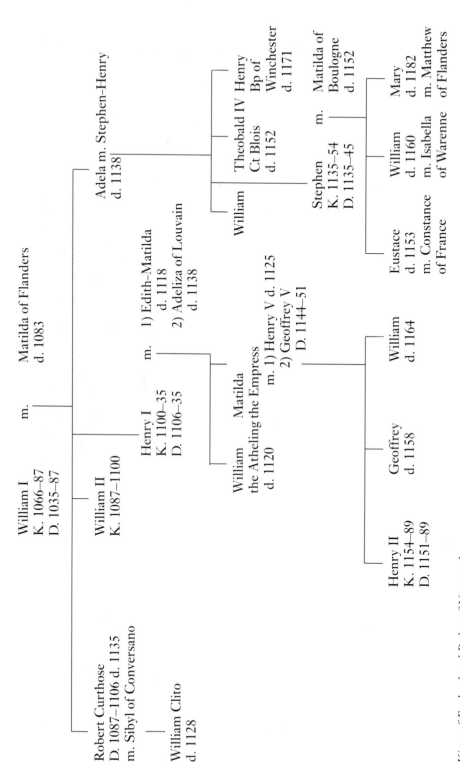

Kings of England and Dukes of Normandy.

Henry I mourning the death of William the Atheling. (BL MS Claudius DII, f. 45v)

number of ladies was, according to William of Malmesbury, 'not for the gratification of the flesh, but for the sake of issue', and he certainly succeeded in that aim.[4] Some of his offspring played a notable role in the reign of Stephen, not least his sons who became earls: Robert of Gloucester and Reginald of Cornwall. It is ironic that such a prolific father could only have two legitimate children, and one of those a girl. The girl was Matilda, and in 1114 she was married off impressively to the Holy Roman Emperor Henry V, thirty years her senior. It was as great a match as any English princess ever made, and not surprisingly she would hold on to her title of empress for life. In 1120, though, she was in Germany and seemed irrelevant to the question of the English and Norman succession.

By this period of the Middle Ages, legitimacy had become more important as a bar to succession, and therefore Henry's illegitimate sons seem never to have been seriously considered as his successors either by their father, by themselves, or by anyone else, though Robert and Reginald were responsible adults who would build good reputations as military leaders. Henry's immediate hope of a solution seemed the most sensible one: to marry again. He chose as his second wife the young Adeliza of Louvain. Unfortunately for Henry, and perhaps for England and Normandy, the marriage proved barren. It can at least be said for Henry that he does not seem to have contemplated the possible, if cynical, solution of casting off Adeliza for a new wife. Of course it could be that, despite his many children, Henry himself had become impotent.

At any rate Henry must gradually have come to the view that he would not have another legitimate son. He may have looked at his illegitimate sons and his legitimate nephews and wondered about the future. He was a good father to his illegitimate sons, and both Robert and Reginald owed their initial rise to prominence to his generosity. Did Henry wonder if Robert in particular might not be material for the throne? He never declared so, but by giving him marriage to the heiress to the Gloucester lands he did build him into a possible contender, and helped unwittingly to provide serious problems after his death. Without Robert of Gloucester there would have been no civil war.

He may similarly have looked at his nephews, in particular at Stephen of Blois. Stephen was only the third son of Stephen-Henry, Count of Blois. His mother was Adela, daughter of William the Conqueror and sister of Henry I. The older brothers were less known to Henry. The eldest seems to have had some defect, and was discarded by his own family for the succession to the county of Blois, which went to the second son, Theobald. Theobald was a major figure in northern Europe, and was in 1135 considered by the baronage for the succession to Normandy and perhaps England. But Henry I was more attached to the third son, Stephen. This was because Stephen had been sent to his court as a youth. His mother obviously hoped that he would be favoured by his uncle, and this proved to be the case.

Indeed, the younger fourth son, Henry of Blois, also received favours from Henry I, whose concern for members of his family was one of his few likeable traits. The young Henry of Blois had been destined for the church, though he was as unsaintly and 'unmeek' as it might be possible to be. He was tough, aggressive, bullying and blustering; a perfect politician, which in essence is what he became. His career, though, began as a monk in the prestigious abbey at Cluny, and he proceeded, through his uncle's favour, to become abbot of the ancient house of Glastonbury in 1126, which in opposition to the current views on church reform, he retained when appointed as Bishop of Winchester in 1129.

The older brother, Stephen, was given equally impressive assistance for a worldly career. He received vast estates in England and Normandy, including the honors of Eye and Lancaster in England and the county of Mortain in Normandy, as well as the lands of William Talvas in the south. In addition he was provided with a rich heiress as wife in Matilda of Boulogne whom he married in 1125. She was the daughter of Eustace III of Boulogne, and brought that county into her husband's collection.

Henry of Blois, Bishop of Winchester. This twelfth-century enamel shows Henry kneeling, with a crosier. The inscription round the edge reads: '. . . Henry, alive in bronze, gives gifts to God. Henry, whose fame commends him to men, whose character commends him to the heavens, a man equal in mind to the Muses, and in eloquence higher than Marcus (Cicero)'.

Such favours, as with Robert of Gloucester, and probably just as unwittingly, built another possible contender for the crown. Without these grants in England and Normandy, Stephen would never have been a serious contender for the English throne. Presumably Henry thought his illegitimate sons and legitimate nephews would honour his wishes and support his choice. In practice what he had done was to build up potential rivals for the crown and produce the raw materials for the making of civil war in both England and Normandy.

THE EMPRESS MATILDA

Henry I himself never seems to have given any encouragement at all to either Robert or Stephen or any nephew or illegitimate son to see themselves as successors to the crown, until perhaps the very last moment, when he may have changed his mind and favoured Stephen. In fact, Henry was now offered what seemed a lifeline of escape, though none could have thought it ideal.

In 1125, unexpectedly, the Emperor Henry V died, leaving Matilda a widow. Since the death of her brother, William the Atheling in 1120, she was Henry's only surviving legitimate child. She had no children, but she was still quite young. Henry began to toy with thoughts of a second marriage for his daughter.

The wedding of Matilda and the Holy Roman Emperor Henry V, which took place at Worms in 1114. Matilda was eleven years old. (Corpus Christi College, Cambridge, MS 373, f. 95b.)

The seal of Henry I.

Like the subtle politician he was, he thought he might tie up several problems in one solution. He had for some time been seeking an alliance with the county of Anjou, which had been threatening the stability of Normandy.

Henry I had himself won the English throne against the odds as a younger son. His oldest brother, Robert Curthose had become Duke of Normandy; the next in age, William Rufus had gained the English throne. When Rufus died, Henry had acted fast and won the crown at the expense of Curthose, just returning from the First Crusade. The relations between the brothers had remained difficult until 1106 when Henry defeated and captured Curthose at the Battle of Tinchebrai.

From that time on Curthose had been kept in prison, where he still languished and would until his death in 1134. But Curthose's son, William Clito, had evaded Henry's clutches and become a rival to his uncle in Normandy. That was too good an opportunity for Henry's enemies abroad to resist, and in particular Louis VI, King of France, had taken up the case of Clito. Henry needed allies against Louis and William, and the powerful county of Anjou was perhaps the most hopeful. Thus he had married his only legitimate son, William the Atheling, to Matilda of Anjou. The prince's death had of course brought that match to an end, and the alliance. Now Henry thought about marrying his daughter to Geoffrey, the son and heir of Fulk V, Count of Anjou.[5] This would give aid against Clito, a husband to Matilda, and quite soon it was hoped a son to them, a grandson to himself, who would inherit England and Normandy. In fact, this did eventually come about, but not in any way that could possibly have been predicted in 1125.

The marriage plans went ahead. Henry met and approved his intended son-in-law. The young Geoffrey was a bright and precocious youth, who showed his ability as a teenager in intellectual discussion, answering questions put to him by Henry to test his judgment. Henry was 'affectionately attracted by his wisdom and his responses'. He was also a comely and promising young warrior, his face at the ceremony 'glowing like the flower of a lily, with rosy flush'.[6] He was indeed nicknamed 'pulcher', or handsome.[7]

At Rouen on 10 June 1128 Henry knighted the young man, who thus probably acquired the arms of England as his own.

> On the great day, as was required by the custom of making knights, baths were prepared for use. . . . After having cleansed his body, and come from the purification of bathing, the noble offspring of the Count of Anjou dressed. . . . He wore a matching hauberk made of double mail, in which no hole had been pierced by spear or dart. He was shod in iron shoes, also made from double mail. To his ankles were fastened golden spurs. A shield hung from his neck, on which were golden images of lioncels. On his head was placed a helmet, reflecting the light of many precious gems, tempered in such a way that no sword could break or pierce it.

Thus clad, he showed his agility and ability by leaping on to the back of his beautiful Spanish horse, without having to use the stirrups. The *History of Duke Geoffrey* goes on to describe a tournament in which the young Angevin hero participated, joining the weaker side, striking blows with lance and sword, pressing on 'more fiercely than a lion', killing the giant Saxon on the other side. It is difficult to believe all the details in this account, but shows that Geoffrey was viewed as an heroic military figure.[8]

Then at Whitsun, on 17 June, in Le Mans, the marriage ceremony was performed by the bishop of that city, though Geoffrey was still only fifteen. A herald announced the coming ceremony in the streets so that all would attend. John of Marmoutier describes the celebrations, 'both sexes reclining to eat a varied meal'. He says the rejoicing continued for three weeks, and every knight who had attended went away with a gift from the king.[9] There was further celebration when the couple reached Angers: the citizens rushed out to meet them, bells rang, churches were hung with curtains outside, and clerics sang hymns in the streets. They were also welcoming their new count in Geoffrey. The young man's father went off to marry Melisende the heiress to Baldwin II, King of Jerusalem. In time Fulk succeeded Baldwin on the throne. His son Geoffrey was left in the West to take over as Count of Anjou.

Henry's decision was that the succession should pass to his daughter Matilda. Probably his longer-term intention was that the crown should pass to his grandson by Matilda.[10] He was less enthusiastic about giving any rights to the new son-in-law. Later, Geoffrey would claim that certain promises had been made to him, not only about gaining a hold on named castles on the southern Norman border, but

An enamel of Geoffrey V, Count of Anjou, standing with a sword, showing heraldic designs on his cap and shield. This brillantly coloured enamel is held in the Musée de Tessé at Le Mans.

also about joint rule with his wife in England and Normandy. However, Henry seems carefully to have excluded Geoffrey from any provable claim.

What the king did, was to insist that the leading barons, ecclesiastics and officials in England and Normandy should take an oath to accept Matilda as his heir. There are records of oaths taken in 1127, 1128 and 1131.[11] Henry was doing his best to guarantee her right to succeed him. Henry was no fool, and must have realized the difficulties in his choice. There was no tradition of female inheritance of the throne in England or Normandy, and it was later clear that a number of the oath-takers were reluctant. Roger of Salisbury claimed that when he first took the oath to support the widowed empress, the king promised that he would not marry her without their consent and this was a condition of the oath. Roger's argument was that the marriage to Geoffrey of Anjou had been made without the consent of the barons, prelates and officials, and was therefore invalid. What he is voicing is clearly a view, felt if not expressed at the time, about Henry's preference for Matilda. Many clearly thought that when she married, her husband would be likely to become the ruler in England and Normandy, and therefore it was important that her husband should be acceptable to the leading men of the land.

When Geoffrey of Anjou was named as the husband there was some hostility to the choice. Anjou may have been less of an enemy to Normandy than had once been the case, but the two provinces had never been great friends or allies, and there was plenty of past antagonism to fuel hostility. Geoffrey's father, Fulk V, had fought against Henry I at Alençon, and alongside Louis VI against him at Brémule. When Geoffrey later invaded Normandy, the enmity of the local populace soon became clear; the Angevins were taunted as 'Guiribecs', which was something akin to the Cornish term of abuse for outsiders as grockles.[12] How the chronicler Orderic would rejoice over the fact that they caught dysentery and trailed diarrhoea behind them during their unpleasant retreat.

There was no enthusiasm whatever for England to be ruled by such an outsider, and this probably explains why Geoffrey himself never made any serious attempt to have direct rule over the kingdom. Indeed, Henry I himself seems to have become estranged from his son-in-law. Soon after the marriage, Matilda abandoned the marital bed and returned to her father. The problem was partly political, in that Geoffrey claimed possession of the promised southern Norman castles which Henry retained, and partly personal. Most accounts accept that the married couple did not get on very well, but we have no insight into the marital chamber. When Matilda left her husband, Henry of Huntingdon says that she came to England with her father, and only after a council had spoken in favour of her being 'restored to her husband, the Count of Anjou, as he demanded', was she sent back.[13]

In short, Matilda's rights to the English crown were pressed by her father, but were never very certain to be enacted. As a female with an unfavoured husband, her chances seemed questionable. Of course the oaths taken to her mattered in the context of twelfth-century beliefs, and would cause problems, since virtually every person who took the oath would later stand accused of perjury. But even Henry's own hopes must have been unsure, or he would not have needed to have the oath repeated on three occasions.

The most likely explanation of all this, as suggested above, is that what Henry I and most of his barons hoped, was that Matilda would have a son who would be old enough to rule when Henry himself died. The real factor which undermined Henry's plans was not Matilda's flaws as a successor, but his own death in 1135. This is also suggested by Matilda's own apparently surprising lack of action in 1135. She made no attempt to come to England, and made no overt claim to the throne. It does not appear as if she had seen herself as her father's heir, or had been planning to take over the kingdom and the duchy. As yet her sons were not old enough to rule; Henry had been born in 1133 and Geoffrey in 1134. And although Henry I had to some extent recognized her position, through the oaths, and through a nod to her rights in some of his late charters, he had not given her any definite role in government such as would suggest he expected her to take up the reins of rulership. In 1134 Matilda had been seriously ill, and her survival was probably deemed uncertain. Henry had been training her into a position of queen mother rather than of reigning queen, but with his death those plans had all gone awry.

KING STEPHEN

When Henry made his last crossing to Normandy, there was an eclipse with stars around the sun, and then a terrible earthquake, which the chronicler William of Malmesbury saw as omens of evil to come.[14] On 25 November 1135, Henry I rode

This badly eroded statue on Rochester Cathedral is probably a representation of King Stephen. It is similar to statues on the cathedral at Chartres, in the territory of Stephen's family.

into his castle at Lyons-la-Forêt, some 20 miles east of Rouen. It was one of the many centres he used for his hunting expeditions. He sent out various of his huntsmen to take up their stations ready for the next day's sport. Clearly he was well and planning his normal active life. But Henry of Huntingdon says he had 'partaken of some lampreys [an eel-like fish], of which he was fond, though they always disagreed with him, and though his physician recommended that he abstain, would not submit to his good advice'.[15] In the night he was taken ill, and for six days lay on his bed, gradually weakening. He fell into a fever, and it became clear that he was dying. Henry made confession to the Archbishop of Rouen, and gave out his last instructions. He wanted Robert of Gloucester to take money from the treasury at Caen to pay off his soldiers and household servants, and for gifts to the poor, which apparently was not done.

As the night of Sunday 1 December drew on, Henry breathed his last. Hugh, Archbishop of Rouen, and Audoin, Bishop of Évreux, made the lords and officials who were present swear to accompany the body back to the coast for burial in England. On the Monday they set out first for the cathedral at Rouen. That night an embalmer, working in a chamber within a corner of the cathedral, opened up the swollen body, cleaned it out, and filled it with sweet-smelling balsam. It was covered in salt and sewn up in ox hides. The entrails went in an urn to be buried at Notre-Dame du Pré.

Henry I with his prelates. This is one of four representations of Henry I in the contemporary chronicle of John of Worcester. (Corpus Christi College, Oxford, MS 157, ff. 382, 383)

A band of clerks and knights, lesser men, accompanied the remains in a bier to Caen, where it rested in the choir of Saint Stephen's. They had to wait four long weeks for a suitable wind to convey them to England. Christmas had passed by the time they sailed. Gentle winds carried them across the Channel, and the body was taken on to Reading Abbey, where it found its last resting place.

The chaos which ensued, perhaps the nearest to genuine anarchy which the period produced, demonstrated the need for an urgent decision over the succession, and the need for an effective ruler. There were disturbances and some lords took advantage of the situation to pursue their own interests: 'every man now seeks to plunder the goods of others. . . . The Normans abandon themselves to robbery and pillage . . . greedy brigands rush out, ready for evil'.[16] Another writer said: 'each man, seized by a strange passion for violence, raged cruelly against his neighbour . . . bringing to naught the enactments of law . . . they seized the chance of vengeance'.[17] Succession by a minor or a woman did not at the time seem the answer to such a situation. Hardly a soul spoke out for Matilda to succeed either in England, or in Normandy.

The Norman view on the question of the oath and the succession was not unlike that in England. The Norman barons ignored the claims of Matilda and Geoffrey, and thought first of the old king's Blois nephew, Theobald, now himself a count, an established ruler and man of substance. After an assembly at Neubourg which decided in his favour, Theobald was invited to become duke.

However, the man who seized the initiative was Theobald's younger brother, Stephen, now Count of Mortain and Boulogne. He was in Boulogne when he received the news of Henry's demise, and decided to sail at once for England. It is clear that Stephen at least had thought about the succession, and was ready to make his move. His motives may have been concerned more with the enduring enmity between Blois and Anjou, than any personal animus against Matilda. If he could gain England and Normandy, then control of those areas would be denied to the Angevin count. We know that Stephen's mother received a letter from Abbot Peter the Venerable, in response to her own immediate request for news on the death of Henry I. The presence soon after the deaths of both Theobald in Normandy and Stephen in England, show the Blesevins' high interest in the succession.[18] The *Gesta Stephani* says that some of the leading men in England had bound themselves to the house of Blois while Henry was still alive.[19] Stephen's county of Boulogne gave him an ideal position from which to make the crossing, and he sailed at once from Wissant, despite the promise of bad weather. For speed, he travelled with a very small retinue, not waiting to collect a force. On the morning of his arrival in England there was a storm with thunder and lightning, which William of Malmesbury took to presage evil, but for the time being at least the heavens seemed rather to be smiling on Stephen.

No one knew quite how to act. They had been used to the firm and ruthless hand of Henry I. There were prejudices against Matilda, which held back any great desire to see her or her husband prosper. There was no obvious candidate in England, and here was the king's favourite nephew taking just the sort of decisive steps which they would wish to see in a ruler. There was, says the *Gesta Stephani*: 'no one else at hand who could take the king's place and put an end to the

The town of Canterbury, showing the castle and the cathedral. (Corpus Christi College, Cambridge, MS 26, f. i.r)

dangers'.[20] One by one the obstacles were removed from his path. At first, though, he was refused entry to Dover and Canterbury, both held in the name of Robert, Earl of Gloucester.

It is interesting, given the modern view of Stephen, that in 1135, the chronicler Henry of Huntingdon could see him as 'a resolute and audacious man'.[21] Another might have been daunted by the unfriendly initial reception, but Stephen knew clearly what a successful claimant needed to do. He must hold London and Winchester, and he needed to be anointed and crowned if possible by the Archbishop of Canterbury. Stephen soon achieved all three.

There can be little doubt that Stephen's model for his early behaviour as king was that of his admired uncle, Henry I.[22] Henry had also gained the throne by prompt action in an uncertain situation. In London Stephen was welcomed; the citizens came out to greet him 'with acclamation', as though they had recovered Henry I in him, and that before he had made any agreement.[23] But their attitude was also affected by promises of privileges which he alone could grant, as well as promises about London's status. As Count of Boulogne he had a significant say in allowing privileges for trade through that city, which was also the major route for trade from England to Flanders. Stephen showed wisdom and shrewdness in London. He seems to have been prepared to recognize London as a commune, a status awarded to many cities in this period throughout Europe. The citizens would reward him by consistent loyalty throughout the reign. They took an oath to aid him with their resources and protect him, an oath to which they faithfully adhered. His conduct in 1135 compares very favourably with that of Matilda six years later. London was secured. At any rate, the citizens, probably revelling in

The coronation of Henry I, in 1100, took place in London only two days after the death of Henry's brother, William Rufus, in the New Forest.

their new status as members of a commune, called an assembly at which his birth and character was praised, and elected Stephen as king, the first in the realm to do so.

He moved on to Winchester, still the site of the national treasury though London was overtaking fast as the chief city in the land.[24] By this time Stephen was accompanied by a band of supporting knights. It is usually said that Stephen gained Winchester through the offices of his brother Henry. Henry was indeed

Bishop of Winchester, and at this stage a supporter of his brother's claims. The bishop came out to greet Stephen, along with some of the leading citizens. The *Gesta Stephani* hints that Winchester may also have been granted commune status by the aspiring monarch.[25] But chronicle descriptions of Stephen's arrival in Winchester suggest the major officials there trusted Stephen rather than his brother. It was to him in person that the two major officials, Roger, Bishop of Salisbury, and William Pont de l'Arche, insisted on handing their keys. No doubt they were looking to their own futures, and it may be that Henry had helped to persuade them, but there is no evidence to that effect. The bishop had even attempted to bribe William to hand over the keys to the castle, which contained the treasury, but he had refused to do so except to Stephen.

Stephen also persuaded the Archbishop of Canterbury, William of Corbeil, to carry out the coronation. William was an experienced prelate, who knew well the wishes and actions of Henry I. He therefore hesitated to overthrow those intentions. On the other hand, the kingdom needed a ruler – no one else seemed to be seeking the position – and everything was pointing towards Stephen as the man for the moment. The support of the Bishop of Winchester helped to make up his mind. Henry of Blois gave his guarantee that Stephen would keep the oath he now made to restore and maintain the freedom of the church, promises which Stephen later incorporated into the Charter of Liberties issued at Oxford.[26] Much has been made of these promises, as if they were unique, and that Stephen was particularly wicked in breaking them. The fact is that every king since the Conqueror had made such promises on his accession, and none had kept them fully. Indeed, Rufus, Henry I, and later Henry II broke them in much more obvious and dramatic manner than Stephen.[27]

The *Gesta Stephani* says that Stephen's supporters had to try hard to persuade the archbishop.[28] William of Corbeil indicated that he would not act lightly or in haste, and the counsel of all was needed: 'it is fitting that all should meet together to ratify his accession'. They responded that Henry himself knew they all swore unwillingly, and that they would not keep the oath. They also said that on his deathbed the king had 'very plainly showed repentance for the forcible imposition of the oath on his barons'. They pointed out the need for 'a man of resolution and soldierly qualities' to save the kingdom which was being 'torn to pieces'. Then Hugh Bigod, an important baron of East Anglia, together with two other unnamed knights, swore on oath that they had heard from the lips of Henry I in Normandy that he had changed his wishes over the succession; that he released those who had taken the oath from their obligation, and no longer wanted Matilda and Geoffrey to succeed, but preferred his nephew Stephen.

Later, when the succession was discussed before the Pope, it was claimed that Bigod's oath was invalid because he was not present at the death. It is probably true that he was not present at the last, but it does not altogether invalidate his oath, especially given the bias displayed on both sides in the arguments before the papacy. According to John of Salisbury, at the hearing before Innocent II, Arnulf, Archdeacon of Sées and later Bishop of Lisieux, stated that 'King Henry had changed his mind, and on his death bed had designated his sister's son Stephen as his heir'.[29] This may have simply been based on Bigod's oath, but it still shows that a respected cleric accepted that oath, as apparently did the Archbishop of Rouen, also present at the death. Bigod had almost certainly been in Normandy, and almost certainly attended upon the king. Not only he, but two other knights, were prepared to swear the oath. What they swore is patently possible given the known situation: that Henry 'had changed his mind, and . . . had designated his sister's son, Stephen as his heir'.[30]

Geoffrey of Anjou had quarrelled with his father-in-law, 'had vexed the king by not a few threats and insults', and Matilda had finally sided with her husband against her father.[31] Henry of Huntingdon says there were several disagreements between Geoffrey and Henry, 'fomented by the arts of his daughter', angering the king to the point where they contributed to his final illness.[32] It is extremely likely that Henry felt angry and hostile to them, and made some such comment about the succession. Since 1128 the political reason for making the marriage in the first place had been neutralized by the death of William Clito at the siege of Alost. Henry may well have been regretting his decision to marry Matilda to Geoffrey.

Bigod gained nothing from his oath; in other words he had not made a deal with Stephen over it, nor was he alone in making it. The supporters of Matilda before the Pope never said that the content of the oath was inaccurate, only that Bigod was not present at the last moment. It seems highly likely that Henry had made some such remark to Hugh. The Archbishop of Canterbury was convinced, and so were two clerics who were at the bedside, the Bishop of Évreux and the Archbishop of Rouen, both of whom supported Stephen as king. The Archbishop of Rouen actually represented Stephen before the Pope in 1139. Of the five earls present, four became supporters of Stephen though the fifth was Robert of Gloucester. The evidence on the whole argues for an acceptance of Bigod's oath as genuine.[33]

The archbishop accepted this oath and went ahead to arrange an immediate coronation.[34] The ceremony was carried out on Sunday 22 December 1135. Stephen was anointed king, with the implicit support of the church and nation. According to William of Malmesbury there were not many nobles or prelates present, though the *Gesta Stephani* says he had universal approval.[35] When Henry was buried at Reading on 4 January 1136, his crowned successor attended the solemn occasion.

Stephen's success in England fostered his acceptance in Normandy as well. The very assembly of Norman barons which proposed to his older brother Theobald that he should be duke, was informed that Stephen had gone to England and was already accepted there as king. It was enough to make them reconsider, and they now had to back down and ask Theobald to withdraw his claim to Normandy. They wanted to join the bandwagon for Stephen; they did not want separate rulers for England and Normandy, with all the risks of divided estates and loyalties which that entailed, the effects of which they knew only too well from the squabbles which had attended the period of Robert Curthose's rule as duke. They were 'determined to serve under one lord on account of the honors which they held in both provinces'. Orderic says that Theobald was 'offended' at being overlooked, since he was the older brother, and stormed back home with a bad grace.[36]

England and France in the twelfth century.

Stephen's success had been misleadingly easy. The underlying problems had not all disappeared. It remained for him to prove that he could be an effective king. In that case most opposition would fade away. In the next two years, modelling himself on the early actions of Henry I as king, he did his best to give law and order and crush opposition. He had mixed success, but on the whole succeeded in England. His friendly, engaging personality helped to win men over. Not unlike his eventual successor, Henry II, he had something of the common touch, and 'by his good nature and the way he jested, sat and ate in the company even of the humblest, earned an affection that can hardly be imagined, and already all the chief men of England had willingly gone over to his side'.[37] Although some showed reluctance, and some hesitated, the barons of England came round to acceptance of Stephen. His success here is demonstrated by the list of barons who witnessed the acts of his Easter court.

When even Robert of Gloucester came to court, his achievement was almost complete.

The *Gesta Stephani* says that Robert had hesitated, and that in 1135 others had suggested to him he ought to claim the throne. Robert had resisted that temptation, but suggested that his sister Matilda's son, the child Henry, should have the crown. However, he made no move to that end, and after several summonses from the king by messages and letters, he turned up at court after Easter. It was an important gain for the king, and he showed the earl special favour, so that he 'obtained all he demanded' in return for his homage.[38] William of Malmesbury, writing as the apologist of Robert, says that he had secretly intended to help Matilda and was biding his time, planning to work for her on the English nobles, 'pretending to share their breach of faith'.[39] He claims that the earl only did homage 'conditionally, that is to say, for as long as the king maintained his rank unimpaired and kept the agreement'. No doubt this was the earl's private thinking, but one can hardly imagine it was part of an overt deal with the king. The earl had seen the way things were going, and must have thought it likely that unless he urgently made his peace with Stephen his lands in England and Normandy might well be forfeit. It is significant that he made no open move to aid Matilda and Geoffrey for two years. Like others, he had come to see that at least for the time being, there was no real alternative to accepting Stephen as King of England and Duke of Normandy. Stephen then made a triumphal progress through England, demonstrating the strength of his support, and everywhere he was given an enthusiastic reception.

We shall not examine the events of the first two years in any detail in this chapter, which is concerned with the causes of the war, but one point needs to be made. Stephen did reasonably well in dealing with the early rebellions and invasions in England. He put down the two earliest rebellions with alacrity. An army acting on his behalf defeated the Scots in the Battle of the Standard. His hold on the crown was confirmed by a letter of congratulation from the papacy. The majority of the barons of England accepted his rule, and most were indeed to stay loyal even after the war began. The civil war would not have happened had Stephen not built up a strong party of support ready to back him against Matilda's challenge.

But there were also ways in which his success was less complete. There were always some dissident barons, and he never crushed them all. The Scottish invasion was dealt with decisively, but the Welsh and Norman borders were not. Matilda's husband, Geoffrey of Anjou, grasped the castles on the southern Norman border which were claimed as her dower. He supported the rebellion by William Talvas, which increased the pro-Angevin hold on Normandy. He made annual invasions of Normandy. Stephen's expedition to Normandy in 1137 failed to dislodge him, though a treaty was made between them. On the Welsh border, English baronial forces suffered two setbacks, and Stephen was not able to alter the position much. The point is that where Stephen failed to achieve absolute success, he left a gap in his authority. This left hope for Matilda. She had been slow to act in 1135, and might have lost her chance for good, but Stephen's incomplete success over the next two years, allowed her to consider her claims again. Thus a war of succession became possible.

THE TENURE DEBATE

There has been a long running attempt to see the civil war of Stephen's reign as caused by the uncertainty of rights to inherit land. In simple form the argument runs: men could not be sure that their sons would inherit their lands and they wanted to remove this uncertainty. Matilda and her son stood for the direct descent by heredity from Henry I, and the outcome of the war was a victory for hereditary right. S.E. Thorne opened this debate, in 1959, by questioning Maitland's view that the Norman Conquest had established fees in England as being heritable.[40] Thorne believed this did not happen until the twelfth century. He based this on the twelfth-century need for consent from others with an interest in an estate, and argued that the change did not occur until after 1200. R.H.C. Davis presented the view that the crown itself had not been hereditary and that the civil war was an attempt to establish the principle that it should be.[41] He argued that the nobility wanted their own estates to become hereditary, and therefore favoured a monarchy which stressed the same point.

The most detailed contribution to this complicated argument, was made in a series of articles by J.C. Holt, beginning in 1972.[42] It is impossible to summarize these articles quickly, but to an extent Holt agreed with Thorne that the hereditary claim to property had been established gradually after 1066. He argued that it was the working out of this process which caused the discontent that broke out into civil war. His subtle point was that it was not inheritance which was at issue, but the rules of inheritance, the question of who had the best right. He saw the key period as that of Stephen's reign.

Henry I with his knights; another of Henry's visions, as represented in John of Worcester's chronicle. (Corpus Christi College, Oxford, MS 157, ff. 382, 383)

Meanwhile, in 1974 Edmund King added a new dimension to the debate.[43] He suggested that the examples Holt had given were not typical, but all came from cases where inheritance was disputed. His view was that problems over tenure did not cause the anarchy, or prolong it, neither matters of heredity nor rules of inheritance; that the civil war was a political crisis, and not a tenurial one. The debate has continued with several interesting further contributions, but we can end it at this point.[44] The general conclusion of historians since that time is that tenurial instability was not a prime cause of the civil war. In general the principle of hereditary succession to estates was established well before 1135. There had been a period of uncertainty in England, but not because of vagueness over rights of heredity so much as over the problems caused by the revolution in land holding that was the Norman Conquest, and the matter of establishing hereditary right over acquired properties.[45] It took a generation or two from 1066 to regain a feeling of normality. Of course there would always be disputes to land, and those 'disinherited' by Henry I were bound to seek means of recovering their lands, but it was hardly the prime cause of war in England. In any case there is never any question of hereditary right being absolute. Royal decree could always override hereditary right, for example on the grounds of treachery. The civil war was not caused by uncertainty over noble rights to acquire estates by hereditary right, but it was caused by the uncertainty of how the crown should pass from holder to successor. Henry II's claim, for all his blather about being the legal heir, was a direct blow against the right of a son (William of Blois) to inherit the crown from his properly anointed royal father.

ROBERT, EARL OF GLOUCESTER

By 1137 there was hope for the Angevin cause in Normandy, but little hope in England. In the kingdom Stephen seemed to have brought law and order: 'already England was gradually settling into its accustomed peace and its wonted tranquillity'.[46] No major English noble had declared openly for Matilda. Geoffrey of Anjou was not prepared to send or pay for any large force to go to England; he wanted to concentrate on exploiting his claims in Normandy. Matilda therefore had neither the resources nor the men for any military campaign in England. She had begun to consider her rights, and was preparing a case to put before the Pope. She may have received some secret promises from England, but realistic chances did not seem great.

One event above all others improved Matilda's hopes, and therefore made a military attempt to gain the English throne possible. What really caused the civil war of Stephen's reign was the sudden declaration of Robert, Earl of Gloucester, in 1138. Writing later, offering Robert's own justification of his actions, William of Malmesbury claimed that Robert had always supported his sister, but other accounts suggest otherwise, and it seems likely that Robert had actually been opposed to her marriage to Geoffrey.[47] Robert had come to Stephen's court; he had accompanied the king to deal with rebellion. He was in Normandy during the 1137 campaign, when his aid would have been crucial to Geoffrey of Anjou, but he made no move to give help. The evidence is that during the first two years of the new reign, Robert was more concerned about his own estates and his own position than that of his half sister.

Why did he change his mind? Again, William of Malmesbury, his apologist, and an unreliable witness because of his bias and tendency to distort, tells us of Robert's long-held intention to desert Stephen, and is the only one to report an incident which he suggests caused Robert to change sides.[48] Despite the bias this may well be the case; we have no other explanation. Unfortunately we have no other account to balance the picture, and William does not fully explain why Stephen attempted to have Robert ambushed (assuming that he did). Until that time, Robert had little cause to complain. Despite his tardy acceptance of the new monarch, Stephen had confirmed all his estates and had heeded his advice at the siege of Exeter.[49] Nevertheless, he may have been discontented at having to play second fiddle at court to those whom Stephen had better reason to trust, including the Beaumont twins.

According to William of Malmesbury, the king, through his lieutenant, William of Ypres, laid an ambush against Robert which failed, but which persuaded Robert that he could not trust Stephen. Clearly there were developments of which we are not aware. We can only speculate. There is little question that no love was lost between Stephen and Robert. They had quarrelled over their respective status at the time of making the oath to Matilda. No doubt they were jealous of Henry's favour each for the other. It was probably this hostility to Stephen as a person which had most dictated Robert's reluctance to accept him as king, rather than any great love for Matilda.

From William of Malmesbury's attempt to report the earl's own motives, it would seem that he had never accepted Stephen without serious reservations, and was always ready to desert him. From Stephen's point of view, he was always distrustful of the earl, who was never likely to enter the circle of advisers closest to the crown. William of Malmesbury, on the ambush incident, puts a telling phrase into the king's mouth: 'when they have chosen me king, why do they abandon me?'[50] It suggests that his motive against Robert was fear of treachery, not unlikely given his attitude. Davis, probably correctly, believed that Robert's desertion of Stephen stemmed from the ambush incident, and was also connected to the divisions within Stephen's army in 1137.[51]

Why Robert failed to join the Angevins during Geoffrey's 1137 invasion remains a mystery, but suggests he was still preparing to make the move after Stephen had openly acted against him. We know that Stephen's 1137 expedition was ruined by arguments between his Norman barons and his Flemish mercenaries. Davis' suggestion is that it was Robert of Gloucester, the leading Norman baron, who particularly objected to the trust Stephen placed in William of Ypres. William of Malmesbury's account suggests that William of Ypres was responsible for the attempt to ambush Robert. It is impossible to give a definite account of what happened here, but our suggestion is that Robert of Gloucester was in contact with the Angevins and Stephen had been warned that he might desert. William of Malmesbury says that 'a rumour was flying over England that Robert, Earl of Gloucester, who was in Normandy, was just on the point of siding with his sister'. There is also evidence, in two chronicles, that Geoffrey of Anjou

made some sort of approach to Robert, and according to one that he persuaded
him to make the move.[52] William of Ypres was instructed to prevent Robert
joining the Angevins, and the ambush had this intention. Robert was unhappy
over the prominence of William of Ypres, and his reservations were shared by
many of the Norman barons who had rallied to Stephen. The ambush failed.
Stephen's expedition was halted because of the differences in the army.

Robert was now ready to change sides. In 1138 he finally issued a *diffidatio* or
defiance, that is he renounced his former allegiance to Stephen. Just after
Whitsun:

> he sent representatives and abandoned friendship and faith with the king in
> the traditional way, also renouncing homage, giving as the reason that his
> action was just, because the king had both unlawfully claimed the throne and
> disregarded, not to say betrayed, all the faith he had sworn to him.[53]

William of Malmesbury also claims that Robert produced a bull from the Pope
bidding him to obey his oath. It is one of the many occasions when one doubts the
veracity of this partisan chronicler. All our evidence is that to this point the
papacy fully accepted Stephen as king and would not surely have countenanced
any kind of rebellion against properly constituted authority. Innocent II 'in
friendly letters confirmed his occupation of the kingdom of England and the
duchy of Normandy'.[54] Alberic of Ostia, a papal legate, came to England in 1138
and helped to make the agreement with the Scots of that year, showing nothing
but friendliness to the new king.

There must also be some doubt about the legality of the *diffidatio*, not a process
ever recognized in England. But whatever the legal niceties, its impact was clear.
It was in effect a declaration of war. The king could now take as forfeit Robert's
lands. The earl's only practical hope of retaining his lands in both England and
Normandy was to throw all his weight behind the efforts of Matilda and Geoffrey,
and to open up the war in England. If he acted quickly, he knew he could rely on
the men from his own estates to support him. What Robert of Gloucester's move
meant was that Matilda now had a ready-made party and army in England. The
earl's move was equally important in Normandy. Altogether, it was Robert of
Gloucester who caused the civil war in England by giving Matilda an army to
back her claims. Until then she could not have mounted a military effort to
support those claims. Geoffrey of Anjou showed no intention of using his own
resources to back a war in England. Matilda had a small force of her own, led by
Alexander de Bohun in Normandy, calling himself '*cohortis comitisse primipilus*'
(the chief centurion of the countess' force), but it was a force in no way adequate
to mount a campaign in England.[55] It was only when Robert of Gloucester
brought his considerable power into her camp in 1138, that Matilda could
realistically contemplate a war for her succession in England. The evidence points
to Robert of Gloucester rather than Matilda as the person who determined in
1139 that there should be war in England.

CHAPTER 2

The Two Sides

Before Robert of Gloucester's defiance in 1138, few men had cared to oppose Stephen openly. But there had been rebellions of the kind that were typical at the beginning of a new reign, borne out of frustrations built up under the previous monarch and now loosed to test out the new regime. However, in 1138 there was a different kind of rebellion, with the suggestion of some concerted plan. There can be no certainty about the motives of the new rebels, but circumstantial evidence strongly suggests that the supporters of Matilda were beginning to harden their intentions into action. Once Robert had made his declaration, the leading figures in the looming war, on the Angevin side, were prepared to come into the open. It was the formation of this Angevin party which made the civil war inevitable.

Before 1138, there had been a general acceptance of Stephen's succession, but there was also latent resentment. The actions of the king during the years between 1135 and 1139 provoked some men to move into opposition. Some rebelled openly, others began preparations to join Matilda once she entered the country.

At the same time, although there was probably a majority of men who accepted Stephen with resignation rather than enthusiasm, there was also a hard core of strong royal supporters, those who were especially favoured by the new king and had gained from their association with him, those who had their own reasons for hostility to the old regime of Henry I, or dislike of his daughter or son-in-law.

The attitude of those only loosely committed to Stephen was crucial to the war which followed. For one reason or another, some of the most important among them would change sides and influence the direction of the war. Already, by 1139, some of these attitudes had been formed by the events of the early reign. Previous historians, notably Davis, have tended to see every move of Stephen in this period as a 'mistake', because it aroused some opposition. The fact is that any decisive act was bound to cause some opposition; this was hardly a new factor with Stephen. The hostility caused by Henry I's ruthless and often harsh treatment of his leading barons had aroused far more resentment than Stephen's measures ever would. But Henry had been more fortunate, at least in England, to have no leading figure who unified such resentment. The point is that Stephen did act decisively in the years before the war began, and that should not be viewed as mistaken policy, but it did provoke opposition and helps to explain the formation of the warring parties.

EARLY REBELLIONS

There were two early rebellions against Stephen, by Robert of Bampton and Baldwin de Redvers. Robert was 'a knight not of the lowest birth or of small landed estate'.[1] However, according to the same chronicler, he was a lover of wine and of food, given to drunkenness and gluttony. Robert of Bampton's anger was directed not so much against the king as against Glastonbury Abbey, which won a dispute against him over land at Uffculme. But the Abbot of Glastonbury was of course Stephen's brother, Henry of Blois. Robert felt desperate enough to turn to open rebellion immediately after Henry I's death, acting with aggression and cruelty. When summoned to the new king's court, he did turn up, albeit reluctantly and with a scowl on his face. Judgment was given that he must hand over his castle to the king, and the disposal of all he possessed should be put at the king's discretion. Robert had at first accepted Stephen, and done homage to him. Now, in the presence of the king, he accepted the judgment of the court.

But immediately afterwards he stole away on horseback, strongly garrisoned Bampton, and plundered the countryside around. As a result his castle was declared forfeit. Stephen himself led a force to Bampton, in Devon.[2] His troops blockaded the castle and captured a man trying to slip over the wall and get away. He was hanged before the castle wall, at which the garrison decided to surrender. Stephen therefore captured the castle and sent its garrison into exile; Robert himself had already fled. It was a relatively unimportant and isolated rebellion, but Stephen had dealt with it promptly, as was his wont, and effectively. The forfeited lands were awarded to Henry de Tracy, who remained a fervent and active supporter of the king. Robert of Bampton figures no more in history, except that the *Gesta Stephani* says he 'met a dreadful end among strangers'.[3] Some of Robert's men found refuge at the court of the King of Scots.

The second, and more dangerous rebellion was that of Baldwin de Redvers. Although both rebellions preceded the outbreak of war, it is notable that the leaders were both west country barons. The civil war itself would take on something of a regional nature, and the west country would always be Matilda's main base. This is well known, but is always assumed to be because of the role played by Robert of Gloucester. So far as is known, however, neither of these two early rebels had any close connection with the earl, though the *Gesta Stephani* makes a veiled hint that someone with the king's own force at Exeter had encouraged Baldwin's revolt. As the editors point out, Robert of Gloucester seems the most obvious candidate for this role.[4] But there is no similar hint about Robert of Bampton. The two rebellions may just be coincidence, but possibly there might have been some particular cause for discontent in that area. Perhaps, for example, the famines and shortages of the period had hit that region hard. Regions where discontent against a given regime is especially strong have always been an important feature of English rebellions, and the regional discontent found in the west country and to a lesser degree in East Anglia, should not be ignored in this period.[5]

Baldwin de Redvers, 'a man of eminent rank and birth', was suspicious of the new king, and one of the few major lords not to come to his court or make any

The matrix of the seal of Exeter (reproduced in reverse), showing the castle, c. 1200.

agreement with him.[6] Perhaps the arrival of Robert of Gloucester at the court in 1136 swayed Baldwin; at any rate he made approaches to the king, but found that he had delayed too long. Stephen chose to make an example of him. It was probably not as bad a decision as it is usually represented. By this time Stephen had the declared allegiance of virtually the whole of the English baronage. To make an example of the one laggard would be commonly seen as sensible, and might be compared with Henry I's treatment of Robert of Bellême. Stephen did crush Baldwin's rebellion and capture his castles. It is true that Baldwin then joined the Angevins abroad and fought alongside them throughout the war, which incidentally is not so very unlike the conduct of Robert of Bellême against Henry. What if Stephen had made terms with him in 1136? Almost certainly Baldwin would still have been one of the first to join Matilda when she arrived. The conclusion must be that Stephen did not lose much by acting harshly.

The way in which Stephen's actions in this episode have been treated is very strange. Stephen acted promptly, effectively and successfully. When Henry I had done much the same against Robert of Bellême, no one accused him of weakness. Stephen refused the approaches from Baldwin. The latter, not surprisingly, then fortified Exeter against the king, collecting provisions of all sorts in the castle, 'a royal possession on which he had laid hands'.[7] Stephen heard about this while still at Bampton, and came fresh to Exeter from his triumph there. The king at once sent ahead a considerable force of 200 cavalry, which rode fast through the night. Baldwin was annoyed because the citizens of Exeter had themselves sent an appeal against him to the king; yet another city which gave its support to Stephen. On the next morning Baldwin came out of the castle determined to plunder and burn the town, but the king's advance force galloped in at that moment 'with glittering arms and standards waving in the air'. Stephen himself arrived not long afterwards, and the citizens came out to welcome him with gifts and receive him within the walls of Exeter.

Exeter was an important city, seen then as the fourth in the kingdom, benefiting from local farming and fishing, and with its own flourishing trade. Baldwin, his family, and the garrison which was sworn to resist to the last, were shut up within the castle. From the walls they taunted the royal forces. They shot down arrows, and sometimes made sorties into the town. But Stephen wore them down. He captured an outpost, broke the bridge which gave access from the town to the castle, and built timber counter fortifications. Armed men crawled up the mound against the castle, stones were thrown against it using hired experts, and in the meantime miners set to work. Baldwin's nearby castle at Plympton sent to the king, seeking terms for surrender, which Stephen willingly accepted. That castle was razed to the ground, and Baldwin's lands were devastated, his sheep and cattle collected for the king's use.

Alfred fitz Judhael, a man of Baldwin's, came secretly into Exeter with men in disguise and managed to get a message through to Baldwin to give him encouragement. The garrison made a sortie and managed to carry Alfred and his men back inside the castle. It was a slight blow to the royalist force, but Stephen himself was not greatly concerned and remained in good humour. He said the more of his enemies who were locked up together in one place the better. But the siege had dragged on for some three months and was proving expensive.

Then suddenly things brightened for the king. It was a hot summer, and the springs which were the water supply of the castle, and which had always bubbled away merrily, dried up. The chronicler saw it as 'the operation of divine power'.[8] Men and horses within would not be able to survive. For a time the troops of the garrison were driven in desperation to drink wine; they had to make their bread using wine instead of water, and even used wine to boil food. When the royalists threw in lighted torches in the hope of burning the wooden throwing engines or the timber buildings within, even the torches were put out with wine, but eventually the wine gave out too.

The two leading men in the garrison then came out to seek terms from the king. Henry of Blois advised his brother to refuse an agreement, which he did. The bishop's uncharitable feeling was that the two men looked thin and wasted, 'their lips drawn back from gaping mouths', suffering from thirst and must be close to surrender. When the king turned down the appeal, Baldwin's wife came to him, barefoot, her hair loose over her shoulders and in tears begged for mercy. He received her with kindness, but still refused to give terms. There were relatives of Baldwin and his men in the king's army, and those who had connived at the rebellion, and they now also approached the king and argued for mercy. They said it would be an act of royal clemency to accept surrender. They pointed out that Baldwin and his men had never sworn allegiance to him. They also said that everyone would be glad to see the end of the siege. The author of the *Gesta*

Stephani, himself an ecclesiastic, is clearly of the opinion that the bishop was right and that no mercy should have been shown, and others agreed.[9] This point could be debated *ad infinitum*, and most modern historians have taken the bishop's side. However, looking at the matter from the angle of common practice in war at that time, let alone the merits of showing mercy, there seems no disgrace or mistake in agreeing terms. Whether vicious reprisals would have served Stephen's cause better can only be a matter of opinion. To agree terms should normally be seen as the ideal victory for a besieger. The garrison could honourably be allowed to go, as was the case here, and in an internal disturbance, where the ruler wanted to become the authority over the defeated that was usually wise policy. In other words it was no doubt true that the garrison would have been forced to yield unconditionally before long, but whether that would have been a greater gain is dubious. Victory through agreed terms was a perfectly acceptable means of success. The main point is that Exeter Castle was now in the king's hands.

Baldwin, who may not have been in Exeter himself all through the siege, had escaped to the Isle of Wight, where he possessed almost the whole island according to the *Gesta Stephani*, including the castle at Carisbrooke, whose defences he himself seems to have improved.[10] He also had access to ships, referred to as a 'huge pirate fleet', with which he began to interfere with cross-Channel trade. Stephen was not dismayed. He left Exeter in the hands of his brother and moved on to Southampton, where he gathered a fleet to continue the fight against Baldwin.

No further fighting proved necessary. Baldwin de Redvers came to the king and submitted. It seems that the water supply at Carisbrooke had also dried up in this exceptional summer. The original well of the castle may still be seen, but it is not the one shown to tourists which operated during the time of Charles I's captivity there and which is driven by donkeys. The older well is a simple shaft protected by a plain iron grid. Baldwin had broken no oath to the king, but he was not able to persuade Stephen to recognize his holdings. He left, landless, for the continent, and sought refuge at the court of Geoffrey of Anjou. Execution of such opponents was not the common practice of that age, so there is no reason to condemn Stephen for leniency. He had achieved his ends in the manner normal to the time. Baldwin had twice been forced to move on, and all his lands were now at the king's disposal, including the two vital castles at Exeter and Carisbrooke. Soon the embittered baron was active against Stephen, first in Normandy, and later when the opportunity offered, in England.

There was a second region which created problems for Stephen both before and after 1138, and that was East Anglia. To be more precise there was one troublesome prelate, Nigel, Bishop of Ely, and one troublesome lord in East Anglia, who was a constant source of difficulty. The latter was Hugh Bigod. After the death of Henry I, and after giving his important oath with regard to the king's last wishes which had helped Stephen to gain the throne, Hugh took possession of the castle at Norwich at some time in 1136. However, when Stephen came to deal with it, he professed to have no intention of rebellion and handed the castle to the king, albeit reluctantly. Whether there was some genuine uncertainty about the possession of the castle, or whether Hugh had thoughts of rebellion and changed his mind, remains uncertain. Perhaps he believed the rumour of Stephen's death, perhaps he hoped to receive a reward for his oath, but if so he was disappointed. He was to remain to the end of his long life a difficult and vexatious man, always feeling cheated of Norwich Castle, and never the happy subject of any king.

It was not Stephen but Matilda who rewarded Hugh with the earldom of Norfolk at a later date. At any rate, Stephen's response had probably antagonized this volatile lord. According to *The Book of Ely*, which should be the best informed source on the subject, there was also a rebellion by Nigel, Bishop of Ely, before 1139, which the king put down. Nigel seems to have been involved in a northern plot involving the Scots, which he betrayed. The devious behaviour of Nigel underlines the wisdom of Stephen's measures in 1139. It may also suggest a more widespread discontent in East Anglia, as in the west country; they were the two regions most consistently opposed to his rule. One notes that the narrations of most detail of sufferings in the period are found in East Anglian chronicles from Huntingdon and Peterborough. The cause of the regional discontent is quite possibly the most obvious; that it was a region suffering worse deprivations than others through natural and man-made causes.

WALES

There was also trouble for Stephen on the borders with both Wales and Scotland in the first years of his reign. This too was almost a traditional test for a new English monarch. There were raids over both borders. Stephen had mixed success in dealing with the two areas, but his actions in both cases determined certain positions of the local lords in the civil war, and are therefore important to our present concern.

The Welsh border was notoriously difficult to deal with. None of the kings since the conquest had really solved the problem, and none would completely, until Edward I at the end of the thirteenth century conquered the principality. William the Conqueror had established certain trusted lords on the marches, notably Roger of Montgomery, and given them greater powers of independent action than barons elsewhere. This policy had been followed ever since. These Norman lords had begun to take over areas in Wales under their own authority. One chronicler wrote of Wales, that 'depopulations and depredations never cease'.[11] Already therefore much of southern Wales was in the hands of Norman lords who operated without much reference to any overlord. But the independent Welsh were given to frequent raids across the border, destroying houses, killing people, capturing animals and taking plunder.[12] They would then return to their own land. Retaliation was less effective, because of the problems of the Welsh countryside, and the Welsh custom of moving house from winter to summer lands. It was normally difficult, if not impossible, to bring the Welsh to battle. The usual consequence for the Norman lords and their kings was frustration. Both Rufus and Henry I had failed to achieve much against such methods. In 1095 Rufus lost men and horses in one expedition to Wales, and in 1097 failed to bring the enemy to book. Similarly in 1114 Henry I could get little satisfaction from his invasion. Stephen did no better, but probably no worse either. There were some minor defeats for Anglo-Norman forces in Wales, but these were almost certainly from the Welsh practice of ambushing armies, rather than from defeat in set battles. Under Stephen, as under previous kings, such advances as were made by the Normans in Wales were made by individual marcher lords on their own behalf.

At the very beginning of the new reign, and almost certainly from the action of marcher lords rather than Stephen, on 1 January 1136, the Worcester continuator says there was a battle in Wales in Gower in which 516 men were killed on either side. He does not say which side won, but it was probably a successful ambush by the Welsh. He says the bodies remained on the field and were left to the wolves. On 15 April, this time in what is described as an ambush, the Welsh, during a raid into English territory, caught and killed the Norman lord, Richard fitz Gilbert. The body was carried to Gloucester where it was buried. In the same year, in October, an English force was involved in another bloodletting, deeper into Wales, in Cardigan. Again the chronicler speaks of many deaths, but without specifying on which side.[13] This must have been a force sent on a punitive expedition and probably by Stephen. The same chronicler suggests that the 'English' in 1137 had more success, when the Welsh suffered at the hands of Normans and Flemings, though the Flemings also suffered deaths, and Payn fitz John was killed and again buried in Gloucester. It reminds us that the west country barons often had a large interest on the nearby Welsh marches. Those in the area who opposed Stephen did not seem to do so because of any reaction to Stephen's efforts or lack of them in Wales. So far as can be seen, they made progress with their own interests in much the same way as they had done for nearly a century past.

Stephen is generally accused of failure in Wales, but as pointed out already, it was similar to the failures of his predecessors, and in these cases early in the reign, the blame can hardly be laid against the king. Stephen's attachment to the fitz Gilbert family stemmed from these disturbances, and they mainly remained loyal supporters. Richard fitz Gilbert's brother Gilbert was made Earl of Pembroke in 1138, and a third brother, Baldwin, fought alongside Stephen at Lincoln and even made the battle speech for the king. Stephen in these years was winning loyal support as well as making enemies. Once the civil war began, Stephen was unable to take action in Wales, since his routes there were blocked by the swathe of Angevin territory in the west country. But men like Robert of Gloucester did not allow their interests to be neglected, and even made new gains.

SCOTLAND

Much the same might be said of the Scottish border, where, however, Stephen had more obvious success. David, King of Scots, raided over the border into England almost straight away, at Christmas 1135. He captured five towns in Northumbria: Carlisle, Wark, Alnwick, Norham and Newcastle, but failed to take Bamborough. He was probably surprised by the speed of Stephen's response. The Scots had arrived before Durham, which they proceeded to besiege. The English king gathered a force together quickly and rode north. When David knew of this, he abandoned further aggression and made terms.

King David seems to have been one of the few early in Stephen's reign who acted overtly in favour of the Empress Matilda: 'he received from the chiefs and nobles of that locality vows and pledges of fidelity to his niece'.[14] He was the brother of Edith-Matilda, the Empress Matilda's mother. One notes that by the time of the Battle of the Standard, the king was advised by men who had fled from Stephen in England, including Eustace fitz John, who had taken with him control of the castles of Alnwick and Malton. By the Treaty of Durham of 1136, Stephen confirmed David's son, Henry, as Earl of Huntingdon, and gave him Carlisle and Doncaster. The other captured towns were restored to Stephen. David was married to the daughter of the English Earl, Waltheof, which gave him the claim to Huntingdon.

Prince Henry of Scots now joined Stephen's court and was present at the important Easter session, and later in London. Some English nobles were angered by the favour shown to the Scots, and later David ordered his son home after insults had been offered him. But Stephen's first encounter with the Scots had shown firm military action, and a restrained statesmanlike settlement.

David showed little gratitude for the generous settlement. He pursued the typical raiding policy of the Scots into the border lands, which were not yet firmly attached to either kingdom. He invaded no less than three times in 1138. English chroniclers show the current national hatred for the raiders. Atrocities real or imagined are retailed in minute detail: the ripping open of pregnant women, the tossing of children's bodies on the points of spears, the killing of priests, the rape of matrons and virgins.[15]

To face the third invasion of late July, with Stephen occupied in the south, a northern army was raised. It was called into being by Thurstan, the ageing Archbishop of York, and led by a group of northern nobles including Walter Espec, 'an aged man full of days . . . huge, with black hair, bushy beard, large eyes, and a voice like a trumpet'.[16] Before the battle the northern English army was joined by a force of household knights sent by the king and led by Bernard of Balliol. Forces also arrived from the midlands, from Derbyshire and Nottinghamshire, with Geoffrey Halsalin, Robert Ferrers and William Peverel. The English army took with it an Italian-style carroccio, a cart with a large pole fixed to it. To the pole, which was a ship's mast, were attached the relevant banners of the northern churches, and at the top a shining silver pyx containing the host. It would be a rallying point in the battle, and was also a good propaganda symbol; the English were fighting for the church, indeed the archbishop had organized parish priests to lead their flocks to the fray. But this should not be allowed to give a false impression. There were local levies, but the English force contained the best trained forces of the day, mounted knights and trained archers, and proved better disciplined in the battle than their opponents.

The morning of 22 August saw a thick fog covering the low hills on the broad plain north of Northallerton, just east of the modern A167 where the battle monument is not quite accurately placed. The Cistercian monk Ailred, from nearby Rievaulx, gives a good balanced account of the battle which ensued. The

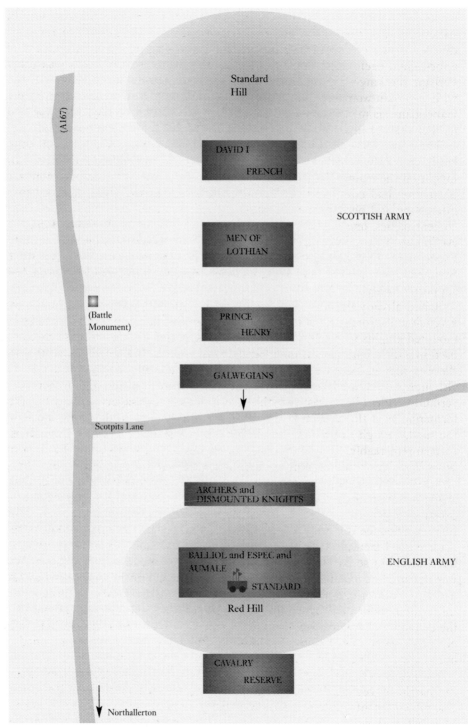

The Battle of the Standard, 22 August 1138. This is based on the proposition that Red Hill rather than Standard Hill was the rallying point for the English army.

patron of his monastery, Walter Espec, was one of the English commanders, but Ailred had also lived for a time at the court of the King of Scots and therefore had divided loyalties. According to him the Scottish force was larger. As they approached each other through the fog, the Scots to some extent panicked. Perhaps the king's prestige had been dented by a recent scandal involving him with 'a certain woman'.[17] David had a sensible plan of battle, but when the tough Galwegians claimed it was their right to be in the van, he changed his mind and let them have their way. It was a serious error.

The English army formed a defensive position on the slopes of a hill, and a battle speech was made by one of the leaders from this hill. But the battle was fought on the mainly flat land which dominates the area.[18] We do not know who, if anyone, had command of the English force, but they were arrayed in an interesting and perhaps novel fashion. Given the shrewdness and awareness of current tactics, one might suggest the leader of the household force, Bernard of Balliol, as the mind behind the formation. Ailred emphasizes the role of Walter Espec, while Orderic suggests that William of Aumale, soon to be rewarded by Stephen with the earldom of York, was the commander. William was to be a loyal supporter of Stephen.[19]

It had already become customary in the armies of the preceding reign for English and Norman armies to dismount a considerable proportion of their mounted knights to fight on foot in battle.[20] Here though, they seem to have been used in a different manner, interspersed with archers. It is possible that this was the way they had been used at Tinchebrai, Brémule and Bourg-Théroulde, but although dismounted knights were used in all those battles, and archers were certainly evident in the last two, the descriptions do not suggest exactly the same formation as at the Standard. Here they seem to have formed a front line across the field, though quite how the mixing was organized we cannot know. It is a pattern remarkably like that used by English forces much later on in the Hundred Years War. We should also understand that the bows at the Standard were almost certainly what we know as longbows. Given the composition of this particular army, it is not likely that they were primarily crossbowmen; they were most probably northern English levies. The planning of the English formation has further evidence of shrewdness. The standard on the carroccio, as suggested, made a good tactical point in the battle, and a good morale booster. It was not a novel idea, but so far as we know it had never been used in England before, and was not used again. It had been employed on the continent, and seems to have had an Italian origin. Why it appears in this particular battle is a mystery. The third point about the English force is its use of a tactical reserve. The horses of the dismounted knights were led to the rear, away from the battle, so they would not be disturbed by the noise and killing. But some men were still retained on horseback. This gave the force more than simply defensive power.[21]

With their recently altered battle plan put into effect, the Galwegians opened the battle by recklessly charging on foot against the English. It was an ill-disciplined infantry attack by less well-armed troops, and it proved disastrous. Men fell as they ran, hit by the archers confronting them in the English front line, so that they were 'destroyed by arrows'.[22] The Lothian chieftains were cut down. Their men fled 'like hedgehogs with spines, so were the Galwegians with arrows'.[23] Too late the king tried to emulate the English tactics by ordering the knights with him to dismount and halt the English; they could not turn the tide. Prince Henry of Scots did lead a flanking cavalry charge, but it proved a forlorn hope. They were beaten off. The battle had lasted a mere two hours. Only the infantry van of the English force had really been called upon to fight, except that the English cavalry may have played a part in holding off Henry, and certainly engaged in the pursuit. In any event the English tactics had succeeded brilliantly.

There is a tradition that the bodies of the dead Scots were buried on the field, and there is a modern track called Scotpits Lane. It is said that buried weapons have been found there. When I visited the battlefield with a group of students, we met an elderly local man who claimed that the story of findings was true. If the tradition is correct, it poses a problem for siting the battle, which is normally said to have occurred on the small hill just north of Standard Hill Farm, while Scotpits Lane is to the south. One would expect to find Scots killed on the field to be north of the hill, and further to the north beyond that if killed during the flight. It is just possible that the bodies of some of Prince Henry's cavalry had fallen in the southern position and were buried there. But another possibility is that our tradition of the battle site is incorrect, and that the hill used in the battle was the slightly more southerly Red Hill, in which case Scotpits Lane could well mark the position where Scots died as they attacked the English line, or as they turned to flee. This also fits better with the distance from Northallerton of 2 miles, given by Richard of Hexham.[24] Of the possibilities the second seems slightly to be preferred, but one always recognizes that any such tradition as that attached to Scotpits Lane or to Standard Hill Farm might be inaccurate.

The Battle of the Standard was a great success for the northern English. It was also a great relief to Stephen. From his point of view, his own absence from the field was a loss, as his prestige would surely have been much increased had he commanded such a victory. True he had sent the force under Bernard Balliol and thus played some part in the battle, but it did not have the same cachet as a personal part in the victory.

Nevertheless, the effects of the Standard were important on the formation of sides in the civil war. Following the victory, Stephen again showed his statesmanship in the settlement made with the Scots. As so often with Stephen, his best moves have been damned by historians. In this case he is condemned for his leniency in the second Treaty of Durham, of 1139, for not giving Carlisle to Ranulf, Earl of Chester. The earl did have a claim to the place, and obviously felt very strongly about it, but Stephen's decision had much to recommend it. Ranulf's claim in the first place was not watertight, and had already been turned down by Henry I. The claims of the Scots were stronger. In any case the king had to consider the settlement in a broader context. Stephen sought a permanent settlement, and the Scots were more likely to accept a long-term arrangement that was not vindictive. Therefore, despite the raid and the battle, Henry of Scots was confirmed as Earl of Huntingdon, and of Northumbria, including Lancashire north of the Ribble. This was sensible rather than weak; recognizing good Scottish claims to hold the areas, but stipulating that they were held from the

English crown and would retain their English law. The barons of these areas were to do homage to Prince Henry, but saving their fealty to the English king. Stephen also demanded four hostages. He did make some alterations to the previous settlement, keeping Newcastle as well as Bamborough, and dividing the former earldom of Huntingdon. This latter was another statesmanlike move, intended to mollify Simon de Senlis who had a claim to the Huntingdon earldom. What was separated off were the lands of Northampton, of which Simon was made earl. It is odd how the successes are ignored. Simon remained loyal to Stephen for life, and proved there was wisdom in Stephen's settlement.

In the event the settlement did not achieve all that Stephen hoped, but it was surely a commendable attempt to make a sound border peace. One is more inclined to blame David for not keeping to the new settlement. One cannot even give him the excuse of close kinship to the Empress Matilda as justification, though this is often done. He was in fact uncle to Stephen's Queen Matilda as well as to the empress. He would later again link forces with the Angevins, particularly as the empress' young son grew towards maturity. Nevertheless, the Scottish king was barely concerned in English events for several years, and through the whole of the reign the threat from north of the border was much diminished.

However, it remains true that Ranulf, Earl of Chester, was angered by the settlement and it drove him to oppose the king. Ranulf de Gernons (the mustachioed) was a vitriolic individual. He moved gradually into the Angevin fold, but was never greatly trusted there either. The springs of his attitude were his personal and family lands. He had never forgiven Henry I for taking the lordship of Cumberland and Carlisle from his father in 1120, even though on the reasonable grounds of rebellion against the king, and even though Henry I had restored the valuable earldom of Chester to him. Davis assumes that had Stephen given Carlisle to Ranulf all would have been well, and he would have fought for the king 'with his life'. [25] It is unlikely that the temperamental earl would have stayed loyal for long to anyone, and such a move would have certainly antagonized the Scots, and almost certainly have caused greater conflict with them than was to be the case. For Stephen it was hardly an easy decision, but in the circumstances he had made the right choice, though its consequences were not as he hoped. Nevertheless, even if David proved an unreliable ally, and even if Ranulf eventually turned away from him, the Battle of the Standard had been an important success. Most of the northern barons in England would remain on Stephen's side through the English war, and appreciated the regime which had brought one of the greatest English military victories against the old enemy, and something akin to peace to a very troubled frontier.

NORMANDY

The other major border problem of the early part of Stephen's reign was in the end probably the most vital. This was the conflict between Normandy and the territories commanded by Matilda's husband, Geoffrey, Count of Anjou. Geoffrey was still a young man, born in 1113, and was vigorous and ambitious.

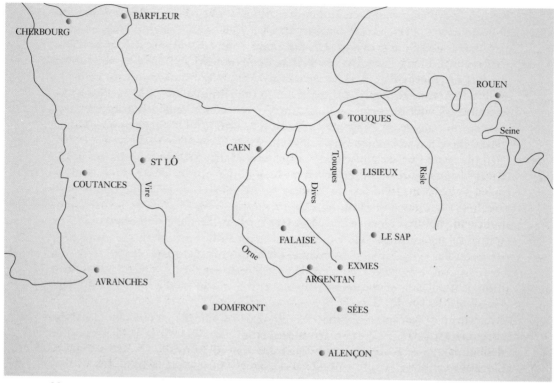

Normandy in the twelfth century.

His father's conquest of Maine, long a bone of contention with the Normans, had brought the Angevins to the Norman border.

The marriage to Matilda, the Angevins hoped, would bring control of Normandy to the house of the Plantagenets. Henry I had promised several castles on the southern Norman border as the empress' dowry, but had refused to give them up while he lived. This, not surprisingly, had annoyed Geoffrey, who first demanded them, then sought to take them by force. In the last year of Henry I's life, it had led to a border war between the king and his son-in-law, and this time Matilda had sided with her husband.

On Henry's death, Matilda had not made a strong effort to gain England, but Geoffrey had made sure of his Norman castles, which from then onwards he strongly garrisoned. Probably Geoffrey calculated that gradually he would need to take a firm grip on individual Norman strongholds, and win over the hearts of their masters, before he could hope to rule Normandy. Such an explanation makes sense of the relative inactivity in 1135. The few castles he claimed and took, were to be the base for a remarkable effort at the conquest of the duchy over the next decade. He also gained the support of William Talvas, together with his castles, since the Bellême lands which William claimed for himself had been given to Stephen by Henry I. But at first Geoffrey's hopes of success did not appear to be high. Even without Stephen's assistance, the Norman lords seemed easily able to stop the Angevin.

On 21 September 1136 Geoffrey crossed the River Sarthe and entered Normandy. The war he had started against Henry I in 1134 would continue against his successor Stephen. Accompanying him was a large force, including William Talvas, William, Duke of Aquitaine, Geoffrey of Vendôme, and William, son of the Count of Nevers. They besieged Carrouges, which was taken in three days. Écouché was burned and destroyed, so that its inhabitants fled from the flames. At Asnebec, Robert of Neubourg made terms with Geoffrey and surrendered the castle. Geoffrey approached the castle at Montreuil, which Richard Basset had newly fortified with stone walls. The invaders attacked but failed to break in, and had to abandon the attempt. But at Les Moutiers-Hubert Geoffrey was again successful against the castellan, Paynel, who was defeated in a fight and captured along with his castle. Painel and thirty other captive knights were ransomed for a good profit.

As the invading force advanced on Lisieux, the Normans, on Stephen's behalf, sought to halt them with a hastily gathered army. Additional defenders were thrown into Lisieux under the command of Alan of Penthièvre. Waleran of Beaumont, Count of Meulan, led the field army to face the enemy. Orderic says that when the Angevins approached, the garrison at Lisieux, and especially the newly arrived 'Bretons' panicked and burnt the town.[26] It seems more likely that it was done deliberately to deny its provisions and shelter to the invader. Orderic somewhat illogically continues in praise of Norman courage at being prepared to destroy their own town rather than 'bowing their necks to the yoke of foreign dominion'.

Geoffrey turned aside from Lisieux and went instead to Le Sap, where he attempted to capture the castle. Orderic says the place was named after a tall silver fir tree which had once stood near the church in the village. Fires were started by both sides, and in the confusion that same village church of Saint Peter was burnt down. The castle was stormed, and the garrison overwhelmed.

But the thirteen-day campaign, successful to this point, had been wearing. The invaders had faced constant harassment from the local people. The Angevins were accused of committing atrocities, attacking priests and churches, but in their turn were sniped at and sometimes killed. Orderic admits that Geoffrey tried to restrict the damage, and forbade the desecration of holy objects, but says that he could not keep his men in order. Then on 1 October Geoffrey himself was wounded at Le Sap, when a javelin thrown at him pierced his right foot. It was ironic that it occurred on the very day that his wife, the Empress Matilda, arrived with reinforcements. At dawn the next day, badly wounded, Geoffrey decided to return home.

Such a raid inevitably required that the invaders should live off the land. The Angevins had killed flocks and herds, and eaten the meat half cooked or raw, and without salt or bread. There was plenty of food from the harvest, but not enough cooks who knew how to prepare it properly. Also, it may have been plentiful, but it provided an unbalanced diet. The consequence was the common plague of medieval armies, dysentery. The result is best described in Orderic's vivid account:

as a result of carelessly devouring uncooked food after desecrating consecrated buildings, by God's just judgement almost all suffered from dysentery; plagued by diarrhoea, they left a trail of filth behind and many were barely capable of dragging themselves back home.

The Normans made some efforts to attack the retreating Angevins, who were presumably easy to trail. But the Normans were surprised by the speed of the march, which shows a disciplined retreat rather than the humiliating flight at which Orderic hints. A few knights tried to block the crossing of the Don, but failed, though they did take some captives and some of the baggage train. The campaign had generally been a success for Geoffrey, and one must not be misled by Orderic's distortions, though his picture of the ailing Geoffrey catches the final miserable stages of the expedition 'carried home pale and groaning, lying in a litter', his baggage with his robes of state and precious vessels stolen along the way.

Normandy seems to have suffered more painfully, and for a longer time, from the death of Henry I than England. Probably the duchy had been less securely governed in any case. Henry's rule may have brought peace to England through his last years, but it had seen almost constant warfare in Normandy. Geoffrey's invasion and devastation had done damage to the districts he had traversed. Some Norman lords had taken matters into their own hands; and at least two, William Talvas and Roger of Tosny, had seen their lands put under an interdict for acts against the church. The year 1137 also proved to be one of drought, with a water shortage.[27] It was certainly time for Stephen to intervene and restore ducal authority. Towards the end of March 1137 Stephen crossed to Normandy, landing at Saint-Vaast-la-Hougue. It may sound a long time, but in effect Stephen had taken a year to settle his English realm, not an unconscionable age, and prepare for a major Norman expedition, which was not an unreasonable amount of time.

Now he raised a force, including chiefly Flemish mercenaries. He hoped to settle his relationship with Louis VI, King of France, and with his own brother, Theobald, Count of Blois. He also, of course, had to deal with Geoffrey of Anjou. One good sign was that Geoffrey's ally during the 1136 invasion, William of Aquitaine, had undergone a change of heart. He had made terms with the King of France, arranging for his daughter Eleanor to marry Louis le Jeune, the son and heir of Louis VI. He then undertook a pilgrimage to Compostella where he died. Geoffrey had lost one important ally.

Following the itinerary of Stephen given by Robert of Torigny, which is preferable to that given by Orderic Vitalis, though the latter has generally been adopted by historians, we see Stephen undertaking several other tasks before attempting to engage with Geoffrey, Count of Anjou.[28] The king's first effort was to deal with rebellion by Rabel de Tancarville. Three strongholds belonging to the baron were attacked and taken: Lillebonne, Villers-Chambellan and Mézidon. Another rebel, described by Orderic as a brigand, was Roger le Bègue, in the Evrecin. Stephen attacked his castle at Grossoeuvre, and forced it to surrender, so 'the region enjoyed peace for a little while after great oppression'.[29] Others soon showed themselves ready to make their peace with him. Next to do so was his brother Theobald, whom he met at Évreux. The latter had harboured resentment over losing Normandy to his younger brother, but the two now met, and Stephen promised him a pension from his English revenues if Theobald would agree to give up any claim he had, and recognize his brother. Theobald accepted these terms.

Stephen then sought to make an agreement with the old King of France, Louis VI. They had a meeting on the Norman border, and it was agreed that Stephen's son Eustace should do homage to Louis for the duchy. Stephen was now officially recognized by Normandy's suzerain, and his position in the duchy seemed unassailable. In quick time, Stephen had settled two major relationships in a manner favourable to himself.

The expedition looked well on the way to being a triumphal success. But Geoffrey of Anjou was less tractable. Indeed, in 1137 he once again invaded Normandy, and it looked as if battle might determine their respective claims. However, while Stephen had been making the above arrangements, trouble had already been brewing between his own people. His chief military lieutenant was the Flemish noble, William of Ypres, and Flemish mercenaries made up a good proportion of the force brought from England. The Flemings, and probably the pretensions of William of Ypres in particular, seem to have irritated the Normans. The Norman nobility expected to be given priority at the duke's court over an illegitimate Fleming and his mercenary following. Throughout the campaign there was bad feeling between the two groups. Some of the local nobility just packed up and went home.

We have reports of two incidents which fuelled a more serious break. The first, which we have already examined, saw Robert of Gloucester, probably contemplating desertion, being ambushed on the orders of William of Ypres. Robert escaped and for a time brooded over his future action. The second incident, which may have been related, saw a brawl between the Norman and Flemish troops which broke up the army.

Geoffrey of Anjou had come into Normandy in May 1137 with an even greater force in May, obviously meaning to provoke Stephen. He brought devastation to the Hiémois, and fired Bazoches-au-Houlme, where sixteen people sheltering in the church were burnt to death. Monasteries agreed to pay protection money to the Angevins to prevent themselves suffering a similar fate – which sounds not unlike the *tenserie* levied in England by individual barons later during the wars. With the king engaged in negotiation, William of Ypres had sought battle, but lacking support from the Normans, had turned back to join the king. Stephen was still attempting to win over Norman support, and had success at least with Rabel de Tancarville, Rotrou of Mortagne and Richer de l'Aigle.

Stephen still aimed to bring Geoffrey to battle and now moved southwards to Lisieux where he assembled his force again, ready to besiege one of the castles which Geoffrey had taken over, and where he hoped to bring the Count of Anjou himself. It was at this moment that the incident of the brawl occurred at Livarot, near Lisieux. For some reason one of the Flemings made off with a barrel of wine which belonged to a squire of the Norman lord, Hugh of Gournay.[30] It was spark enough to fire the scarcely suppressed hostility between the Normans and the

Flemings. There was a violent brawl in which men on both sides were killed. Various of the Norman nobles took this as sufficient excuse to collect their men and leave without a word to the king. Stephen of course was furious. He chased after them as far as Pont-Audemer and did persuade some to return to the army, including Hugh of Gournay and some other 'hot-headed youths'. [31] But although he restored some sort of order, Stephen had to abandon the idea of a battle. How many men he had lost is not clear, but in any case he could hardly rely on the divided army. Given this situation, he made the best of it he could. There were negotiations with Geoffrey of Anjou, and a three-year truce was agreed, with Stephen to pay a pension to the count. [32]

The conclusion of the Norman expedition was disappointing, but by no means disastrous. Before leaving, Stephen dealt with further disturbers of the peace in the duchy. He destroyed the troublesome castle at Guitry in the Vexin, and caused the death of another troublemaker in Richard Silvanus in the Avranchin. This shows that during his visit, Stephen moved about widely, seeking to restore order; he was 'extremely active and vigorous' throughout the campaign. [33] Stephen had made good terms with the King of France, and had reconciled his brother. As for the Angevin threat, the truce simply delayed any final outcome, but Geoffrey did not seem to have made much progress in 1137. Stephen's arrival in Normandy had prevented the second invasion having as great a success even as the first. Geoffrey in two years had made a little progress, but not much beyond his initial base. Nor was he to make much for years yet to come. Stephen did not come back to Normandy, but until 1141, his position was well defended by those he appointed to the task, including William de Roumare, Roger of the Cotentin, and Waleran of Beaumont. Any threat for Stephen from France seemed further diminished when Louis VI died in the summer of 1137, leaving his mild mannered son to succeed as Louis VII, under the tutelage of Stephen's brother Theobald. Through the rest of the reign Stephen would generally have the support of Louis VII against the Plantagenets. But the events in Normandy had begun to draw a line between opposing elements. Stephen had brought some sort of order, but what had occurred confirmed that the worst threat came from Geoffrey of Anjou, and those who opposed Stephen in Normandy were Geoffrey's natural allies. The expedition had shown that if the Normans had little liking for Geoffrey of Anjou, they also felt little loyalty towards Stephen of Blois.

THE EMPRESS MATILDA'S PARTY

It was only when Robert of Gloucester made his defiance that Matilda's support in England became clear, but those who then joined her cause had for the most part been already inclined towards her for her father's sake, or had been alienated by the actions of Stephen in the early part of his reign. There were two main strands to the support: a personal support for those who were to remain loyal to her, and a support which depended largely on Robert of Gloucester's affinity, whose ties to the earl brought them inevitably on to the side he supported in the war. Some of course fell into both categories. Outside of England there was also

The twelfth-century Exchequer Building at Caen.

the important inclination towards her cause of her uncle, David, King of Scots, but for the time being that was not a very active support.

In England, initially, there were really only three great men who sided with Matilda, and an interesting trio they make. Robert of Gloucester's position we have already discussed. He was perhaps the eldest of Henry I's illegitimate sons, known first as Robert of Caen, or sometimes Robert fitz Roy. His mother may have been Sibyl, the daughter of a citizen of Caen. He had been made Earl of Gloucester by his father in 1120, on marrying the heiress Mabel, daughter of Robert fitz Hamon who was holder of the honor of Gloucester, becoming probably the wealthiest of all the English nobility. He also held considerable estates in southern Wales and western Normandy. There seems to have been mutual love and respect between father and son, and Robert did better than most bastards. He was strongly attached to Henry I, and was present at his father's death. He is generally seen as a worthy man of his age, though his self-interest has become clearer more recently, and the rose-tinted view of his chronicler, William of Malmesbury, is more apparent. Even so, once he had committed himself to his half sister, his loyalty and devotion were admirable. And it is worth pointing out that, however biased, William of Malmesbury was one of our greatest historians, and he could admire Robert as his 'well-beloved lord'.[34]

The other two, who would be loyal to Matilda throughout their lives were Miles of Gloucester and Brian fitz Count. Both had connections with Earl Robert, but both probably took their position from a loyalty to her in person. Brian fitz Count was also probably illegitimate, the son of Alan IV Fergant, Duke of Brittany. He was distantly related to the empress. He was an able and literate man, who corresponded with such as Gilbert Foliot and Henry of Blois. He even wrote a work justifying his actions in support of the empress, reported but unfortunately now lost.[35] His fortune had been made by Henry I, who gave him in marriage the heiress, Matilda of Wallingford.[36] Like several of the Empress Matilda's supporters he had interests in Wales, being Lord of Abergavenny, as well as holding the honor of Wallingford in Berkshire. In May 1127 Brian and Earl Robert had escorted Matilda on her journey to Rouen in preparation for her marriage to Geoffrey, and it is tempting to think of their long-term alliance being forged on that occasion. There were some hints that Brian's feelings for Matilda went beyond those of a loyal subject, but any embroidery of this suggestion can only be fictional. There is, though, a charter of Matilda referring to 'the love and lawful service' of Brian.[37] So far as one can see, Brian had accepted Stephen's accession, but was ready to join Matilda as soon as she made any move to claim her rights.

The third of the group was Miles of Gloucester. His motives are hidden from us. If anything one might have expected him to stay with Stephen, though like the others he owed a debt in his rise to prominence to the old king, Henry I. Stephen, so far as we know, had done nothing at all to antagonize Miles. Indeed, the reverse was true. Miles had done very well from Stephen and had every reason to be grateful. He continued, as his father had done, to act as sheriff of Gloucester. His possessions in Brecknock, Hereford and Gloucester were confirmed and he was given Gloucester Castle to hold, perhaps in the hope that he would prove a counter to Robert. In a dispute, Stephen favoured Miles and his son at the expense of Gilbert de Lacy and Geoffrey Talbot. In 1138 Miles acted as welcoming host to Stephen in Gloucester, and he had also been of military assistance to Stephen, notably at Shrewsbury. His position in relation to Robert of Gloucester was ambivalent. As castellan of Gloucester Castle he could be seen as a natural rival to Robert as much as an ally. He was powerful enough not to be forced into joining Matilda against his will, and cannot be seen therefore as simply being obliged to follow where Robert took the lead. Nor, so far as we can see, did Miles have any particular attachment to Matilda, though his initial rise had certainly been thanks to her father, and as we have seen he had been chosen as one of the men to escort her for her wedding. The *Gesta Stephani* says that Miles was 'unquestioning in his loyalty to King Henry's children'. After Matilda's arrival in England, she spent most of her time at Gloucester under Miles' protection.[38]

Whatever the reason, an attachment to Matilda existed. Miles, like Brian, had surely been in contact with Robert of Gloucester before Matilda arrived in 1139. We can take William of Malmesbury's word for it, that Robert had been doing some secret canvassing before he made his move. He knew that he could expect help from certain quarters. His immediate actions on arrival in England in 1139, show that he anticipated the assistance of both Brian and Miles. The implication is that they had conspired in advance of Robert's open declaration, and together had prepared plans of action. The Worcester continuator does indeed refer to such a connection, saying that Miles and Robert had conspired to invite the empress to England, though he is surely incorrect in stating that Miles made any open declaration at this time.[39] Robert had not moved blindly and spontaneously. We may suspect that the plan was for Robert to bring Matilda to England, and then the others would come into the open, as indeed happened. Davis suggests that Miles may only have made up his mind to support Matilda because of the arrest of the bishops in 1139, but he had no particular connection to any of the bishops and was not an outstandingly religious man. A likely explanation is that Matilda, Robert, Brian and Miles respected each other and had bonded together in a determination to oust Stephen.[40]

Miles was perhaps the most able military leader of the trio, all of whom were good commanders. He was intelligent and decisive in his acts. The probability is that Robert of Gloucester knew his man and made efforts to ensure that Miles ended on the right side. This sort of persuasion is suggested by the later apparently unsolicited act of Brian fitz Count, who in return for Miles' aid at Wallingford, made a gift to him of his lordship in Wales, a highly unusual act in this period. It looks as if Robert and Brian were both desperately keen to make sure that Miles stayed in the imperial camp. All three of these supporters of Matilda held considerable lands in Wales, which gave another strong motive for acting together.

At the opening of the war, Matilda's support consisted of little more than these three men and their followings, though there were others in rebellion against Stephen for their own reasons, who would naturally side with Matilda, as well as men who were still uncertain which way to jump. Matilda's support was relatively small, confined mainly to a group of barons whose chief holdings were in the west country and Wales. But they had the advantage of making a geographically compact group for military operations, and the perhaps greater advantage of being exceptionally able military leaders. Matilda was fortunate at least in the quality of the men she had attracted to her side.

STEPHEN'S SUPPORTERS

Stephen apparently had a much broader support. He had the advantage of being the anointed and crowned king. Therefore, military action against him was rebellion; legally and morally unacceptable. But as war approached, men asked themselves narrower questions about their loyalties. There were many who hesitated to oppose a king, but who were not especially eager to fight for him either. Stephen, like Matilda, in the end, would have to rely on those who were really committed to his cause. More men stayed at Stephen's court than joined the empress, but unlike her, he could be less sure in those around him – which of them were to be trusted.

As the reign progressed, certain men came to the fore in the royal circle as being especially favoured and trusted by the king. Stephen also worked to establish a rather different network of control to that of Henry I. Stephen's preference was for placing great responsibility on the leading magnates. He did promote men, but he relied chiefly on top ranks of the existing nobility. Under Stephen there were not the type of 'new men' favoured by Henry I, often nobles

The seal of King Stephen.

but of small standing previously. The number of new creations of earls made by him, clarifies this policy. There has been some debate over the real strength of some of his appointments – were they really all earls or were some only given county territories? The likelihood seems to be that they were truly intended to be powerful men in their own regions, and that included being powerful militarily. Of course in some areas where he failed to establish full power his appointees failed to establish their authority too. But it is probably fair to say over all that Stephen's earls were the backbone of his support. These men were all of existing high rank, though some had not previously held earldoms.

However, in the war which followed, Stephen's chief military lieutenant was not an earl, but William of Ypres. William was, though, Earl of Kent in all but name. It is uncertain why he was not created an earl; perhaps because he was an outsider and virtually a mercenary, perhaps because it was felt the creation would antagonize the Count of Flanders. William of Ypres was to remain in something of an exceptional position throughout the reign. As an illegitimate descendant of the Counts of Flanders, son of Philip of Ypres and grandson of Count Robert the Frisian, he had twice sought to become Count of Flanders himself, and twice failed, during the period which saw the fall of one dynasty of counts and the rise of another. He had been imprisoned for a while, released and forced into exile in 1133, and became a captain in the employ of Stephen. His position as trusted adviser of the king made him an object of jealousy and scorn, and he seems to have aroused particularly strong feelings as we have already seen in Normandy. But he was an experienced and able military commander, a man of high noble rank in Flanders, and one of Stephen's most loyal supporters.

At the heart of the new regime was a noble family which Stephen much favoured, and who like William of Ypres, aroused resentment and jealousy. These were the Beaumonts: the twin sons of Robert, Count of Meulan, and their relatives.[41] Count Robert had been a faithful servant, almost a friend, of Henry I, and had become a wealthy and powerful baron in his own right. His broad estates were divided, when his twin sons came of age, the English section in the main going to Robert who became Earl of Leicester, the Norman part to Waleran, who succeeded to his father's title as Count of Meulan. Their younger brother, Hugh, became Earl of Bedford through Stephen in 1137, while their cousin Roger had been Earl of Warwick since 1119. Gilbert of Clare, made Earl of Pembroke by Stephen in 1138, was their brother-in-law. A number of other relatives also held important posts in the church in England and Normandy. Although already holding a great deal of land, the Beaumonts still owed a debt to Stephen for various appointments and gifts, including the earldom of Worcester to Waleran, probably in 1138. The twins' mother had remarried, to William of Warenne, Earl of Surrey, and her child by the new marriage became William III, Earl of Surrey.

They proved, at first, enthusiastic supporters of Stephen. Waleran had once, as a young man, rebelled against Henry I and fought a losing battle against the king's men at Bourg-Théroulde. He had been defeated, captured and imprisoned, and though later released, could never have been entirely trusted by Henry I. He threw himself into supporting the new king. The twins gave invaluable aid to Stephen in the first years. Robert's loyalty in the end outlasted Waleran's, though from neither of them did it outlast the reign. But in the period before the civil war began, the Beaumonts seemed the mainstay of the regime, to such an extent that many believed they had undue influence over Stephen. It is clear that their position was resented by others, who felt the Beaumonts were usurping their own position, including Robert, Earl of Gloucester, the richest English magnate, Roger, Bishop of Salisbury, the head of Henry I's English administration, and probably Henry of Blois, the king's brother. The English and Norman nobles who gave Stephen his central support proved to have less military ability than those supporting Matilda. Stephen's war in England was conducted primarily by himself and William of Ypres, though others carried on the defence of Normandy, including Count Waleran.

At first the leading ecclesiastics in England, and the leading administrators, gave the king their services, but in few cases was this from outright loyalty. William of Corbeil, Archbishop of Canterbury, who had crowned Stephen, only lived until 1136. The election that then occurred caused difficulties for Stephen. It is thought that his brother, Henry of Blois, desired the archbishopric. The election was delayed for some time. In the end it took place without Henry being present. This has generally been presented as a deliberate ploy to get him out of the way while it occurred. This view seems doubtful. Had Stephen ever attempted to get his brother elected as archbishop, there would certainly have been an outcry, and it is unlikely that the papacy would have approved. The

The seal of William of Corbeil, Archbishop of Canterbury.

election which took place in 1139 was perfectly proper, in the presence of the papal legate Alberic of Ostia, who outranked any churchman then in England and whose views must have been predominant in the procedure followed. An excellent candidate was chosen in Theobald, Abbot of Bec. The election was at Westminster, and Henry of Blois was only at Saint Paul's nearby. To claim that the abbot of the prestigious house of Bec, which had already produced two great Archbishops of Canterbury in Lanfranc and Anselm, was a nonentity and unworthy is just ridiculous.[42] It would be difficult to find a more deserving candidate, and he was undoubtedly a better choice than Henry of Blois in the circumstances. If Henry nevertheless resented his exclusion, as he may have done, the fault is with him and his ambitions. Henry's actions in due course would demonstrate less than wholehearted support of his brother, though this did not become entirely apparent until after the arrest of the bishops.

THE ARREST OF THE BISHOPS

Stephen's standing in the church was to be greatly diminished by his action in 1139 of arresting three of the English bishops; those of Salisbury, Ely and Lincoln. We are moving towards the opening of the war, and this was an event which very much helped to draw the lines for that conflict. The three bishops were virtually in control of Henry I's administration by the time of that king's death. Their adherence to

A bishop's crosier from the mid-twelfth century.

Stephen in 1135 was vital, but their loyalty thereafter was open to question. Many at the time saw them as overpowerful, and even William of Malmesbury, no friend of Stephen, thought that in 1139 they got what they deserved.

This is not a case where one can determine finally rights and wrongs. We shall never know for certain how far the bishops had involved themselves in the conspiracy of Robert of Gloucester, but Stephen certainly believed they were so far in that they constituted a serious danger. The *Gesta Stephani*, whose author was either a bishop or close to one, seems to accept that the suspicion is correct, and writes that Roger 'was suspected of betraying his king and lord, and giving support to the Angevin party'.[43] His action against them, therefore, had the intention of gaining control of the valuable castles they held between them. He afterwards claimed that he acted against them as holders of castles and not as bishops. He won his case to the extent that the papacy never took direct action against him over the matter.

The leader of the bishops was Roger, Bishop of Salisbury. He had long been a valuable servant to Henry I. In his earlier career he had been a poor priest at Caen in Normandy. It was said he had first come to the king's attention when Prince Henry was campaigning in Normandy, and had turned aside for mass at the church where Roger was priest, and the latter had shown how quickly he could get through the service so that Henry could continue with his hunting: 'they

Said to be the head of Roger of Salisbury, Salisbury Cathedral.

claimed that a more suitable chaplain for military men could not be found'. He was then taken on in the prince's entourage, and 'although he was practically unlettered, he nevertheless so shrewdly managed things by his natural astuteness, that within a short time he became dear to his master and conducted his most confidential affairs'.[44] Other evidence associates him as a priest with Avranches in western Normandy. He soon became Henry's chancellor, benefiting from his master's rise to the royal throne, and was made Bishop of Salisbury in 1101. During the king's absences in Normandy, Roger was at times responsible for the government of England, acting as a viceroy. Roger was certainly one of those rather worldly clerics whose abilities lay in efficient administration rather than spiritual example. We know that in 1139 he had a mistress, Matilda of Ramsbury, who was holding Devizes Castle in his name. The bishop also had an illegitimate son, Roger, by Matilda of Ramsbury, who was employed within the administration as a chancellor. He is called Roger the Poor, though the reason for the nickname is not known. From his age it seems likely that he was conceived after Roger became a bishop. It is possible they had a second son, called Adelelm, who was also a royal servant as a treasurer.[45] Both Roger the Poor and Adelelm were given archdeaconries in Salisbury, so Bishop Roger was guilty of yet another ecclesiastical abuse, that of nepotism.

The two other bishops involved in the 1139 incident were also relatives of Bishop Roger; his nephews Nigel and Alexander. The word nephew in the twelfth century was often a euphemism for son, but in this case they probably were

Old Sarum, motte and ditch, Roger of Salisbury's castle at Salisbury.

genuinely nephews, the sons of the bishop's brother, Humphrey. They had both been excellently educated, and had attended the cathedral school at Laon. They also benefited from the patronage of their uncle, both gaining archdeaconries in Salisbury, before going on to their bishoprics. Alexander became bishop of the large and wealthy see of Lincoln in 1123, and Nigel, having been a royal treasurer, was then appointed to the bishopric of Ely in 1133. Nigel is also thought to have been the author of the work known as the *Constitutio Domus Regis* (The Composition of the Royal Household), written probably early in Stephen's reign. To complete the circle of this amazing family group, we must mention Bishop Nigel's son, Richard fitz Nigel, who also became a treasurer, and Bishop of London, and was author of the famous *Dialogus de Scaccario* (Dialogue of the Exchequer).[46]

Stephen inherited the services of this powerful family group. They virtually ran the English administration, and had enriched themselves further during Henry I's reign, possessing between them great wealth, and some of the most important castles in the country, including Sherborne, Devizes, Malmesbury, Salisbury, Ely, Sleaford and Newark. Although Henry I had received good service from the group, there is the possibility of some change in Bishop Roger's standing, and he may have lost something of his apparently unassailable position. One could also suggest that Henry I was mistaken in allowing such a tight-knit group so much power at the head of affairs. It certainly posed a serious problem for his successor. Stephen had not the same reasons to receive their gratitude, and

The remains of Sherborne Old Castle.

would never be able to trust them as Henry had. It would have been in his interests to break up their hold on government, even if they gave him no obvious cause. In the event they gave him very good cause indeed, by conspiring with the pro-Angevins before the civil war broke out. Evidence was brought to Stephen on this account, and it was good enough to convince him. It is inconceivable that he would have acted without good grounds, as he is often accused of doing. We cannot prove the matter either way, as is so often the case with conspiracies, but the evidence strongly hints at the intention of Roger to join the Angevin party. It was also said that, although he had the favour of King Henry I, his own affection had been more for the king's children; one assumes by that meaning Matilda and Robert. The chronicler also suggests that Roger avoided offending Stephen on the surface, but secretly kept faith with Henry's offspring. At the same time he was surrounded by a 'numerous bodyguard of troops', and was filling his strong and newly fortified castles with weapons and supplies 'on a very lavish scale', which suggests preparations for immediate use.[47] Orderic writes that 'he was suspected of betraying his king and lord, Stephen, and giving support to the Angevin party. He was backed by his kinsmen and accomplices'.[48] William of Malmesbury reports that a group of laymen, who resented the bishops' power and wealth, came to Stephen and told him the three were planning to hand over their castles to Matilda when she arrived. William says that Stephen was slow to be convinced because he had previously favoured them.[49] The *Gesta Stephani* identifies Waleran of Meulan as the spokesman of the lords against the bishops, and says that the bishops were plotting 'against the majesty of the crown'.[50] The author, in a somewhat obscure passage, seems to condemn the Beaumont twins as being like 'the sons of Korah' (a good match perhaps for a daughter of Zelophehad), who would be swallowed up for opposing properly constituted authority.[51] It has also been seen as significant that a cleric patronized by the Beaumonts, Philip of Harcourt, became chancellor after the fall of the Salisbury group, but it only demonstrates the favour in which they were held, not the motive for the arrest.

Both Orderic and the author of the *Gesta Stephani* suggest that what followed was set up deliberately, but the incident sounds like a spontaneous event of which the king took advantage. It is notable that, despite their accusations, the various sources cannot agree on who was responsible for starting the trouble. An assembly of magnates, an interesting constitutional meeting, met at Oxford in June 1139.[52] The three bishops also set out to attend, though Roger had experienced some foreboding of evil and been reluctant to go. A quarrel broke out between the men of Bishop Roger and those of Alan of Penthièvre over their respective lodgings. Others suggest that the Beaumont twins were also involved. It started off with the followers shouting abuse at each other, and ended with swords being drawn. In the fight several men on both sides were killed, but by William of Malmesbury's account, Alan's men suffered most and 'the bishop's men did not gain their victory without loss of blood'. The king, on the legally justified grounds that the peace of his court had been broken, demanded that named castles be handed over as guarantees of their future behaviour. The bishops refused, and therefore he arrested the two who were present, for breaking the peace. Although the author of the *Gesta Stephani* says the court was made up of the 'ill-disposed', he nevertheless shows that the king did not act hastily, but first called a council to determine action against the bishops, and the result suggests that there must have been quite a wide consensus of opinion against them.[53] Roger of Salisbury and Alexander of Lincoln were taken into custody; Roger arrested in the court, Alexander rooted out of his lodgings. Bishop Nigel had not reached Oxford, and was lodging in a nearby village. News of the affray was brought to him and he immediately rode for a safer haven in Devizes Castle, which was held for his uncle, Bishop Roger. There Nigel prepared to defend himself, even devastating the country round about in true military fashion. If there were no conspiracy involving the empress, it seems odd that he should have chosen to go to this west country fortress, which was Bishop Roger's and not his own, since Oxford was not particularly close to it, and that he should act in such a provocative manner. After all, there could be no charge against Bishop Nigel with regard to the affair at court. Orderic says he fled because he was 'conscious of his own guilt'.[54] The charge against him was rather open rebellion against the king.

Stephen then pursued Bishop Nigel to Devizes. He took with him Roger the Poor in chains, and his father Bishop Roger not chained. Salisbury, Sherborne and Malmesbury Castles were surrendered to the king, but Devizes prepared to resist. William of Malmesbury says that Bishop Roger undertook voluntary fasting to persuade his nephew to surrender.[55] However, Orderic says it was the king who threatened to starve him unless the castle was handed over. Stephen also set up a gallows and threatened to hang Roger the Poor before the walls, knowing that his mother, Matilda of Ramsbury was within. A rope was fastened around the unfortunate chancellor's neck and he was led towards the gallows. She reacted immediately, jumping up and calling out: 'I gave him birth, and it can never be right for me to cause his destruction'.[56] She at once sent a messenger to Stephen and agreed to surrender the castle 'she was holding'. Stephen then took Bishop Alexander off to his own area, where he handed over the keys to Newark and Sleaford Castles after Stephen threatened to starve him unless he gave them up. It took prayers and tears from the bishop before his garrison at Newark gave way.[57]

Stephen claimed that he had arrested the three not as bishops, but as 'sinners against the pacific office of a bishop and suspected enemies of his peace and public order, until by the restoration to Caesar of their castles and those things that belonged to Caesar, the king was safer from suspicion of rebellion [the charge alleged against the bishops] and his country was more tranquil', though the author himself clearly opposed such action against bishops.[58] Henry of Blois criticized his brother for his action against the church, and shows how little Stephen could expect from Henry. The bishop spoke in support of the freedom of the church, but perhaps with the bitterness of a man disappointed in not getting the archbishopric. He said of the arrested bishops, 'it was not for the king to judge them, but for the canon law'.[59] Bishop Henry then called a council at Winchester for the church to debate the question. There he condemned his brother of a 'lamentable crime', in a speech given in Latin, and sought to get a general condemnation.[60] Stephen did not turn up in person, but sent representatives. His case was put by Aubrey de Vere 'a man practised in many kinds of cases', in a mild and restrained manner, though others present shouted insults at Bishop Roger.[61] Aubrey said that it was not the first time that Bishop Roger's men had caused trouble at court. It does indeed seem odd that these bishops were accustomed to coming to court accompanied by their own private armies. Aubrey said that it was the bishops' men who had attacked the others in the brawl, inspired by Bishop Alexander's long-held hatred for Alan of Penthièvre. He now openly accused Roger of favouring 'the king's enemies', and said that when Matilda arrived 'he would take her side together with his nephews and his castles'.[62] He said that Roger had already refused entry at Malmesbury to a royal force under Roger Mortimer.

Bishop Roger blustered in his own defence, and said if he did not get satisfaction from this court, he would go to a higher one. Bishop Henry demanded that Stephen reinstate the bishops and abide by church law. But the Archbishop of Rouen arrived at the council and spoke in the king's defence. He subtly undermined the bishops' defence of the three prelates, saying that 'he would allow the bishops to have their castles if they could prove by the canon law that they were entitled to have them'.[63] Of course it was clear to all that canon law provided no defence for such a position. The archbishop added a further telling point: that even if the bishops should hold the castles, yet they 'ought to hand over the keys of their fortifications to the disposal of the king, whose duty it is to fight for the peace of all'; it was the right of the king to have castles rendered to him.[64] The bishops, having handed over their castles, were released, 'downcast and stripped of all their empty and ostentatious splendour, to hold their church property in the simple fashion that befits a churchman'.[65]

Bishop Roger was a broken man who played little further part in affairs. Bishop Alexander seemed reformed by the episode and henceforth acted as a loyal bishop to the king; Bishop Nigel on the other hand, bided his time before openly joining the Angevin party. A further council was held which ruled that all the military possessions of the bishops should properly now be in the king's hands. Stephen had survived the incident. He was not censured officially, and not excommunicated. Apparently voluntarily, when it was all over, he put off his rich royal robes, and 'with a contrite heart, humbly accepted the penance enjoined for his fault'.[66] The bishops' castles remained in his hands. As the civil war loomed, the possession of these vital fortifications was a boon to his position. It also meant that Stephen could reconstruct his government. This has always been seen as a disastrous moment because he lost the services of so many experienced administrators. In practice it also had many advantages. It was not difficult to find trained administrators, men like Philip of Harcourt. What Stephen was now able to ensure was that his administrators were loyal men, dependent upon himself. At the same time there was a purge of sheriffs, and those with connections to the Salisbury group were removed. It has often been argued that Stephen's sheriffs were military as well as administrative appointments, as were his earldoms. Given the critical nature of the situation, it seems a very wise move to make sure that these vital positions were filled by men who could be trusted.

THE BREAKDOWN OF PEACE

Although the civil war did not begin properly until Matilda and Robert of Gloucester arrived in England, the fighting had already started in a series of spontaneous rebellions against the king. At least this is how the disturbances are usually seen, and no doubt some of them were purely coincidental risings. But a different picture can be presented over the majority of the rebellions which began in 1138 and 1139. Robert of Bampton, the earlier rebel, was a west country lord, and indeed his fortification of Castle Cary, became a bone of contention in the new wave of revolts. Even the rebellion of Baldwin de Redvers might come into this same category, with his strong attachment to Henry I which was transferred to his daughter Matilda. It was said that his revolt in the first place had been encouraged by the Angevin party, who then let him loose on Normandy. The *Gesta Stephani* saw the rebellions as like the hydra of Hercules: 'when one head was cut off two or more grew in its place'. Yet this gives a misleading picture of the period, as if it is all confusion without any coherence. The rebellions can be viewed as part of the conspiracy in favour of Matilda which predates even Robert's declaration of defiance in 1138, let alone his arrival in England in 1139. The suggestion is that most of these risings were coordinated as the first efforts in the war for Matilda's succession.

This thesis seems underlined by a study of the people and places of revolt. The vast majority of the places concerned were in the west country, and the vast majority of the rebels had strong connections with Robert of Gloucester. The

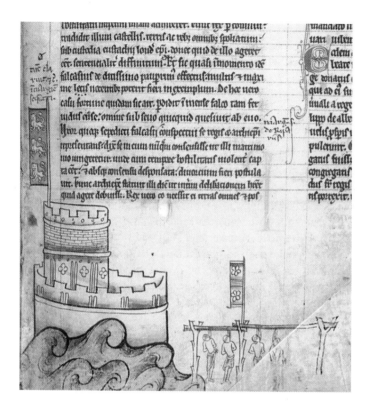

Bedford Castle, showing the tower. This represents the events of the siege of Bedford, under Henry III. (Corpus Christi College, Cambridge, MS 16, f. 64r)

view can also be contested that Stephen's reaction to this outburst of trouble was a meaningless rushing about hither and thither. He was well aware of the significance of the risings, and his reaction was militarily competent. In fact, during the period of more than a year between Robert's defiance and his appearance at Arundel, Stephen had virtually crushed the opposition which had raised its head to that point. What he was doing was seeking to enforce the forfeiture of Robert of Gloucester's lands in England, and he had very nearly succeeded. Only Bristol stood out strongly in defiance, and by 1139 Stephen had isolated it. In many ways what we are examining here is the first campaign of the civil war, and certainly the rebels of 1138 to 1139 were declaring their stance for that combat.

The revolt at Bedford was early, and rather outside the group we are looking at, but worth a moment of our time, because of the men involved. Stephen had made the youngest Beaumont brother, Hugh, Earl of Bedford, and obviously meant him to have Bedford Castle, which he saw as royal. It was held for the king by Miles Beauchamp, and Stephen made a placatory offer to him of honours and gifts, which was refused. Miles saw Bedford as an hereditary possession. Although it was Christmas, Stephen mounted a force and angrily went against Bedford. Stephen used archers to attack the vulnerable points, harassing their lookouts. Royal guards were posted by the exits, and ordered to keep watch at night.

Engines were built and used to throw stones against the stockade and the wall. Having set up the blockade, Stephen left his men to carry it through. It was a model siege, lasting five weeks, by which time the garrison was prepared to surrender.

The reason that Stephen was not in the north for the Battle of the Standard was the outbreak of serious revolt in the west, initiated by Geoffrey Talbot. Robert made his defiance in May; and as Henry of Huntingdon says: 'after Easter the treason of the English nobles burst forth with great fury'.[67] This outbreak almost coincided with Robert's defiance, and the timing is surely no accident. Geoffrey Talbot took over Hereford and defied the king. As so often, the citizens of the town welcomed Stephen, who recaptured the castle when the garrison, seeing the size of his army, surrendered. Geoffrey had fled to Weobley, and Stephen followed and captured that also. Both places were then garrisoned by the king. After Stephen had gone from Hereford, Geoffrey returned and fired the town. John of Worcester says that he then joined Robert of Gloucester at Bristol. Robert cannot have been there in 1138, but there is little reason to doubt that Geoffrey Talbot aligned himself with the Angevin party.

A little later he appeared at Bath:

> where little springs through hidden conduits send up waters heated without human skill or ingenuity from deep in the bowels of the earth to a basin vaulted over with noble arches . . . [where] the sick from all over England gather to wash away their infirmities in the health-giving waters . . . to see the wondrous jets of hot water and bathe in them'.[68]

The wonders of Roman Bath had not altogether vanished by the twelfth century. Geoffrey, accompanied by his relative Gilbert de Lacy, attacked the city with scaling ladders. A surprise sortie by the bishop's men captured Geoffrey; they fettered him, and threw him in a dungeon. Under a guarantee the bishop came for talks, but they treacherously took him prisoner and threatened to hang him unless Geoffrey was released. This was done, much to the chagrin of Stephen.

Meanwhile, on the Welsh border, four castles at Overton, Whittington, Bryn and Ellesmere were held against the king by William Peverel, but although we lack narrative detail of the events, they were also taken over by the king. Nearby Shrewsbury also revolted under William fitz Alan, who was a nephew by marriage to Robert of Gloucester, having married his niece Christina. Shrewsbury was besieged by the king in August, and was stormed. William fitz Alan and his wife and children had escaped, leaving the siege to his unfortunate uncle, who refused the offered terms. When Stephen captured Shrewsbury, as allowed by the laws of war to a victor who had taken a castle by force, he hanged or otherwise executed the garrison of some 93 men and its commander, Arnulf de Hesdin.[69] As a result of this ruthless treatment, other castellans came to the king at once to hand over their keys. Again, this region of rebellions is consistent with our thesis, being in the west country and on the Welsh marches.

A whole host of smaller castles, dependent on Bristol and Robert of Gloucester, joined the revolt: Castle Cary now under Ralph Lovell, Harptree under William

Dover Castle, with ships in the background. (Corpus Christi College, Cambridge, MS 26, f. i.r)

fitz John, Dunster under William de Mohun, and Wareham under Robert fitz Alured; and another group associated with the Welsh marches, including Dudley and Ludlow. There can be little doubt given the geographical positioning of these places, and the political, feudal and personal links between most of them and Robert of Gloucester, that this was no accidental rash of rebellions, but a declaration in arms to accompany the defiance in words by their absent leader in Normandy.

Stephen chose to deal with the western rebellion, while leaving his wife to look after the more isolated problem at Dover. He went to Bath and ordered some improvements in the defences. Then he went on to Bristol on what was clearly part of a reconnaissance expedition. Some advised him to besiege the place immediately, but it was very much a matter of opinion which strategy was best. Stephen's choice was probably the wisest, and came near to success. Bristol was a powerful place and would not be easy to take. Stephen's decision was to capture the surrounding hostile fortifications one by one and gradually isolate Bristol. A siege of Bristol would have much more chance of success if friendly fortifications nearby were neutralized, so that supply and reinforcement would be that much more difficult. Therefore, the king attacked the important castles at Castle Cary and Harptree. These were held by Ralph Lovell and William fitz John, whom the *Gesta Stephani* says:

> were bound to the earl [Robert] by ties of friendship, firmly united with him by pledge and oath, and so much his allies by compact and homage that as soon as they learned he wished to rebel against the king's power, they joined in his rebellion promptly and by agreement.[70]

They ravaged the country around in order to obstruct Stephen.

Castle Cary stood on an impressive mound, and had a stone keep. Stephen starved it into submission. Nowadays it is a quiet and ignored site, the mound remaining, but only grassy heaps marking what was once a great castle. Stephen moved against Castle Cary more rapidly than its garrison expected. He set up engines and shot in fire and stones. Food ran short and the garrison surrendered on terms. They were also disappointed that despite his defiance, there was no sign of Robert of Gloucester. This comment in the *Gesta Stephani*, is probably the secret behind the rash of rebellions at this time.[71] The rebels of 1138 had expected, and probably been promised help from Normandy, but nothing had arrived so far. They had put themselves out on a limb. Then Stephen turned on Harptree. He considered building a counter castle, but decided it was not necessary, since his force at Bath could deal with it. Later, when the king was passing nearby Harptree, en route to Bristol, the garrison decided to make a sortie and attack his army on the march. They tracked him on his flank, thinking he did not realize. Then suddenly, Stephen turned his force and attacked Harptree with a cavalry force which reached the gates quickly. They took the remnants of the garrison by surprise, set fire to the gates, and placed ladders against the walls. The small rump of a garrison could not hold off the energetic attack, and Harptree succumbed. The king garrisoned it with his own men. Stephen also seems to have captured the four castles of William Peverel, as well as Wareham.

In 1139 Ludlow was taken. It was here that Henry, Prince of Scots, who had been brought to England by Stephen and was assisting the king at the siege, was nearly captured by a crow. This was an engine consisting of a sort of large fishing rod on a balance, with a hook on the end, which caught hold of the prince. However, he seems to have escaped its clutches. Henry of Huntingdon says that Stephen himself rescued the prince.[72]

Dover also fortified itself against Stephen. This would seem to be well beyond the pattern suggested above, but in fact it was not. Dover was Robert of Gloucester's, and held for him by Walkelin Maminot. Stephen's Queen, Matilda, blockaded the castle from the land side, and sent to Boulogne for aid from the sea. The blockade was thus closed. Stephen, meanwhile, had persuaded Robert of Ferrers, whom he had made Earl of Derby, to intervene. He was Walkelin Maminot's father-in-law, and managed to get the castellan to yield. Henry of Huntingdon says that Walkelin surrendered when he heard the news of Stephen's success and harshness at Shrewsbury.[73] In the south-east region, Leeds Castle in Kent had also revolted, but was taken for the king by Gilbert of Clare.

In 1139 a new rebel emerged in the west country in William de Mohun, who 'stirred up a mighty rebellion against the king'.[74] He held, and indeed had built, Dunster Castle, which he had filled with armed infantry and cavalry. He raided around with his troops. Stephen realized that it was a strong site, and built a counter castle to contain it. When the king needed to move on, he delegated command of the siege to Henry de Tracy, to whom Stephen had granted Barnstaple. The details of what followed are not given in any source, or we might have an additional battle to add to the few we know of in the period. At any rate Henry seems to have defeated a sizeable force of the Angevin supporters, and captured 104 knights, in a 'cavalry battle'.[75] The effect of that battle was to settle the problems caused by William de Mohun, and by other opponents of the king, including William fitz Odo. Henry also probably captured Torrington Castle for the king.[76]

The pro-Angevin castles around Bristol had been systematically reduced. The pro-Angevin rebels had been defeated in turn. Geoffrey Talbot was at large, but had suffered severe setbacks. The expected arrival of Robert of Gloucester had been too late to coincide with the outburst of rebellions in 1138 to 1139. Almost certainly, Robert's delay of some sixteen months between his defiance and his arrival, had been due to his need to see to his interests in Normandy and to persuade the empress to come to England, rather than to any dilatoriness on his own part, but Angevin interests were at a very low ebb by the time Matilda arrived at Arundel in 1139. As Davis says, Robert 'had lost nearly all his lands in southern England'.[77] It seemed only a matter of time before the last stronghold, Bristol, also fell into the king's hands. Stephen seemed to have little to fear. The first stage in the conflicts of the reign had been a very definite royal victory. As a result, Stephen probably became over confident.

CHAPTER 3

War

With the landing of Matilda at Arundel, the civil war may be thought to have begun, though as we have seen, the 'rebellions' of 1138 and 1139 seem to have been a concerted, if abortive, attempt to back Robert of Gloucester's defiance. Indeed, at the time, Matilda's arrival did not seem as noteworthy an event as it did afterwards. Stephen probably did not anticipate that it would have any great effect on the military situation, and he may have been right. It was the arrival of Robert of Gloucester which had the greater impact from this point of view. One doubts that Stephen would have arranged Robert's journey with an escort to Bristol or anywhere else in England. Events which seem puzzling to us, often make better sense if we try to block out knowledge of what happened afterwards, and try to see with the eyes of someone there.

In order to understand the civil war, we need some knowledge of the state of warfare by 1139, the developments in technology, and thinking which affected it. We need to know something of the tactics of dismounted knights, of the kind of arms and armour now favoured, and of the current state of fortification. So, before we tackle the events of 1139–40, let us turn aside to consider these matters briefly.

The experience of both Stephen and Robert of Gloucester, was of warfare as members of the household of Henry I. Both had fought for him. Both were therefore fully aware of the kind of methods used by the King of France and his allies. Both had some experience of the kind of war waged by Geoffrey of Anjou, and perhaps felt some resentment against him for his conflict with Henry in 1134–5. Both were grandsons of William the Conqueror, and were aware of the significance of the fighting methods of the Normans. No one in this age was ignorant of warfare in the East and of the crusades. Indeed, Stephen's father had fought in the First Crusade, where he is generally said to have disgraced himself by his flight from Antioch. I have argued elsewhere that this has been greatly exaggerated.[1] Count Stephen-Henry had been a highly respected leader of the crusade, indeed elected as its chief by the leading crusaders themselves. The problem had arisen during his own illness, which only his enemies sought to question, and had happened because of a particularly good relationship which he had built up with the Byzantine emperor. Some letters of the count back to his wife, Adela, give his own account of affairs. He did not flee in a cowardly manner. He did decide to return home, falsely believing that all was lost. It was a realistic assessment of the situation as he then knew it, and largely dependent on the fact that the Byzantine emperor chose not to assist the crusaders at Antioch.

Stephen-Henry had gone to seek aid for a desperate situation. When the emperor refused aid, having no army behind him, Stephen-Henry had no chance of breaking through to what seemed in any case like a lost stronghold. The comments by Anna Comnena on the incident need to be treated with caution, since she was chiefly concerned to protect her father's reputation. Only afterwards did it look like cowardice because the crusaders won a great, if unlikely, victory. Nor should we be too ready to believe waspish comments by unfriendly chroniclers, in particular by Orderic Vitalis, who pretended to knowledge of conversation between Stephen-Henry and Adela in their bedchamber, 'between conjugal caresses'. Was the chronicler hiding under the bed to obtain this information? What we truly know is that Stephen-Henry did return to the Holy Land, and then bravely fought in the continuing conflict, and lost his life in doing so. We must not forget that in the twelfth century most men were very provincial in their outlook; virtually all outsiders had to be ridiculed. Thus a Norman, perhaps especially if he himself were an outsider from England, like Orderic, was contemptuous of people like Geoffrey of Anjou, or Stephen-Henry of Blois. The English, even if they were of Norman origin, were equally contemptuous of the Scots, the Welsh and the Irish. The nearest neighbours were usually the most despised. Stephen-Henry was almost certainly much maligned over this episode, and undeservedly so, but his son Stephen knew of the sneers and the criticism, and it affected his view of warfare. He would not want to be seen as a coward, or give any excuse for such comment against himself.[2]

At the same time, like almost everyone else in the West, Stephen admired the achievements of the great crusaders. To what extent battle tactics and fortification methods of the East influenced development in the West remains controversial, but it is impossible not to believe that those crusaders who returned had not been affected by their experience, which included contact with Byzantine military methods, as well as those of the Saracens.

By the 1130s, the association between England and Normandy was a long-standing one. Only for relatively brief periods since 1066 had the two regions been separated. Both had been ruled together for some time, at least during the reigns of William I, William Rufus and Henry I. The troops which the kings used and the military system they depended upon, was largely Norman in origin, but had also been influenced by Anglo-Saxon traditions. The idea of agreed quotas for military service had been gradually introduced to England. The ruler, as king or duke, could call on military service in defence of the realm or duchy. In England the ruler had been able to hammer out individual deals with the magnates, to gain military service from the men of the magnates for national purposes.

Fundamentally, Stephen's plan of military organization seems to have been to treat earls as military governors acting on his behalf; thus he selected men of military ability and aristocratic standing, rather than officials. A large number of new earls was appointed during the crucial four years from 1138 to 1142, the only period of his reign when Stephen made a large number of appointments. The strategic placing of many of these earldoms is significant, including border regions such as Yorkshire (1138), Pembroke (1138), Worcester (1138/9), Northumbria (1139), and Herefordshire (1140), together with vital areas bordering on Angevin territories, such as Wiltshire (1140) and Cornwall (1140). Not all of these men were able to establish themselves, but the intention is clear: to have loyal men of ability in vital military regions, apart from the dubiously loyal Henry of Scots in Northumbria. They were also to be men of sufficient social standing to command respect in their regions and act with a degree of independence. William of Ypres was also given an equivalent position to that of an earl in Kent, an essential area to protect, because of its cross-Channel significance. And even the interior earldoms must not be left out of the military equation; no area was safe to neglect in a situation of civil war.

Royal control was important, and this was especially noticeable in the system of fortifications that had developed since 1066. Stephen was prepared to delegate a degree of power to his earls, but he expected to have rights over the royal castles, usually the key castles in a time of war. By the time of the Conquest, the Normans possessed castles in the duchy, used both as military centres and as residences for families, dependents and garrisons. They had developed both stone towers and the earth and timber fortifications, which we call motte and bailey castles. Excellent illustrations of this type of fortification, developing throughout northern France at the time, are found on the Bayeux Tapestry, both in Normandy and in Brittany. Naturally, when the Normans invaded and conquered England, they developed such castles there too. In fact, because Edward the Confessor had lived for some time in Normandy, and had a number of Normans whom he favoured in England, a few of these castles had been built in England even before 1066. But after 1066 they mushroomed, until the whole country seemed to be smothered with mounds and moats and baileys. England was now governed from, and by, castles.

The motte and bailey at Dinan, from the Bayeux Tapestry. The illustration shows the outer ditch and rampart, the motte, with a wooden stockade around the top, and a wooden keep.

The motte and bailey castles at Dol and Rennes in Brittany, from the Bayeux Tapestry. The castle at Dol (left) has a gatehouse and both are depicted with a bridge leading into the keep.

This is one reason why siege warfare was so far and away the most common kind of war in this period. Battles were very rare: only two major ones in a reign of constant border invasions and civil war, plus a few lesser skirmishes which we might just consider as battles, on the Welsh border, or at Wilton. There were no battles at all fought in Normandy, though from 1135 there was nearly constant war for a decade. Battles were very risky, their outcome very uncertain. No one risked battle unless fairly certain of victory, and to find two commanders in that frame of mind was not very common. Most good commanders avoided battle so far as possible. It has been said before, but it cannot be emphasized too greatly, since readers coming from other periods of history are often hard put to understand twelfth-century warfare unless they appreciate this basic fact. There was no disgrace in avoiding battle in most circumstances. Of course, war could have many aims: conquest, survival, expansion, defence, power, punishment, booty, order – and many others. The achievements and successes of war depended on the aims, as did the method of fighting. For example, in a war of conquest, one needed to establish firm authority over a region, and castles were extremely useful for that, defending against a hostile local population, and giving a secure base to conquering troops. In the Welsh border wars, where the Welsh aim was often to raid and collect booty, castles had a different use, more for containing mobile troops who could emerge to cope with raiders, often when on their way home.

With the dominance of siege war, the significance of the castle is only too obvious. The normal type of castle was the earthwork motte and bailey castle of the Norman period. This consisted typically of a large Christmas pudding shaped mound of earth, the motte, plus a larger and flatter mound which was the bailey. The motte was the chief defensive section of the castle, and could usually only be entered by a wooden bridge crossing a ditch of moat round the foot of the motte. The flattened top of the motte was protected by a palisade, and within that, built

Bayeux Castle, from the Bayeux Tapestry. The castle belonged to Bishop Odo of Bayeux, for whom the tapestry was made. The castle, seen here on the right, appears to have more elaborate decorations, including carvings of animals at the entrance.

on the top of the motte, was a tower keep. Within the keep lived the lord, his family, some retainers, and an armed garrison to defend it. The flattened mound of the bailey was also usually surrounded by a ditch or a wet moat, and a palisade, and any entrance would be defended. It would contain various buildings of use in the castle, probably some dwellings for lesser folk, store places, stables and so on. If a motte and bailey castle were attacked, the bailey would be defended, but usually the last ditch defence would be from the keep on the motte.

Archaeology has shown that there was in fact a variety of motte and bailey designs. That described above is typical but by no means universal. There were earthwork castles without mottes, castles with two mottes, castles with two or more baileys and so on. It all reminds us that although there was a model within men's minds, castles were generally built for individuals, and men have always fancied making improvements to their homes, or changes to suit themselves, or changes based on new fashions of which they had become aware.

Castles were certainly affected by fashions and by changes in ideas about defence. They were symbols of power and status as well as homes and fortifications. Therefore, lords liked their symbols to be up to date and impressive: they might improve the motte, add another bailey, or especially change the wooden palisades and keeps for stone ones. The Normans had been perfectly capable of building in stone, and there were stone towers in Normandy before the conquest, and early on in England. The two earliest in the kingdom, begun in the reign of William the Conqueror, were the White Tower in the Tower of London, and Colchester Castle. At first stone castles in England were scarce. Motte and baileys were cheaper to build, and quicker, and suited a situation of conquest and emergency. But as the disturbed condition eased, more castles were built or rebuilt in stone, both by the king and by the lords. By 1139, it was becoming rare to undertake any new building which was not mainly in stone, though the new disturbances of the civil war meant a temporary return to some motte and bailey construction.

Because castles had become stronger, with improved defences such as better gatehouses, towers built into the walls, battlement walks and so on, sieges tended to take longer. It was still possible, but less easy, to take a castle immediately with a storm attack. Therefore, castle besiegers had also to develop their techniques. Improvements were made in throwing engines for hurling stones and javelins. We do not know when the trebuchet was first introduced, but it may just have been at this time; certainly already men were interested in being able to throw heavier stones, further and with more force. The ballista and the mangonel were commonly used, as were great wooden towers on wheels for approaching walls. Mining was a common method of bringing down defences, and the throwing of fire often used to destroy gates or internal buildings. It was during Stephen's reign that Greek fire was first used in a siege in western Europe.[3] Improved archery was also important in sieges, both for attack and defence. And besiegers, having often to spend a lengthy period reducing a castle by blockade, made life more comfortable and more safe for themselves by constructing siege huts to live in, and counter castles to give protection. Speed, surprise, and originality of method by a commander, remained important, and we shall see a good deal of improvised and clever tactics in the sieges of the civil war.

Although battles were rare, they did occur, and the Battle of Lincoln in particular is a key moment in our story. It is no longer commonly believed by historians that medieval battle tactics were primitive or non-existent. But the Battle of Lincoln has not been analysed very closely with a view to studying the tactics.

As fortification provoked changes in siege war, so improvements in arms and armour led to changes in battle tactics. Armour was gradually becoming more elaborate. It was still, by 1139, not unlike the armour used in 1066, but there had been some changes. More men were usually now well armoured, and included more mercenary troops than had previously been the case, on horse as well as on foot. The ring-mail hauberk, tunic shaped, was the fundamental garment; men now tended to add additional pieces to protect legs or arms or chest. The helmet might still be in the conical shape of the familiar Norman style, but helmets covering more of the head and face were developing, and may have encouraged the need for more clothing to distinguish the knight from his fellows.

Our period seems to be the one when heraldry was beginning, though its rules were not yet developed, as later they would be. This development began in France but was soon taken up throughout Europe, with social as well as military connotations. The enamel in the museum at Le Mans of Matilda's husband, Geoffrey of Anjou, is one of the most famous early examples of heraldic dress, and as I have argued elsewhere, may have derived from the coat of arms of the English kings as used by Henry I. Both his cap and his shield have a device with lioncels which are obviously similar to the lions of England.[4]

There were also developments in the major arms used. Swords were now made in larger numbers by experts, well balanced, sharp; some of the best swords

Early heraldic style shields depicted in an illustration from the Stephen Harding Bible. Although this represents a biblical scene and the shields do not belong to medieval knights, still the style of decoration is clearly heraldic; note the chevrons. The illustration is one of the very earliest pieces of evidence for the beginnings of heraldry. (Bible de Saint Étienne Harding, MS 14)

ever made. Lances were used, and seem to have been growing in length, with great emphasis on balance, as the cavalry charge was perfected. Longbows were being used more than previously, and crossbows were becoming familiar weapons.

In a war against the infidel, there was every encouragement to kill the enemy. In a civil war, the fighting could often be bloody, but there was every reason to capture rather than kill enemy knights, for ransom, and as a sign of tit for tat mercy. There was also good reason to treat the native population with care, since one might hope to govern the same people afterwards. In any case war between Christians was viewed as a different matter to war between different faiths. The church condemned war between Christians except on very good grounds, and could normally only approve of one side's actions, for example, if fighting in self defence or in defence of the church. The arguments for what was or was not a just war were more than simply theories; men cared about seeming to have justice on their side, and war propaganda formed an important part of the whole picture. Knights saw themselves as Christian warriors, and other knights, even those fighting on the opposite side, as members of a class, a brotherhood; therefore mercy was normally to be praised, and death in war was much less common in this period in the West than in most other circumstances.[5]

THE ARRIVAL OF MATILDA

There can be little doubt that Robert and Matilda planned a war to win the succession, but Stephen and his friends may not have realized this at first. Robert's defiance had been taken as a declaration of war, and Stephen had already started the process of taking over his forfeited lands. Stephen was also aware of the threat posed by Robert, and had set up a guard on the coast, 'closing the harbours by a very close watch'.[6] He did not mean to be caught unawares by the landing of an invasion force.

But Matilda's plans were not yet clear. She held virtually no land either in England or in Normandy, since Henry I had neglected to give her this vital base for taking over power, assuming that she would take over the royal lands. She held only those few castles in Normandy mentioned above. Her appearance in England was neither illegal nor necessarily a threat. The fact that she arrived at Arundel made it look even more normal, in that she received an invitation to the place from her step-mother Adeliza, widow of Henry I and now married to the lord of Arundel, William of Albini. William of Albini was with Stephen and had shown no signs of disloyalty; indeed, he was to remain at least nominally a royalist. Then again Matilda was a woman, and although this had been a disadvantage with regard to the succession, it gave her certain privileges in polite society. Stephen had no grounds for arresting her or otherwise ill treating her. Again, when we look through the eyes of contemporaries, Stephen was presented with a much more difficult and delicate situation than normally seems to be recognized, and it is not at all clear that he acted badly, mistakenly or stupidly. In some ways, the less he provoked Matilda's hostility, the less likely she was to cause trouble. If she could be persuaded to accept the new regime, he would have won a major battle.

Of course, if we look through Matilda's eyes, we see a very different picture. Two facts allow us to believe this. Firstly, she came in the company of Robert of Gloucester, who had already begun a war. But secondly, and it would take time for this point to be clear to her enemies, she was clearly behind the sending of Baldwin de Redvers to Dorset, and Baldwin came in very hostile fashion, seeking to establish a maritime base for the Angevin cause.

Baldwin de Redvers had good cause to oppose Stephen. His offer to come in peace to the king, albeit late in the day, had been rejected. He had twice rebelled in 1136 and twice been defeated, losing both Exeter and the Isle of Wight. Since then he had joined up with Geoffrey of Anjou and been encouraged to cause trouble for Stephen in Normandy. Now he came to reclaim his lands in England, and to help the cause of Matilda and Robert. He landed first at Wareham, which had belonged to Robert of Gloucester but had been captured by Stephen. Baldwin arrived at about the beginning of August 'with a fine and strong body of troops'.[7] He does not seem to have been able to use Wareham except for landing, and moved on to nearby Corfe Castle, where the ruins still dominate the surrounding countryside from their imposing hilltop site.[8] Here he was admitted. Stephen, with his usual promptness, learned of the arrival and came to besiege Corfe. But no sooner was he there than news came of the imminent arrival of Robert of Gloucester and Matilda, and Stephen realized he must give priority to the Arundel landing.

Corfe Castle.

Again, Stephen took precautions against a new invasion. He also had forces at sea, and ordered 'a careful watch, night and day, on all the approaches to the harbours'.[9] The same source says he was watching 'over the pacification of the kingdom with the greatest soldierly skill'. But he did not prevent the landing. To be fair, Arundel is not the most obvious of landing points for an invasion, and the force that arrived was more of an escort than anything else. Presumably none of the major ports was open to Robert and Matilda, so they preferred to slip in to Arundel. William of Malmesbury says Robert had come 'with a far smaller military force than that with which anyone else would have ventured on so hazardous a war'. They were accompanied by just 140 knights, one of whom was Guy of Sablé.[10]

They slipped into Arundel on 30 September 1139, opened to them by Adeliza of Louvain; 'welcomed as if merely guests'.[11] Arundel is hardly a port; it stands near the sea and is approached by the River Arun. Its position has never allowed large ships to come close, but the nature of its approach is excellent for a secretive entry by a smallish group. It is also a very strong castle on a good defensive site, not easy to approach by land. It is situated on the edge of a rise of land which stands above the very flat, watery meadows, crossed by streams, which run down to the sea. The motte, which existed in 1139, is still impressive, though practically all of the buildings around have been rebuilt. In the old entrance building on the approach to the motte is a chamber over a gateway, and this retains the name of 'Matilda's chamber', though whether she ever used it is impossible to say. The Worcester chronicler suggests that Stephen was angry that his watch had failed and Robert and Matilda had managed to land at all.[12]

The arrival of Robert, as the *Gesta Stephani* says, was the signal for his supporters; 'all who secretly or openly favoured the earl were keener than usual

Matilda's chamber at Arundel, an exterior view. The chamber is immediately above the central gateway. The motte at Arundel lies to the right of this photograph.

An interior view of Matilda's chamber at Arundel.

and more eager to trouble the king'.[13] But Stephen's readiness was soon apparent, in that he used the troops with him and advanced straight on Arundel, while Matilda was still within. Robert of Gloucester, however, recognizing that he could not delay, set off with a small escort of about a dozen troops, to reach safer territory. Stephen's subsequent actions are often criticized, but Robert's have never even been questioned. If he expected Stephen to come and attack Arundel, as his rapid move away suggests, what was he doing leaving his half sister behind? Perhaps neither Stephen nor Robert believed that she was the key to the conflict ahead. William of Malmesbury seems aware of some criticism which might be made of Robert on this count, and says he had left her to the protection of Adeliza, who then broke her oath and did a deal with Stephen, but it is a rather feeble defence. It seems as if Adeliza had offered some promise to Matilda, but she told Stephen that 'none of his enemies had reached England by her means', and she was merely being hospitable.[14]

That Stephen saw Robert rather than Matilda as the threat, is shown by the explanation in the *Gesta Stephani* of Stephen's immediate reaction. He came to Arundel, but learning that Robert had escaped, he left a force to blockade the castle, and himself set off in pursuit of Robert, concentrating 'all his efforts on the capture of the earl'.[15] But Robert travelled on quiet side roads and got safely through to Bristol. Stephen then turned back to the trapped Matilda. The same source gives another strange tale, also usually ignored. It says that Stephen's brother, Henry, Bishop of Winchester, 'had all the by-roads blocked by guards, and at length met the earl [Robert], it was rumoured, and after a compact of peace and friendship had been firmly ratified between them, let him go unharmed'. The author asks leave to doubt that such a story of treachery could be true, but gives the reader the impression that he believes it to be so, the bishop then returning to his brother without revealing the secret meeting. If the story is true, then the bishop must bear a great burden of responsibility for the war which followed, for the capture of Robert at this juncture would have given Stephen an unassailable advantage.

The same author then suggests that it was on the bishop's advice that Stephen also made his next surprising move. The writer says that Stephen was keen to press on with the siege of Arundel, but Henry said it was 'wiser for the king himself and more beneficial to the kingdom to let her go to her brother unharmed', and concentrate on attacking Robert. We need not believe that Stephen was a gullible idiot who followed his brother's advice automatically. His preference of Theobald of Blois for Canterbury is sufficient to dispel that idea, apart from his resistance to Henry's efforts in the church council to condemn him for the arrest of the bishops. Neither brother was a particularly straightforward character, and both probably had a healthy distrust of the other's actions. The pact of Bishop Henry with Robert is only a rumour rather than a known fact, but not to be utterly discarded; the advice to let the empress go seems far more certainly known to the anonymous author, who frequently shows himself to possess good information on Bishop Henry. Henry is often held up as the shrewder, tougher, more sensible of the brothers, yet on several occasions he gave advice of dubious benefit to his brother. It is unlikely that Stephen would have accepted the advice if he did not see its merit. As suggested above, he was faced with the dilemma of how to deal with Matilda, and the bishop's advice offered a way out. So then 'an agreement was made, and a truce accepted under sanction of an oath'.[16] It is a pity we are not given the details of this agreement, and no reference is ever made to it afterwards. How wise Stephen was in this episode depends a lot upon what was agreed. Certainly Matilda was granted a safe conduct.[17] William of Malmesbury's reference to a boundary where Matilda was handed over to Robert, suggests some sort of frontier already recognized, somewhere west of Calne. It seems very likely that Matilda had promised not to war against him and broke her promise. That, after all, would seem to be Stephen's main purpose in the move. Even if the agreement were not so specific, that must have been its intention. The *Gesta Stephani* suggests that the point was to put all his enemies in one region, but Matilda was no threat at Arundel, blockaded and isolated. That Stephen had gained something from this agreement is also suggested by William of Malmesbury, no doubt repeating the view of Earl Robert, that Adeliza had somehow been at fault here. William says that she had often pledged her faith, even sending envoys to Normandy, but had now reneged on it 'with a woman's fickleness'. But what 'faith' he refers to is uncertain; whether she had made some new secret pledge in support of Matilda in opposition to her husband's stance, or whether it is the old promise extracted from Henry I.[18]

Stephen was able to pose as a merciful and chivalrous king, as even William of Malmesbury admits, providing an escort 'which it is not the custom of honourable knights to refuse to anyone'. Another gain for Stephen was the removal of the problem of keeping forces at Arundel while Robert was his main target. Arundel was a strong castle, and Henry of Huntingdon points out the king was partly motivated by his knowledge that it would be hard to take. Orderic thought Stephen simply 'foolish', and that letting Matilda go was the cause of the war to come; but he was writing from a distance, from his monastery in Normandy, and ignored the fact that Robert had already escaped. Orderic suggests that the king's enemies should have been cut down with the sword; the mind boggles at what would have been the church's reaction if Stephen had taken that literally, with regard to Matilda![19]

Stephen knew he must fight Robert, but there were still hopes that Matilda might be excluded from the conflict, hopes that were of course to be dashed, though she never actually took up arms. That she meant to join her half brother was no secret. After the agreement, she was escorted by Bishop Henry himself, and by Count Waleran of Meulan.[20] Count Waleran went as far as Calne, and Henry continued to the arranged boundary agreed by the king, presumably as part of the agreement made at Arundel, where Robert met her and took her to Bristol. The west country base for Stephen's opponents was already established.

THE OPENING OF THE WAR

Robert seems to have been disappointed in the number of men who came out in open support. William of Malmesbury, his apologist, says that 'the nobles were

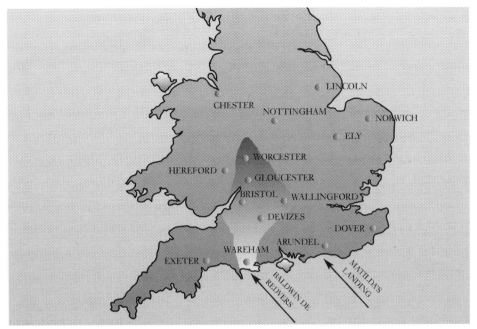

The main war zone, 1139–41.

either hostile or gave no help, apart from a very few'.[21] One immediate ally was Brian fitz Count, who came from Wallingford for a brief meeting with Robert as he made his way from Arundel to Bristol. Another prompt response to the call came from Miles of Gloucester, who gave Matilda his homage, and accepted her into Gloucester, where she chiefly resided during the following years. John the Marshal, who held Marlborough Castle, was another early recruit. It seems that John's rebellion had come just before the arrival of Robert, probably intended to coincide with it. Stephen was besieging Marlborough when he heard of their coming and set off for Arundel.[22]

The position which had emerged in 1138 was now hardened into a stronger reality. Robert of Gloucester was in defiance of the king, and had arrived in England in person to defend his truncated estates. With the arrival of Matilda he could present his defiance as a defence of her claim to the throne, thus giving him a legality which would in her absence have been lacking or at least unconvincing.

Robert had been uncertain of how much support to expect. Now it was clear: Brian fitz Count, Lord of Wallingford; Miles, the castellan of Gloucester; a number of near neighbours in the west country; relatives; and feudal vassals. Not one of the greatest magnates in the land had joined Matilda, apart from Robert himself. The few advantages of the Angevin party were a compact west country base, considerable holdings in Wales which perhaps doubled their territorial base and from which troops could be drawn, though of questionable value for fighting elsewhere than in the border country, a moral argument over the oath and

Matilda's right, and the ability of the trio of leaders. They knew they had the support of David, King of Scots; but for the time being that was an inclination of the heart rather than a solid assistance. Since his defeat in the Battle of the Standard, King David was in no position to give much more than moral support. They could also hope for aid from Geoffrey of Anjou. His part in the end, in carrying on the war in Normandy, proved absolutely invaluable, even decisive, but his contribution to the English war, except indirectly, was negligible.

Stephen weighed up the possibilities and made his decision. He gave his priority to ending the English war, to finishing off the efforts he had already begun against the territories of Robert of Gloucester. His immediate problem was that the return of Robert had reinvigorated the efforts of his friends, and many of the gains which Stephen had made before September 1139 were soon to be lost again. Therefore, Stephen, as usual with undiminished vigour, though he might be forgiven a sigh of resignation at having to start all over again, set about reducing the minor fortresses around Bristol to allow an attack on the final target.

Before that, however, there was another closer target. Brian fitz Count had made his own position clear; he was even 'delighted' by Matilda's coming.[23] The *caput* of his honor was the great castle at Wallingford. The Angevin party had no more easterly stronghold and, indeed, Wallingford could either be viewed as their salient into enemy territory, or as an isolated stronghold. Its isolation made it vulnerable, and strategically Stephen had made a good choice of target. Unfortunately for him, it was a strongly built and strongly defended castle, with a double moat round three of its sides. The surviving foundations are massive, and suggest that this was a powerful structure. It was also under the resolute command of Brian fitz Count, and for all his efforts throughout the whole civil war, Stephen was never able to capture it. Wallingford alone is a perfect illustration of the value of castles in the warfare of this age.

We do not in fact know a great deal about Wallingford Castle. When an opportunity for excavation in the modern period offered, it was refused on the grounds that archaeological ability in castle work was inadequate to tackling the site, which was referred to as 'a unique, uncut archaeological jewel', and the decision was made to delay excavation to a later period. As was claimed, 'there is not another Wallingford Castle'.[24] This came about from plans to build flats and a house on the site in 1976. An earlier dig had established that it had been an Anglo-Saxon settlement, and Domesday Book shows that there had been some destruction of dwellings for the building of the castle.

The castle was built in the north-east corner of the Saxon burh, itself placed on the banks of the Thames at an important crossing place.[25] It is mentioned as early as 1071, and was one of the first Norman castles in England, suggesting its vital strategic position. Basically, it was a typical Norman motte and bailey castle, and was strengthened in stone. But without excavation, and with the knowledge of so many periods of later work on it, including under Henry II, John and Henry III, it is not possible to describe precisely how it appeared in 1139.

At any rate, Stephen's decision was to begin by attacking Wallingford. Brian had a sizeable garrison and an 'impregnable castle' with strong walls. Stephen planned at first to blockade the castle, but soon changed his mind on advice from his barons and decided, that as with Bristol, he was not yet ready for the major challenge.[26] The strength of the place was clear on sight, and it was known that Brian had brought in plentiful supplies, 'enough to last for a great number of years'. The king decided to build two counter castles and leave a besieging force in them while he went to wage war in the west. One of these counter castles either used the church of Saint Peter or was built alongside it.

His first target in the enemy's base region was Trowbridge in the west of Wiltshire and on a route to the far west. It was held by Humphrey de Bohun III, who was married to Miles of Gloucester's daughter, Margaret. The town around the castle was probably the largest in the county. Humphrey was in the conspiracy against the king, and had been advised by his father-in-law to make his castle ready for defence. But en route to Trowbridge, Stephen had two other successes. First, passing by the castle of South Cerney, on the Gloucestershire–Wiltshire border, built by Miles of Gloucester himself, Stephen decided on a sudden attack. He took the garrison by surprise and the castle fell by storm.

Then he approached Malmesbury, a prosperous little town then, with both an abbey and a castle. The castle was well built and held by a mercenary captain, Robert fitz Hubert: 'a man of great cruelty and unequalled in wickedness and crime'.[27] Robert had been employed by the Earl of Gloucester to hold the castle, but soon chose to surrender to the royal army, apparently on the advice of his relative, William of Ypres. Even William of Malmesbury sees merit in Stephen's dealing firmly with this character.[28]

So Stephen approached Trowbridge, with two easy successes to boost his confidence. But his chief enemies now showed their hand for the first time, and their mettle. Miles of Gloucester was to prove the most effective of all the commanders engaged in the early stages of the war, and his death in 1143 was a boon to the king. Now Miles cut across Stephen's rear, and attacked the besieging force he had left behind at Wallingford. He took them by surprise, wounding and killing those who fought him. Others were taken prisoner and chained up. Stephen's initial minor successes had been nullified. It soon became clear that his enemies were too powerful for him to win an easy or quick victory. They would not be lured into a decisive battle, and their major fortifications were too strong to be easily captured. It was likely to be a long war of sieges.

In November 1139 an army from Gloucester attacked the city of Worcester. The Worcester chronicler vividly describes the fears and activities of the citizens in the months preceding this attack, which they had anticipated. Citizens took their furniture into churches for safe-keeping so that the church seemed like a warehouse. The cathedral became like an inn or council chamber, filled with chests and sacks, and the monks' services were drowned by the howling of infants brought into the church by their mothers, as well as the crying of the women. The church seemed stripped bare, since valuable items were pulled down and hidden for safety, including the cross and a statue of the Virgin Mary, along with such things as curtains and vestments.

On Tuesday 7 November, what the chronicler calls the first day of winter, the enemy arrived while the monks were chanting the service of prime. The monks then dressed themselves in splendid clothes, thinking it better to wear them than leave them behind. They made a procession through the city, carrying the relics of Saint Oswald, while the church bells rang. But the attack proceeded, and the garrison of the castle, together with the citizens, resisted. The first attack was beaten off, and then a second was made against the north walls. This time the Angevins broke in and set fire to the houses in their path, so that the flames spread through much of the town. The attackers took away furniture, valuables, oxen, horses, sheep and cattle. Captives were bound in pairs like hounds and carried off so that they could later be ransomed. Then the attackers departed, 'maddened and drunken'.

There had been a great deal of destruction, but the castle had held out. At the end of the month the new earl, Waleran, came to Worcester to view the damage. He was enraged, and made a revenge attack on Sudeley, held by John fitz Harold for Robert of Gloucester. Stephen also came to Worcester and was upset by the injuries the town had sustained. While there he appointed William Beauchamp, the sheriff of Worcester, as his constable to replace Miles of Gloucester.[29]

Stephen made a reconnaissance expedition to the west, but made no attack on either Hereford or Bristol, around which he raided. He did the same near Dunster, 'leaving nothing at all, as far as it lay in his power, that could serve his enemies for food or any purpose'. This was good military thinking in the period, and common practice, but it very much helps to explain the poverty and hardship which accompanied the civil war in England, and especially those areas which bore the brunt of the fighting. William of Malmesbury sums up the situation by the end of 1139: 'so the whole district around Gloucester far into Wales, partly through force and partly from good will, gradually went over to the lady empress in the remaining months of that year'. Of the following year, the chronicler says:

> there were many castles all over England, each defending its own district, or rather plundering it. The knights from the castles carried off both herds and flocks, sparing neither churches nor graveyards . . . pillaging the dwellings of the wretched countrymen to the very straw.[30]

Also of 1140, Henry of Huntingdon, breaking into verse, exclaimed:

> Gaunt famine, following, wastes away
> Whom murder spares, with slow decay.[31]

Stephen had been worried by Miles' activities, but not diverted from his initial target of Trowbridge, which he proceeded to besiege. The king built throwing engines and set up a blockade. But the garrison held out with defiance. The barons who had accompanied him began to murmur, clearly not relishing a long blockade. This was to prove one of Stephen's greatest problems throughout the war. There were more lords who gave him half-hearted support than actually went over to the enemy, but it meant that he rarely had troops he could rely on 100 per cent. It meant also that the morale of his army was often less than that of an enemy which was more unified in its attitude, even if inferior in numbers. Both sides used mercenary troops, but Stephen had to rely on them more, and again this did not improve the morale of the barons with him or his army as a whole. In the end Stephen abandoned the close siege of Trowbridge, though he did not leave it altogether in peace. He put a reinforced garrison into nearby Devizes Castle with the intention of hampering any activity out of Trowbridge. These troops were 'very prompt in battle'; in other words, probably light horse which were mobile.[32] As Leland put it, Stephen could say of Trowbridge: I came, I saw, but he could not add, I conquered.[33]

At the end of 1139 Roger, Bishop of Salisbury, died. He perished of a quartan fever, one which recurred every fourth day. William Malmesbury suggests his health had declined because of the arrest, which had depressed him and led to 'mental suffering'. Comments the chronicler: 'fortune, which had favoured him greatly for so long, finally stung him cruelly with a scorpion's tale'.[34] His death underlines Stephen's achievement in removing the bishops without serious repercussions. Roger left behind at Salisbury considerable wealth in money and vessels of precious metal, and the king used it, not we are told for his armies, at any rate not all of it, but to improve the churches at Abbotsbury and Malmesbury.[35]

Whatever the motive for allowing Matilda to join her friends in the west, Stephen must certainly have hoped to confine conflict to that region, but he was to be disappointed. The west remained the one solid base for Robert of Gloucester. David of Scots remained a brooding threat to the king in the north. But the region which proved most troublesome to Stephen, throughout the war, second only to the west country, was East Anglia and neighbouring districts. The nobility of the region who opposed him were less dedicated to Matilda's cause than the Gloucester coterie, and hence their threat was more intermittent and less coherent, but they caused enough difficulty to divert Stephen from his main target at several vital moments in the war.

Already Nigel, Bishop of Ely, had apparently been involved in at least discussion with men conspiring against the king, and may even himself have acted against him. Stephen had taken no chance with regard to Nigel when moving against Roger of Salisbury in 1139. It was Nigel who had given Stephen the most problems then, preparing to defend himself in arms against the king at Devizes, and only surrendering because Matilda of Ramsbury wished to give way to the king's threats against her lover and her son. Nigel had yielded with a bad grace. With Matilda present and war against Stephen opening up, Nigel came back into the limelight. He now joined the revolt against Stephen, hiring knights and attacking royalist neighbours.

Ely was an ideal base for rebellion. It possessed a castle at Cherry Hill, now in the park close to the cathedral. It was in essence a motte and bailey castle, but improved by Bishop Nigel with stone and cement.[36] There was a second castle at the main entrance to the island, Aldreth. Even better, the isle was isolated by geography. In the twelfth century Ely genuinely was an island, cut off from the mainland by a swathe of rivers and marshes. It was 'impenetrably surrounded on all sides by meres and fens, accessible only in one place, where a very narrow track affords the scantiest of entries'.[37] It was very difficult country to cross. Normal entry to the island was by boat, and easy approach was hard. The nature of the country, and its protection to rebels, had been demonstrated by the rebellion of Hereward the Wake against William the Conqueror. Hereward had finally been flushed out, but only with great difficulty, and he had survived into an obscure end. During the civil war, Ely would twice harbour enemies of the king.

Stephen was probably inspired by a knowledge of the Conqueror's campaign against Hereward, and as usual showed no decline in his vigour against new enemies. Now he set about building a bridge of boats, placed broadside on against each other, supported where necessary on hurdles laid across the marsh. So a timber bridge was constructed over the boats, and his army was transported to the island. Even so, there was difficult ground to cross, and the king had to rely on a monk who knew the area well, showing him a ford through the fens. This was the monk, Daniel, who was later rewarded by being made Abbot of nearby Ramsey Abbey.

Now Stephen's men erupted into the Isle of Ely, capturing Nigel's knights and seizing booty. They also captured the 'small castle' of Aldreth at the entry to the island, with its garrison, where some of Nigel's knights had gone for safety. This castle has not been found, and is not obvious in any present remains.[38] Bishop Nigel, like Hereward before him, managed to elude his enemies by fleeing through the marshes. He fled to Gloucester, 'a poor and humbled man'. Stephen had conducted a rapid and brilliantly successful campaign in very difficult conditions, and had closed down the Angevins' second front, at least for the time being.

Miles, after his victory at Wallingford, returned to the security of Gloucester, where his castle was well stocked and well fortified, and where Stephen's enemies from less secure areas mustered. Miles set about a war of raiding and pillaging against royal supporters in Gloucestershire and Herefordshire, with 'the terrible burning of villages and towns, which he turned into desert land'.[39] That the Angevins had to use such tactics in an area so close to home demonstrates how restricted was their power. Among the places Miles captured was the castle at Winchcomb on 31 January 1140, where some of the garrison afterwards joined him. He also recaptured South Cerney and took Hereford. Miles had little difficulty in recapturing the latter from the small garrison left there, but he failed to take Sudeley.

The primary base of the Angevins in the west was expanding. Stephen himself, held considerable land in the county of Cornwall. William fitz Richard held much from the king, but now William turned against the king. His reasons are unknown, but he clearly had a connection with another of Henry I's illegitimate sons, Reginald. Reginald does not appear to have been one of the initial ringleaders of the conspiracy, but it may simply be that we lack knowledge of his actions. He was to prove as consistent in his loyalty to Matilda as his fellow bastard, Robert. Reginald and William fitz Richard now made a pact. Reginald married William's daughter, and was given entry to the castles which William held under the king in Cornwall. So far as we know this was Reginald's first important link with the county, but it was to become his base for the rest of his life. Reginald's activities in attacking church property soon brought him into conflict with the local church, and the Bishop of Exeter excommunicated him.

Lands mainly under Pro-Angevin control, 1140.

But at first his rebellion looked as if it would be short-lived. Stephen, with his amazingly consistent energy against new threats, brought an army to Cornwall in the summer of 1140, to regain his own lands there. He recovered all the castles which had fallen into Reginald's hands, with the exception of the one Reginald himself inhabited. Stephen introduced his own loyal supporter, Alan of Penthièvre, into Cornwall, gave the recovered lands into his hands, and shortly afterwards created him Earl of Cornwall. Matilda gave Reginald the same title, and the two rivals were left to contest their claims.[40]

In 1140 William of Malmesbury claims that Robert of Gloucester recaptured South Cerney, as well as Harptree and Sudeley, and that he levelled the counter castle at Wallingford. This is almost certainly one of the numerous instances of the chronicler exaggerating the role of his own hero, since, as we have seen, a less biased writer had said that it was Miles who took South Cerney and destroyed the counter castle at Wallingford, though perhaps he could be construed as acting on behalf of Robert. Reginald was made Earl of Cornwall, and William of Malmesbury says that this was done by Robert.[41] No doubt Robert's influence and wishes were regarded, but he could not in any way be considered qualified to create earls, even by his own side. It was Matilda who was claiming royal power in order to make such creations. Reginald certainly proved an effective choice, and was able to push the royal nominee, Earl Alan, out of the county, winning effective authority for himself.

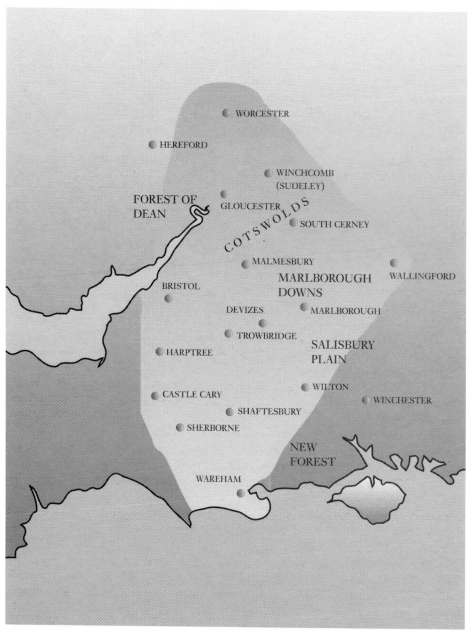

The 1139–41 war zone.

The devious mercenary Robert fitz Hubert, thrown out of Malmesbury by Stephen, and employed by Robert of Gloucester, on 26 March 1140 suddenly seized Devizes Castle from the king. He was said to be related to Stephen's mercenary captain, William of Ypres.[42] William of Malmesbury calls him a blasphemer, saying that he was always boasting that he had once roasted alive eighty monks in a church, and that he would do so again. He wrote that Robert fitz Hubert 'used to smear his prisoners with honey and expose them naked in the open air under the sun, stirring up flies and similar insects to sting them'.[43] The chronicler says Robert's aim was to build a principality for himself, and that he was planning to send for mercenaries from Flanders to aid him. But his career was cut short by John the Marshal, who believed that Devizes should be his. When the mercenary sought to make John agree to submit to him, the Marshal captured Robert fitz Hubert and, when later he refused to give up Devizes, hanged him on the spot. William clearly approved of the execution, though it seems a blatant case of taking the law into his own hands by John the Marshal.

It was still by no means certain that a full-scale civil war would develop. Already in 1140 peace overtures were made, according to William of Malmesbury through 'the legate', presumably meaning Henry of Blois.[44] There was a conference at Bath, which Robert of Gloucester attended on Matilda's behalf, while Henry of Blois, Theobald of Canterbury and Queen Matilda represented Stephen. The stumbling block appears to have been the clerics' demand that the settlement be dictated by the church. Matilda was willing for this to be done, but Stephen refused. The conference, therefore, broke up without a settlement.

Later in the year, Henry of Blois, seeking peace in England, travelled to meet Louis VII and Theobald, Count of Blois, but still without success. Again, according to William of Malmesbury, Matilda and Robert were prepared to accept whatever proposals Bishop Henry brought back (we do not know what they were), but Stephen refused. Virtually throughout the reign the views and aims of Bishop Henry seem to have diverged from those of his brother Stephen. Then, says the chronicler, Bishop Henry abandoned his attempts and sat back 'to see how things would turn out'.[45]

In 1140 Stephen returned to Worcester, and used it as a base for further raids. He also made an attack on Robert's property at Tewkesbury, where the earl's 'magnificent house' was set on fire, along with all the property around it.[46] There was some sort of fighting near Bath on 15 August 1140, but we have very little detail about it. Robert of Gloucester had set out against Bath, one of the few important strongholds held by Stephen in the west. But Stephen had already sent men who probably laid an ambush. Two knights called Roger and John led the royal forces. One of those in Robert of Gloucester's army was Geoffrey Talbot, for whom Stephen had developed a healthy dislike since the previous episode at the same city, when he had escaped the bishop's clutches. In the fighting Geoffrey was severely wounded, and died a week later on 22 August.[47] He was one of the first major casualties of the war, and his death a success for the royalists. The chronicle also says that the clash itself was a royalist victory.

In September 1140 the Angevins made an attack on Nottingham, which like Worcester before it, was sacked. It is a sign of the respective power and aims of the two sides that the Angevins should pursue this tactic. The idea was clearly to try and show Stephen's weakness, but it was not the action of a powerful or winning party. If they hoped to rule over such towns as Worcester and Nottingham, such destructive measures were not likely to aid their cause, so the actions speak more of desperation. At Nottingham, 'the whole city was destroyed by the flames'.[48] Even those in the churches died, as the buildings caught fire and collapsed upon them.

The first year of war had seen little more than the two sides settling down and testing out their opponents. The Angevins had to accept that their loyal territory was very restricted in area. Their main aim must be to seek new allies and increase the territories under Matilda's power. Their main hopes in this respect lay in keeping Wallingford, while building more support in the lands around it, and in opening up another area of war, in which case East Anglia looked the best bet, while keeping touch with the sympathetic David of Scots. They clearly also hoped that Geoffrey of Anjou would succeed in Normandy, and ultimately lend a hand in England.

The royalists had to accept that it was going to be difficult to capture the main bases at Bristol and Gloucester, and even the Angevin outpost at Wallingford had proved impossible to take. It was unlikely that the Angevins would risk a pitched battle, so the probable prospect was for a prolonged and bitter siege warfare. Stephen's aim in this first phase of the war proper, had been much the same as in his earlier operation: to subdue any additional threats to the peace in the country, and to take the lesser fortifications around the major strongholds in the west, with the ultimate aim of besieging Gloucester and Bristol. But as in many wars, fate had a surprise in store for all concerned.

CHAPTER 4

The Battle of Lincoln

Before we examine the details of the only major battle in this civil war, we need to place it in context. We have already considered the development of warfare in general, with a brief look at such matters as arms and armour and siege techniques. But we need to look a little more closely at why battles were fought, and how. We shall then see the significance of Lincoln more clearly. As pointed out above, battles were rare, because of the risks involved; because of the danger of what might happen if defeated. Battle was bound to be chancy, even if one began with all the advantages. There could still be a surprise move, a panic on one's own side, the sudden death of one's leader, the unexpected arrival of reinforcements for the enemy. Any one of a thousand things could undermine even a commander confident of victory. So that although the benefits of victory could be very great, battle was a very high risk gamble, and few commanders in the twelfth century were prepared to take it. Consider the reputation of, say, Richard the Lionheart, always keen for a fight, never afraid of personal risk, yet on several occasions even he turned aside from a possible battle, and the only major battle in which he was involved, at Arsuf, was initiated by the enemy, and engaged at first by his own side against his orders.

Commanders knew that they could gain their ends by other and more reliable means, in particular by siege warfare, winning territory step by step. The occasional setback in this kind of war was to be expected, but it would not cut off one's hopes at a blow. It was highly likely to be successful if you had more wealth and more men, and therefore appealed in particular to kings and superior authorities. But all twelfth-century war was a kind of challenge, and a successful commander could not avoid all challenges and all conflict. In the end he might have to risk battle or even engage in it to overbear his opponent. Therefore, battles most commonly occurred, oddly enough, at sieges. The first challenge was a lesser one: to gain authority over a single place, but if the opponent wanted to dispute that authority he must try to save the place. If the significance of the issue was great enough, this might in the end involve a defending army and an attacking army, and the issue might have to be resolved by battle.

Because of the riskiness of battle, it was also normal to place emphasis upon defensive tactics; it was more important not to lose than it was to win. Battle, like sieges, developed according to changes in technology, and changes in thinking about war. The most important battle-winning force which had emerged in the period just prior to Lincoln, was that of the cavalry charge.

Cavalry of course was not new, but its strength and method of use was. Typically in the past the point of cavalry had been its speed, and so it had been most useful for sudden manoeuvres such as flank attacks, and for pursuit (or escape). The more lightly cavalry was armed, the greater would be its speed. But this also left it vulnerable to attack of all sorts, and horses, however well trained, would find the noise and blood of warfare a great strain, so they might bolt. The most important factor in the changes which had occurred was the social status of the rider. We do not need to pursue in detail the development of what in modern times is usually called feudalism, though it is a relatively modern term and not a medieval one. The change we are interested in has caused some dispute over its timing, but there is no question that it happened. The socially superior class, by the eleventh century, acted as cavalry when at war, and by about this time were beginning to see themselves as knights, with the social and moral code that implies. Once this had happened, the other changes were almost inevitable. This class wanted to be best armed and protected, and could afford to be. They trained their horses and they trained themselves. The armour they wore as it increased in effectiveness, gradually also increased in cost and in weight. As a military group, therefore, this cavalry became more and more exclusive. Special horses were bred and trained for war, needing to be fast enough to move well – so *not* like cart horses – but heavy enough to play their part in battle, and also to carry the armour with which they, as well as their riders, were provided.

No sensible rider wanted his horse always to be weighed down with armour, but it became common practice to arm the horse as well as the man when fighting was likely, including, of course, for a pitched battle. We begin to see what is known as the barded, or armoured horse, as the common type of cavalry mount in battle. This horse would not move especially fast, but it would have reasonable protection and it would have weight. It could now be useful if speeded up and headed against men; it could trample infantry; it could break through their ranks. Thus developed, gradually, the idea of groups of cavalry charging across the field in battle. So effective was this method against forces not accustomed to it, that it helped to win some dramatic victories, as during the First Crusade, or at Hastings. Anna Comnena, the Byzantine chronicler, described its impact upon the Byzantines, who themselves used cavalry and armour, but not in quite the same way. She wrote that 'the first charge of Celtic [Frankish] cavalry was irresistible'; 'a mounted Celt is irresistible; he would pierce his way through the walls of Babylon'.[1]

What made the western cavalry so especially effective was the way they were trained to act as a group. To begin with, this seems to have occurred in small numbers, perhaps ten or twelve together. It was honed by the development of a newly popular sport, the tournament. At first this was mock group warfare rather than individual jousts. Knights from the western world flocked to advertised tournaments in Flanders or France or wherever. They could get rich through them, since one practice was to capture enemy knights and then ransom them. At the peak of the popularity of tournaments, they were occurring somewhere or other at almost weekly intervals. The point about the tournament for us, is that it also provided the opportunity to practise group cavalry moves. At some time

A concerted cavalry charge. This twelfth-century illustration shows lines of knights charging in unison and is important evidence for the development of the concerted charge. (Pierpont Morgan Library, M. 736, f. 7v)

between Hastings and Lincoln, it became the custom to use a large number of cavalry for a charge, in unison, what elsewhere I have referred to as the concerted charge.[2] This is to distinguish it from the small group charge. Now a commander could send in a wave of cavalry: a line right across the field, or a mass attack from one or both wings. At first it was almost like a secret weapon.

As always with new battle-winning tactics, it is not long before someone seeks and finds a response; so it was with the concerted charge. It was powerful, but it had flaws. Once delivered, it was difficult to repeat, since it meant gathering the horses together again in the midst of the turmoil of battle, and finding another chance to give them a clear run. So that if the charge did not decide the battle at once, the opposition was then in a good position to counter. Another flaw was that, although this was an excellent offensive tactic for battle, the cavalry force was not very useful in defence, so that the commander was more or less committed to seeking early means of attack. Another weakness was that, however well armoured, horses could still be wounded, for example in the leg. By aiming at horses, defensive troops, especially if they possessed archers, could halt or weaken the charge before it was even delivered. And horses, after all, are animals, and likely to do unexpected things if hurt or frightened, however well trained; sometimes they bolted, very often they reared, and riders were constantly thrown in the middle of a fight.

One rather unpleasant solution to the problem of how to stop the cavalry charge, was to place objects in the path of the horses, such as caltrops – metal spheres with spikes. This is a tactic mentioned by Anna Comnena, but not so far as we know, used in the West at this time. Another answer attempted in the East was to push forward wagons in the path of the horses.[3] One common answer in the West was increasingly to employ infantry with bows or spears, though this often failed to halt the charge altogether, and such troops tended to be poorly armed and vulnerable to the charge if it reached them.

By 1139, the armies of the Anglo-Norman world had developed their own tactic to cope with the charge. It had been honed through use at several battles from Tinchebrai in 1106, through Alençon, Brémule, Bourg-Théroulde, and as we have seen already at Northallerton in 1138.[4] The Anglo-Norman answer was to use a method practised occasionally in the past for other reasons, of dismounting troops trained as cavalry, to fight on foot. Various examples can be quoted of this use in the past, from the Battle of the Dyle in 891, through Conquereuil, to Pontlevoy. It would shortly also be employed by the Franks themselves on the Second Crusade. But no one used it as frequently and consistently as the Anglo-Normans in the first half of the twelfth century; it was *their* answer to the charge.

On the face of it, there seems to be some illogicality about training and arming troops to fight on horse, and then on the battlefield using them as infantry. Some historians have thought that the Anglo-Normans borrowed the tactic from the Anglo-Saxons, who rode to battle and fought on foot. But this is not the same thing. The troops we are talking about were trained as cavalry, which the Saxons were not. And the evidence shows that the men who practised the tactic for the Anglo-Normans were almost exclusively men of Norman, not Saxon, origin.

A foot soldier with spear.

Economically, in the long run, it did not make sense to pursue this method, but it was an empirical answer to a question which required an urgent response. How do we cope with the mounted charge in battle? What this answer entailed, was to use your best troops to do the dirty work. Archers and missile throwers could obstruct charges, but would not be good at holding their position. The idea of dismounting knights was to use the best armed troops, the best trained troops, the troops with the best morale, and to stand fast against the charge and hold it. Because commanders had soon realized that although the impact of the charge was great, it could be faced and held by determined infantry. Knights were not keen to fight in this way, and protested, for example, to the commander who ordered them to dismount at Bourg-Théroulde. But it was effective and so until a better solution presented itself, virtually every good commander used it.

There were probably some experiments, and at the Standard the archers and dismounted knights were mixed together at the front of the line. But again it had worked. The one disadvantage of this tactic, was that it immobilized mobile troops. It made a good defensive formation, but victory in battle generally required something beyond soaking up enemy offensives. Therefore, most Anglo-Norman commanders only dismounted a proportion of their knights; others were kept on horseback in separate formations, sometimes on the wing, sometimes as a tactical reserve.

This then was the world of war at the time of the Battle of Lincoln. The major new offensive tactic was the concerted charge by heavy cavalry; the main defence against it was to use archers and dismount some of your knights as infantry. But beyond that it still mattered enormously what troops you could raise, from feudal levies to mercenaries, what novel ideas you could introduce, and how good was the morale of your troops. Battle, as always, was a matter of tried and trusted tactics and principles, plus intelligent use of the forces and weapons at your disposal. As medieval commanders knew, it would always remain a risk.

LINCOLN CASTLE

Stephen had made William of Albini, Earl of Lincoln. This was the same William who then married Henry I's widow, Adeliza, and was thus Lord of Arundel at the time of Matilda's landing. But if his wife's allegiance was doubtful, and she either invited or allowed Matilda to enter England through Arundel, her second husband remained loyal to Stephen.

Cronne has suggested that this grant, of Lincoln to William of Albini, enraged both Ranulf of Chester and his half brother, William de Roumare, who believed they had a claim on Lincoln Castle and saw the grant as 'an affront'. Round believed that Ranulf was also motivated by hostility to Henry of Scots after Stephen's Scottish settlement. This was partly over the loss of Carlisle, but also because of a personal antagonism to Prince Henry which had shown itself while the prince was in England at Stephen's court. He had probably been involved in some attempt to ambush the prince, which was one of the reasons King David ordered his son to return home.[5]

If Davis is right, Stephen juggled his earldoms in 1140, transferring William of Albini to Sussex and making William de Roumare, Earl of Lincoln.[6] William de Roumare was half brother to Ranulf, Earl of Chester, both sons of Lucy, who is thought to be the daughter of Thorold, sheriff and castellan of Lincoln Castle. William was the son of Lucy's second husband, Roger fitz Gerold, and Ranulf, the son of her third husband, Ranulf le Meschin, Earl of Chester.[7] Through Lucy, therefore, both had some claim to Lincoln, and William's was the best.

The following sequence of events is uncertain, since there are some discrepancies in the chronicle accounts, and because Stephen visited Lincoln several times, and there is the possibility that the writers mixed up the dates, confused the visits, or repeated events. In 1140 the half-brothers took Lincoln Castle by a ruse. They visited when the best part of the garrison was in the town. They came under the pretext of a social visit to the castellan, sending their wives in advance, to talk and joke with his wife. Ranulf then himself arrived, without a cloak and unarmed, but the men with him carried hidden arms. Once inside, they overwhelmed the guard and took control of the castle. Then they let in William de Roumare, waiting with troops outside.

Stephen came to visit the half brothers in the city, and seems to have accepted their case, moving William of Albini to the Sussex earldom as a result. This was a very special favour to William de Roumare, and makes the subsequent events even more puzzling. The explanation seems to be that William's strong attachment to his half-brother Ranulf, Earl of Chester, overcame any gratitude to the king.

Ranulf, rather illogically, had been enraged by the recognition of the Scots' right to Carlisle, though it was a good claim, recognized previously by Henry I, and though he had played no part in the Battle of the Standard to defend the north against the Scots. Ranulf seems to have been a choleric and difficult man, and William de Roumare, though older, seems to have been dominated by him.

It would seem that the king had taken the castle into his own hands before these events, and that the half-brothers had, therefore, taken it from him. It is not certain what Stephen had gained from the agreement made with them, but William of Malmesbury verifies that a peace had been made.[9]

The citizens of Lincoln soon felt that the half-brothers had exceeded the bounds of the peace, and were treating them harshly, so they sent to the king to come and assist them. They found him in London, where he had intended to spend Christmas. Stephen now decided to besiege the castle, which must mean either that it should have remained in his hands and the brothers had retaken it, or that he demanded they render it to him and they refused. From the uncertain evidence, the former seems to be more likely. Certainly, the taking over of the castle infuriated the king. Orderic wrote that he 'was very angry at the news, and astounded that his close friends, on whom he had heaped lands and honours, should have committed such a crime'.[10]

Stephen came to besiege Lincoln Castle, although it was the Christmas season, and found only a small garrison there which gave him hopes of success. The citizens welcomed the king and let him into the city, so the castle was isolated.

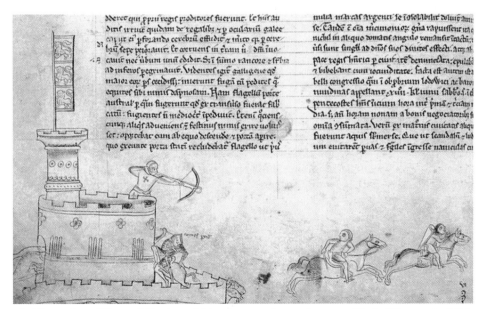

An illustration of Henry III's siege of Lincoln; note the crossbowmen. The building on the left is Lincoln Castle. (Corpus Christi College, Cambridge, MS 16, f. 55v)

They captured seventeen knights who were relaxing in the town. Ranulf had gone, but had left his wife and his half brother William in the castle.[11] No doubt Ranulf had left behind his wife, the daughter of Robert of Gloucester, as a deliberate ploy to encourage Earl Robert to come to the rescue.

Stephen set up throwing engines and began to batter the garrison. Without aid it was unlikely they could survive long. But now Ranulf of Chester decided to throw in his lot with the Angevins, and went for help to Robert of Gloucester, his father-in-law. From the Angevin point of view it was a godsend. Matilda accepted Ranulf's offer of fealty. Ranulf and William together would be powerful new allies, and war in Lincolnshire as well as in the west would greatly improve their chances of success. Robert, therefore, responded positively and raised as large a force as he could, calling up Welsh troops in the process, probably from his own lands and those of his allies.

On the night before the battle, there was a dreadful storm, with hail, rain, thunder and lightning. Then on the day itself, Sunday 2 February, Stephen attended a service, presumably in the cathedral, and was celebrating mass at dawn. According to the ritual, it was the king's role to carry a lighted candle in his hand, but the flame suddenly went out and the candle broke. The chronicler says it was then mended and relit, and with the obvious benefit of hindsight adds: 'which was a sign of course that he would lose the dignity of the kingdom for his sin and at length, when penance had been rendered, by God's favour wondrously and gloriously get it back again'. But Orderic probably voiced most people's thoughts, seeing it as 'a clear omen of misfortune'. According to Henry of Huntingdon, there was yet another evil omen, when during the service, the pyx containing Christ's body broke its fastening, and fell upon the altar; 'a sign of the king's fall from power'. It would not appear that Stephen had much chance of victory![12]

BATTLE

Like many other battles in the twelfth century, Lincoln arose out of a siege. Stephen had only a small force with him, sufficient to besiege the small garrison within Lincoln Castle. Robert of Gloucester led a larger army, intended to relieve Lincoln and not afraid to face Stephen's small force in battle. Stephen was informed of their approach. He was advised to retreat and gather a larger army. The king here made a serious error, probably by allowing feelings to dominate sense. Most commanders would have heeded the advice and avoided battle. But there were special personal reasons why Stephen chose to stay and fight. Of course, he was not keen to abandon the siege; his anger against the half-brothers had not decreased, and one of them was in the approaching army. He was also promised aid from the citizens of Lincoln, which would bolster his army's size. In addition, he may have been influenced by the thought that at last he could get at the heart of the enemy. Through the war to this date, he had always possessed the greater force in the field and the Angevins had assiduously avoided battle. Now before him was the backbone of the enemy military power: the Earls of Gloucester and Chester, along with Miles of Gloucester. Victory for the king

Lincoln Castle and Cathedral viewed from over the river Witham, which the Angevin army crossed. The ground on the other side of the river is the site of the battle.

would put an end to Matilda's hopes. But quite likely the motive which dominated was fear; fear of looking a coward; fear of being tarred with the same brush as his father. The *Gesta Stephani* says 'he refused to sully his fame by the disgrace of flight . . . but went boldly to meet them outside the town'. Orderic says that 'the wilful prince turned a deaf ear to the advice of prudent men, and judged it dishonourable to put off battle for any reason'.[13]

Robert of Gloucester made a diagonal approach to Lincoln from the west, in order to get his army across the River Witham. The course of this river has altered since the Middle Ages, but only a little. The water still meanders across the flat lands to the south and west of the city. Lincoln is one of those cities whose medieval condition is easy to imagine. One can still enter the city formally near the Brayford Pool, from the bustling modern shopping centre, where one faces a medieval stone arch. Ahead and above, silhouetted against the skyline stand the two buildings which dominated the city then and still do, to the west the square bulk of the castle, to the east the soaring towers of the cathedral. They stand at the top of a very steep hill, which made the castle particularly difficult to approach and capture. The city occupied the hill on which the buildings stand. The west wall of the city was the western defence of the castle. At the foot of the western slope is a flat plain, across which wanders the River Witham after its journey through the Fosse Dyke westwards from the Brayford Pool.

The lookout of the royal force in the town, would easily have been able to see the army as it crossed the river by a ford, probably a mile or so to the west of the city, and made its way through marshy ground by the river to the firmer ground of the plain. William of Malmesbury says that the river was swollen by rains so they had to swim across, which would account for the marshy state of the ground

Lincoln city centre, with the entrance to the old city, the Stonebow arch, in the background.

around.[14] The writer in the Victoria County History, with a close knowledge of the area, thought the battle was fought to the north of the city, on the grounds that it was the best direction from which to attack. But given the evidence of the fording, the more likely site is immediately to the west of the walls.[15]

It was Sunday 2 February when Stephen was informed of the approach. He called a council to debate what should be done. The advice was to leave a force to defend the city, but himself to go for reinforcements. As we have seen, he refused to budge. According to Orderic, clerics present advised the king that battle should be avoided because it was Sunday, and that peace negotiations should be initiated, and a truce agreed. Stephen refused to heed the advice.[16]

The king led his forces to stand before the west walls of the city, while the Angevin forces deployed as they arrived to the north of the ford. There was some attempt by the royalists to obstruct the crossing, but it failed. The *Gesta Stephani* gives the impression that the battle followed immediately after the ford crossing was made, but this does not match other accounts, and is probably simply a telescoping of events.[17] Stephen did not make his own battle speech. The scene is beautifully depicted in the pages of the chronicle of Henry of Huntingdon by a line drawing in pen and ink. Stephen, wearing his crown, is shown standing to one side, while the speech was made for him by Baldwin fitz Gilbert, whose

The Battle of Lincoln. Baldwin fitz Gilbert makes a speech for the Royalists. Stephen, the crowned figure, is standing by, listening. This illustration is taken from the chronicle by Henry of Huntingdon, a major source for the events portrayed. Indeed, the section of manuscript shown here contains the account of the battle speech. (BL MS Arundel 48, f. 168v)

brother had been killed in the fighting in Wales at the beginning of the reign. The chronicler says this was because the king was not good at making speeches, lacking a witty tongue.[18] Baldwin, 'a man of the highest rank and a brave soldier', stood upon a hill to make the speech.[19] He began by attracting the attention of all, allowing a telling pause. This suggests that Stephen may have deliberately asked Baldwin to make the speech because he knew him to be an accomplished speaker.[20] According to the chronicler the speech consisted of insulting the enemy leaders, though one suspects the chronicler is having fun at the expense of the nobility through invention rather than repetition. He retailed speeches made on both sides, though he cannot have heard both, and probably heard neither. Baldwin accused Robert of Gloucester of having the heart of a hare. But Baldwin also reminded his own side of the justice of their cause, their numbers and their courage.

For the Angevins, speeches were made by both of the earls; Ranulf first and then Robert. Robert reminded his audience that he was the old king's son, and that Stephen had usurped the crown which should be his sister's. He accused Stephen of bad government, and blamed him for the disorder in the land. On that side insults were also issued: that Earl Alan was guilty of every evil, that Count Waleran was boastful, slow to advance but quick to retreat, that Earl Hugh Bigod was a perjurer, that William of Aumale, Earl of York, had been deserted by his wife because of his intolerably filthy behaviour, and that the adulterer who had carried off the said lady had the gall to be standing alongside the earl in the royalist forces, let alone William of Ypres with his treasons and 'impurities'.[21] When Robert had finished speaking, his army raised a great shout, lifted their arms to heaven and advanced.[22]

As the besieging army facing a relief force, the royalists were in a naturally defensive situation. They had to guard against a sortie from the castle at their rear. Oman thinks the royalists had more infantry, following the words put into the mouth of Baldwin fitz Gilbert by Henry of Huntingdon: 'we are not inferior in cavalry, and stronger in infantry', but both these statements seem wrong. Since the speech goes on to praise the loyalty and bravery of the earls, who all fled, one wonders if the speech as presented by Henry is meant to be ironic. Orderic says that the reverse is true; and all other evidence suggests that the royalists had fewer cavalry. It does seem probable, however, that the royal infantry was better quality.[23] We do not know how good the city militia from Lincoln was, but it was unlikely to be worse than the poorly armed Welsh, 'unskilled and unpractised in the art of war' (at any rate in this kind of war), not generally equipped for fighting in battles.[24] The difference almost certainly was in the Angevin superiority in cavalry; they had come prepared for a battle. Stephen had only his siege army, and had previously had no reason to expect to face a large force. Orderic also says that some of the magnates who were with the king had treacherously sent troops to join the rebels.[25]

The royal force dismounted some knights in the one main division, the king in its midst, himself on foot. He drew these knights in close order around him. The horses were led away to a distance.[26] He meant to lead by example. His own household men protected the royal standard. His left was commanded by William of Aumale, in company with his chief military adviser, William of Ypres. His right was probably led by Hugh Bigod, but contained a whole handful of earls: those of Warenne, Northampton and Worcester (Waleran), as well as Alan of Penthièvre, Earl of Richmond, an experienced captain, no doubt to balance William of Ypres on the left. Both left and right seem to have been cavalry forces, and few in number. Many of the magnates were at Lincoln with only a small proportion of their feudal followings. The royal cavalry formed in two lines 'but this part of his force was small'.[27] It is possible, from Henry of Huntingdon's account, that the cavalry made a line right across the front of the royal force, and were then broken into three sections by the enemy attack.[28]

The Angevin army was probably commanded by Robert of Gloucester. Orderic says he was 'the greatest in the army', and John of Hexham calls him the 'general and organizer of the battle', though Ranulf may not have seen himself as inferior,

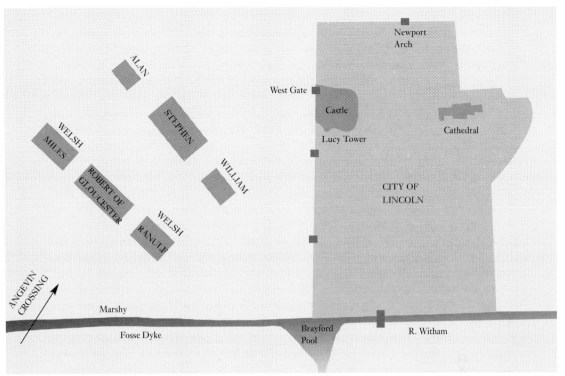

The Battle of Lincoln, 2 February 1141.

and had made the first of their battle speeches.[29] It is not possible to reconcile the various chroniclers' accounts entirely. Some describe both armies in line abreast, some as if in divisions, one behind the other. The most coherent account is that by Henry of Huntingdon. He was also nearest of the main chroniclers to the scene of the battle. We have, therefore, chosen to prefer his account, and where possible to incorporate other information. This suggests that the disinherited formed the left wing of the Angevin force, and faced those earls alongside Alan of Brittany. No leader is mentioned for this division, but Miles of Gloucester, though not an earl, would seem to be the likely name to pencil in. Henry of Huntingdon refers to Welsh on the right flank of the Angevin army, and then speaks of Ranulf's intervention on this wing. This is not the usual decision of historians, but following Henry of Huntingdon, we therefore place Ranulf in command of the Angevin right wing. Since three divisions are clearly mentioned by several writers, this would leave Robert of Gloucester commanding the centre, which would seem to be the natural position. Like the royalists, the Angevins too dismounted some of their knights to fight on foot. Ranulf had also brought with him infantry from Cheshire, most probably archers. It would be wrong to pretend we are certain about the positions in this battle, particularly with regard to the Angevin formation. It is quite possible that the description of ordering, one division behind the other, was the order of march, which as often happened in medieval campaigns, resolved into divisions abreast for battle, van on one wing, rear on the opposite wing. This might explain at least some of the discrepancies in the sources. From the chronicles it is uncertain if the three Angevin divisions were in line abreast or one behind the other. Given the royalist formation, we have preferred line abreast.[30]

One still has to find a position in the van for the Welsh. They were certainly in the van of the Angevin army, and the first to be mentioned as the engagement got under way. Again, following Henry of Huntingdon, we have placed them on the right flank, probably slightly in advance of the main divisions. It is possible from other accounts that a similar Welsh group was placed in the same position on the left flank. Three main Angevin divisions in line abreast seems the most probable formation in order to face the three divisions of the royalists, and we place the Welsh infantry on both flanks, thrown slightly forward. Orderic says the Bretons and Flemings under Alan and William of Ypres faced the Welsh, which implies that they were on the wings. Henry of Huntingdon reports the Welsh advancing from the side, which also clearly places them on at least one flank, presumably the right. Robert of Torigny supports this point, suggesting a Welsh advance from the flank. There does not seem to be agreement among our chroniclers about the formation, so we should remain suitably unsure that we have interpreted correctly. Orderic at least seems to suggest that the Welsh and the royalist cavalry were in the van on either side, and this does match other accounts, and is the one we have chosen to follow. He also tells us that the Welsh were led by Maredudd and Cadwaladr. These are identifiable Welsh princes, brother and brother-in-law of Owain the Great. Cadwaladr married the daughter of Richard fitz Gilbert of Clare, so these men were probably fighting as allies or mercenaries for the Angevins.[31] We conclude that the Angevins had three main divisions in line, with Welsh in advance of both wings.[32] These Welsh levies were infantry forces and poorly armed.

The advancing troops raised their voices in shouts, while trumpets blared, and trampling horses shook the earth.[33] The first action of the battle saw the destruction of the Welsh infantry when they were attacked by William of Ypres and the Earl of York on one side, and Alan of Brittany on the other. This first clash was of brief duration, and the Welsh fled from the field. But the cavalry forces behind them stayed put and now entered the fray. The Angevin left wing, probably under Miles, attacked the royalist forces which included Alan of Brittany. The Angevin cavalry on the right, under Ranulf, must have attacked at the same time, since we are told that their royal opponents were the first to be forced from the field. One account says that Waleran and William of Ypres fled 'before coming to close quarters', which is highly suggestive of an archery attack by the Angevin forces.[34] The royalist cavalry had presumably lost its order in the destruction of the Welsh, and were now themselves an easy target for the Angevin cavalry wings, which broke through and routed them.[35] This was the decisive point of the battle. William of Ypres we know to have been a brave and loyal captain. The fact that he now left the field suggests the hopelessness of Stephen's position. Henry of Huntingdon says that 'as an experienced general he perceived

The wall painting at Claverley Church, Shropshire, shows combat scenes between cavalrymen. These lively paintings probably date from the late twelfth century.

the impossibility of supporting the king'.[36] In fact, according to William of Malmesbury, all six of Stephen's earls fled from the field. Orderic says that William of Ypres and Alan were the first to take flight, and that Waleran, William Warenne and Gilbert of Clare then followed suit.[37] Wise soldiers knew that the king should never have fought the battle; his cavalry numbers were clearly not up to coping with the enemy, and William of Ypres and the others considered that the only option was to flee in order to fight another day. When William left, he obviously considered defeat inevitable. His assessment was not incorrect.

The formation of the two armies, especially that of the Angevins, is uncertain, and so, therefore, must be the exact sequence of events of the cavalry battle, but the final stage is quite clear. Stephen, with his one central division on foot, was now faced by three divisions, 'on all sides', which closed in on him.[38] The situation was graphically described by one writer as being like an attack all round a castle.[39] Some lords had stayed by his side and fought on, including Baldwin of Clare, Richard fitz Urse, Engelran de Saye, and Ilbert de Lacy.[40] Helmets and swords flashed in the air. Shouts and cries echoed all around. The king fought with his sword, men recoiling from his 'terrible arm'.[41] Eventually the weapon broke, and a citizen of Lincoln passed him a weapon more familiar to the Anglo-Saxons than to modern Anglo-Norman armies – a battle axe. Orderic indeed calls it a 'Norse axe', which suggests that the Lincoln militia were not armed in the most modern manner, but in a by now rather antiquated way as infantry forces.[42] Stephen fought on 'like a lion, grinding his teeth and foaming at the mouth like a boar'.[43] At least he did not leave an impression of cowardice, but made a 'strong and most resolute resistance'.[44] The battle axe was also broken in the conflict. At last he was put out of his misery, when one of the opposing army hit him over the head with a rock, which hardly sounds like a knightly action. Stephen was taken prisoner, either by Robert of Gloucester, or by William of Cahagnes. When he came round he kept on complaining that this was not the treatment to give a king, and that his enemies were breaking their faith, to the point where some of them actually burst into tears.[45] The ordinary citizens of Lincoln, however, could expect no mercy. Many were cut down, by 'the just anger of the victors'. As many as 500 drowned trying to escape across the river, more than were killed in the battle. They leaped into any boat they could find until the boats were too full and capsized.[46] The town itself also suffered, with houses and churches set on fire by the victors.

William of Malmesbury says that Robert of Gloucester treated the king well, ordering that he should be kept alive and unharmed, not even insulted.[47] He was taken before the empress at Gloucester, and then on to Bristol, where he was imprisoned. According to William of Malmesbury, because others wanted him closer confined, and because Stephen was found from time to time at night having wandered outside his place of confinement, he was put in iron chains.[48] It sounds like the apologist trying to explain away the fact that his hero, Earl Robert, was keeping in irons the anointed king. But battle was seen as divine decision, and Stephen had lost. One writer, who gave only a couple of lines to the battle, concluded that Stephen had been captured 'by the just judgement of God'.[49]

CHAPTER 5

Matilda's Opportunity

On 3 February 1141 it seemed that England had fallen into the hands of the Angevin party and that nothing could stop Matilda becoming ruler and queen; 'the greater part of the kingdom at once submitted to the countess and her adherents'.[1] Men recalled the fate of Robert Curthose, Duke of Normandy and contender for the English throne. He had been captured in 1106 at the Battle of Tinchebrai, and had been imprisoned for the rest of his life until 1134, losing his duchy in the process. And he had been captured and imprisoned by his own brother, so what chance could there be for Stephen? That indeed is how it seemed to men of the time, both in England and Normandy. The unknown monk who wrote the last part of the *Anglo-Saxon Chronicle* expressed it bluntly: 'when the king was in prison, the earls and the powerful men expected that he would never get out again'.[2]

Almost at once some vendettas were settled and some men dispossessed. Some few did fight on, including Alan, Earl of Richmond, who tried to ambush Ranulf of Chester. But Alan himself was captured, put in chains and tortured in a dungeon until he submitted to Ranulf, did homage to him and handed over his castles. Another result of this humiliation for Alan, was that it also confirmed that his rival in the west country, Reginald, son of Henry I, would keep the earldom of Cornwall.

Another to continue resistance was Hervey, Earl of Wiltshire, married to Stephen's daughter. He was holding Devizes Castle and was besieged in it. He eventually surrendered the castle to Matilda and was banished abroad. To what extent Hugh the Poor resisted is not clear, but he too was turned out of his earldom, of Bedford, and replaced by the pro-Angevin Miles Beauchamp. The *Gesta Stephani* says that he 'became in a short time a knight instead of an earl and instead of a knight a very poor man'.[3] A few men had stuck by Stephen, and had soon suffered for it, others drew a sharp lesson. In England they hastened to join Matilda, and come to terms with her, from Stephen's own brother Henry of Blois, to the castellan of the Tower, Geoffrey de Mandeville. The *Gesta Stephani* sneers at Robert d'Oilly and the Earl of Warwick as 'effeminate' for the speed of their submission, but they were practically trampled in the rush.[4] At first a number of magnates remained in the royalist camp, including Count Waleran and the Earls of Surrey and Northampton.[5] But not for long. Following his deal with Geoffrey of Anjou in Normandy, Waleran had little option but to make his peace with Matilda in England, which he had done by September of 1141.[6] There can be little doubt that Waleran had made his decision by giving priority to his estates over the Channel. For the Angevin party it was, of course, a time of rejoicing: 'to some it was an occasion of festival and seemed the dawning of a new day, as they hoped that an end might thereby be put to strife and war'.[7]

The situation for Stephen was perhaps even blacker in Normandy from the threat posed by the Count of Anjou. Thus, in the end, men equally sought to make their peace with Geoffrey, Count of Anjou, as in England they did with Matilda, even those who had been Stephen's most active supporters, such as Waleran, Count of Meulan, and Rotrou, Count of Mortagne. The church in Normandy followed the example of that in England, and John, Bishop of Lisieux, who had been the leading figure there in Stephen's administration, made his peace with Count Geoffrey, though he would in any case die within a few weeks. Once more it is vital to view things through the eyes of the time. These men were not dyed-in-the-wool traitors, as they have often been presented, they were simply accepting political realities as they appeared to the most sober magnates. That they proved inaccurate in their forecasts, we only know with hindsight. Most men considered that Stephen was likely to remain out of the way, indeed that God had made his judgment upon the king. There was no sense in throwing away lands and position in a hopeless cause. Just as they had flocked to Stephen in 1136 once he had become king, so now they rushed to join the victors of Lincoln and their friends.

The general gloom and depression among the royalists is tellingly reflected by Orderic Vitalis, writing in his Norman monastery. At this moment, with Stephen imprisoned, Orderic felt his life drawing to an end and concluded his lengthy chronicle with a brief personal reminiscence. He tells us of his birth in England at Atcham, his early entry as a boy into the Norman house of St-Evroult, in a country where he did not even understand the language, and they could not pronounce his English name. Orderic was now sixty-six, 'worn out with age and infirmity', and he ruminated sadly upon the fate of kings: 'At this very moment Stephen, King of England, languishes wretchedly in a dungeon'. He saw 'the princes of this world overwhelmed by misfortunes and disastrous setbacks', and took consolation in his religion. So comes to an end this great contribution to our knowledge of the period, and the rest of our tale will be the poorer for lack of his love of detail and human comment.[8]

The Bishop of Winchester was pressured by Matilda and Earl Robert to recognize the empress openly. His attitude before this had certainly given them reason to hope for his support. He had probably been primarily responsible for arranging Matilda's escape from the trap at Arundel, and he had publicly denounced his brother in the church council, after the arrest of the bishops. The *Gesta Stephani* sees the bishop 'dragged this way and that by different hooks'.[9]

The Angevins sent messages to him, and arranged a meeting outside Winchester at the beginning of March. It was on a Sunday, in truly English weather, that the meeting took place. The sky was grey, overcast with clouds, and rain pelting down 'as though the fates portended a change for the worse in their cause'.[10] William of Malmesbury says that Matilda swore 'that all matters of chief account in England, especially gifts of bishoprics and abbacies, should be subject

*The Great Seal of
Matilda, enthroned.*

to his control if he received her in Holy Church as lady, and kept his faith to her unbroken'.[11] Like other details given by this writer, this is open to question. If true, it seems an unwise promise, and one that as ruler she could never keep. The same writer says that all the leading magnates with her, including Earl Robert, made the same vow. Then Bishop Henry agreed to recognize her, provided she did not break the agreement. The *Gesta Stephani* presents Bishop Henry at this point, rather as William of Malmesbury had defended Earl Robert at the beginning of the reign: that he made peace for the time being so that later 'he might assist his brother if a chance were offered'.[12]

On the following day, 3 March, Matilda came into Winchester. The bishop gave her possession of the royal treasury and the keys to the royal castle. Turstin the clerk handed over the royal crown and the money in the treasury. The bishop arranged for the citizens 'at a public meeting in the market place to salute her as their lady and their queen'.[13] So Matilda was recognized as Queen of England at least in one city. Then she entered the cathedral in a procession, accompanied by the Bishop of Winchester on her right, and the Bishop of Saint David's on her left. The nephews of Roger of Salisbury, Bishops Nigel of Ely and Alexander of Lincoln, were also present, no doubt contemplating cheerfully how the tables had been turned. Bishop Henry was also responsible for sending to Theobald, Archbishop of Canterbury, who arrived at Winchester a few days later.

But Theobald was less easily persuaded than Bishop Henry, and deflected the request for his allegiance, saying that it would not be fitting to change so rapidly, and that he would need first to consult with King Stephen. Clearly other bishops also had reservations, and there was an ecclesiastical delegation to the king, which Matilda allowed. Seemingly, Stephen gave his permission to them to break their oaths to him – so at least says William of Malmesbury.[14] Matilda's triumphant Easter at Oxford in 1141 seemed like a repeat of Stephen's five years before.

After Easter a church council was called to debate the situation, which William of Malmesbury himself attended. Henry of Blois, as legate, took the chair, and Archbishop Theobald, together with all the bishops and many other church dignitaries, attended. Bishop Henry held a secret conference with all the bishops, then the abbots, then the archdeacons. No report was published, but it is clear from subsequent events that they favoured acquiescing in the turn of events and accepting Matilda.

Bishop Henry excused his move by saying that his brother had failed to keep his promises to the church, and harped on the arrest of the three bishops in 1139. He told the council that he had often broached the subject with his brother, and won 'nothing but hatred'. Somewhat pompously he declared: 'that while I should love my mortal brother, I should esteem far more highly the cause of my immortal Father'. He argued that the kingdom could not be allowed to stagger along without a ruler, and therefore 'we choose as lady of England and Normandy the daughter of a king who was a peacemaker . . . and we promise her faith and support'.[15] It all sounds rather like special pleading on his own behalf. But from Matilda's point of view, the church at least had been brought over, the first necessity if she were to be crowned.

By the time the empress reached Wilton, her journey was taking the appearance of a triumphal procession. The Archbishop of Canterbury was there to welcome her, and 'a great crowd of people flocked together, so that the town gates were hardly wide enough for the mass which entered'.[16] At Reading again people gathered together, and many came to do homage to the woman who seemed destined to be their new queen. It was at Reading that Robert d'Oilly surrendered his castle at Oxford. Again, at Saint Alban's, great rejoicing and a queen's welcome, and here arrived citizens from London to make arrangements for her welcome in the capital.

Stephen at first was given some comforts and freedom of movement, but was then chained up in a more humiliating fashion. One chronicler says this was because Matilda acted in revenge, 'with a woman's bitterness'.[17] Stephen may have ruminated upon his fate, and no doubt regretted his decision to fight against the odds outside Lincoln.

But the royalist party was not altogether wiped out. This was to prove the reason for the long endurance of this civil war, neither side seemed to have the power quite to finish off the other. And no one would have a better chance of doing this than Matilda in 1141. No major magnate at first stood in the field to oppose the victors. The more enthusiastic supporters of Stephen had shared his defeat at Lincoln, and had either been captured or felt an especial need to placate the Angevins. Only a very few leading figures seem to have continued as royalists without hesitation. In the spring of 1141 that was a very risky stance to take. One of the few was the queen, Matilda, in many ways a more admirable character than her namesake the empress. If anyone saved Stephen's cause it was his wife, even if she were only a figurehead. But she was more than this; she became an active canvasser on his behalf, and a leader of the forces assembled for him. Her partner in this dangerous project was William of Ypres, who showed that his attachment to the royal cause was greater than that of a mere mercenary captain, which is the manner in which he is usually depicted. He was a great noble, Earl of Kent in all but name, and a very experienced commander. Henry of Huntingdon wrote that 'the whole of the people of England accepted the empress as their ruler, with the exception of the men of Kent, where the queen and William of Ypres resisted her to the utmost of their power'.[18]

It is also true that the capture of Stephen was not welcomed everywhere, and did not bring instant peace and prosperity. The English writer of the *Anglo-Saxon Chronicle*, often believed to blame Stephen for causing anarchy and disorder, considered that the king's captivity meant that 'all England was disturbed more than it had been before and there was every evil in the country'. Orderic reinforced the point: 'England was filled with plundering and burning and massacres'.[19] There is a good case for suggesting that the worst disturbances of the reign date from this period. Matilda had seemingly won the war, but like any new ruler she faced disorder unless she could establish herself firmly and quickly.

MATILDA IN LONDON

London had accepted the situation, and admitted Matilda's claims.[20] Henry of Huntingdon suggests that the Londoners, along with the Bishop of Winchester, were among the first to recognize her.[21] Representatives of the city had attended the Winchester council, where they had requested the release of the king, but seemingly accepted that it would not be granted. At Saint Alban's, as we have seen, a deputation from the city came to greet Matilda and arrange for her entry to London, albeit with some reluctance.[22] Here, as with Stephen, Matilda sought to pass her third test. Although not yet crowned, she had won the obedience of the church so that coronation seemed but a formality; she had taken over the treasury at Winchester with very little trouble; it remained only to win over London. She entered Westminster in procession, and remained there a few days dealing with the urgent business of her new realm.

But here for the first time an aspect of her character, which had not so far been apparent, was to let her down. It may be that she had learned certain attitudes from her stay in Germany, where she had been treated with the deference due to an empress. Her retention of that title in later life suggests that she had rather enjoyed the trappings of imperial life. She had been young when sent to Germany, so it would not be surprising if she had imbibed whatever she was taught there in terms of etiquette and treatment of her subjects. It may be that this gave her the haughty appearance which served less well in England. But one senses also a touch of personal character peeping through.

Since the death of her first husband, life had not been easy for the empress.

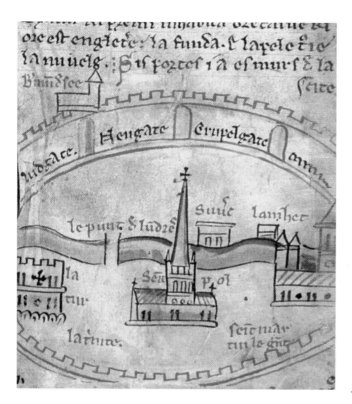

London, showing St Paul's, the Tower, London Bridge, the wall and gates. (Corpus Christi College Cambridge, MS 26, f. i.r)

She had returned from the empire probably without any firm knowledge of what her future might be, and so far as we know, not to seek the succession to the English throne. At that time she had no children, and the move looks very much like a simple wish to return home. She could have stayed in Germany, but presumably did not feel enough attachment to her new country. On her return, she had been married off by her father, with little effort to gain her assent. A boy of Geoffrey's years would hardly have been the choice made by a mature widowed woman.

The new marriage had begun badly and she had temporarily deserted her husband and returned to her father's court. The reason for this separation is unknown. Professor Gillingham has suggested that Geoffrey disliked his wife, and only put up with her for the political benefits; a view which Dr Chibnall seems happy to accept, since she wishes to present Matilda as not being solely responsible for the break.[23] The fact is that no one knows the reason. Some sexual difficulty seems not unlikely, given that he was only fifteen at the marriage, and she had produced no children by her first marriage, made when she also had been very young.

The separation of Matilda from Geoffrey seems to have done the trick. She had then been packed off back to her husband, seemingly against her will, as the result of a decision by an assembly called by her father. That had been a turning point in her affections, or at least in her allegiance, and she now gave her husband support against her father, and the reunited couple produced a whole string of children in quick succession – three sons in four years.

In the last year of his life, Henry I had been at war with Geoffrey of Anjou, and Matilda had taken her husband's part. This period of her life, though, had been dominated by a series of pregnancies, one at least of which was difficult. It may have been weakness from such a pregnancy which prevented her making a stronger effort to seek the crown in 1135.

Her father had made Matilda his heir, and taken oaths from magnates and prelates in England and Normandy to support her succession. When the point came, hardly anyone had kept to their oath. Matilda had been rejected as being a woman and the wife of Count Geoffrey. At last in 1138 she was offered a new chance to claim her succession with the change of heart of Robert of Gloucester. She had been persuaded to come to England and take her chance. But again, though a few had joined her cause, most had ignored her; a second rejection by the English nobility. It was hardly surprising that in 1141 Matilda, elated by the victory of Lincoln, sought to make an immediate impact and gain some revenge for her earlier treatment. What is certain is that she was no meek and mild mouse of a woman, being described by one chronicler as a 'virago', with a deep masculine voice and a very strong personality. She was also 'elated with insufferable pride' from the recent success.[24] She could not have been entirely unlikeable, and inspired strong devotion from some, such as Brian fitz Count, but she had the capacity to speak her mind and upset even those who had given her support.

A coin of the Empress Matilda, struck at the Cardiff mint, showing the Empress, crowned and holding a sceptre.

One of her acts on being accepted into London, was to demand a tax. Matilda's objectives here were almost certainly political, even admirable. They were the same policies which her son, when he became King Henry II, would employ, and which are then generally praised. She rejected Stephen's methods of bowing to citizen desires for commune status, and wanted London to revert to a more lowly position, more amenable to monarchical control. But she upset citizen sensibilities, and pockets, though it was probably not so much the tax as the question of how it should be collected which was the prime issue. A commune controlled its own tax collection. The Worcester chronicler says that she insisted on returning to the laws of her father with regard to London, which almost certainly means she told them she would overthrow Stephen's grant of commune status.[25] The *Gesta Stephani* reveals her attitude to these commoners: 'she sent for the richest men and demanded from them a huge sum of money, not with unassuming gentleness, but with a voice of authority'. The Londoners, like all those facing tax demands, pleaded poverty on account of the costs of the war, and because they had been forced to take expensive measures to combat the threat of the current famine. Later they promised, when peace had been effective and they had prospered, they would be able to pay in proportion to their prosperity. The empress then 'with a grim look, her forehead wrinkled into a frown, every trace of a woman's gentleness removed from her face, blazed into intemperate fury'. She shouted at them that they had paid large taxes to Stephen and had helped him against her, so it was only just that she should demand full payment and not reduce her demands by a penny: 'The citizens went away gloomily to their homes without gaining what they had asked.'[26]

Another disappointed man in London was Henry, Bishop of Winchester. He made a petition on behalf of his nephew, Stephen's son Eustace, as did Queen Matilda, but the empress would give no time to the suggestion, intending to disinherit Eustace. This was more than the bishop could stomach, and he avoided attending her court for several days.[27] It did not augur well for keeping her promises to put governance of the church in his hands. He then met Queen Matilda secretly at Guildford. The empress seems to have upset a number of others, and one chronicler records that she 'alienated from her the hearts of most men'.[28] There is a common belief that she upset her uncle, David, King of Scots, during this period by her behaviour. But in fact she supported his candidate for the see of Durham, William Cumin, against the wishes of the local church, and with unfortunate results for herself in terms of church support.[29]

Through the brief period from the Battle of Lincoln to her stay in London, Matilda had begun to behave like a queen and to call herself a queen, as in charters issued while en route to London, though she also styled herself more commonly 'lady of the English' or 'empress'.[30] She began to dispose of the realm as its ruler. Interestingly she chose to follow Stephen's policy with regard to earldoms, and appointed a number of her own earls, some as rivals to those named by Stephen, as for example William of Beauchamp to oppose Waleran of Beaumont in Worcester, Baldwin de Redvers to Devon, Geoffrey de Mandeville to Essex, Miles of Gloucester to Hereford, and William de Mohun to Somerset and Dorset, all in 1141. It suggests that she at least thought the king's policy had merit.

Although most of the king's supporters had yielded, his wife, Queen Matilda, and his lieutenant, William of Ypres, were still actively preparing to resist the empress. Queen Matilda had sent a request for the release of her husband from captivity to the church council at Winchester, underlining the problem his enemies faced in imprisoning an anointed king. The queen also requested that her son's inheritance rights be respected. One suggestion was apparently that, if released, Stephen should enter a monastery.[31] Again, Matilda showed no restraint in her response, and the queen's representatives were abused and insulted. As a result, Queen Matilda despaired of gaining anything by diplomacy, and sought to achieve what she could through war. From her base in Kent she raised a considerable force under the command of William of Ypres, and began to march on London.

This force then set about the traditional acts of provocation in such a situation, burning and ravaging the countryside surrounding the capital, till it became 'a home only for the hedgehog'.[32] It was enough to sway the attitude of the Londoners, upset by the tax demands, the threat to their status, and the general attitude of the empress. Her manner seemed to offer no hope of mercy or compromise. The projected rule of the Angevins had come to look like 'the tyranny of usurpers'.[33] The citizens decided to throw in their lot with Queen Matilda, who was ranging just outside their walls. They decided to seek the release of the king. They made secret negotiations with the royalists and contemplated 'sedition' against the empress.[34]

Matilda awaited the response to her demands with confidence, but it was misplaced. She was about to settle down to dinner, reclining on a couch, when she heard the sudden loud ringing of bells throughout London. It was the sign of rebellion against her. The citizens took to arms, attacked her followers and opened the city gates. The empress was informed of the situation and she and her close retinue mounted horses and fled. They had barely set out, when a London mob broke into her apartments, and plundered all they could find. Some of the lords who had been with her, sought their own safety rather than hers, and rode off to their own homes. Henry, Bishop of Winchester, was one of those who had followed Matilda to London. The *Gesta Stephani* suggests that the bishop had played a part in plotting with the Londoners. This may relate to the secret meeting with Queen Matilda at Guildford, mentioned by William of Malmesbury.[35] Henry set off back for his diocese to have a rethink about his stance. He claimed that the empress intended to arrest him.

Matilda and Earl Robert made for the safety of Oxford. She had failed to complete the trio of necessary preliminaries to gaining the crown, she had failed to win London, and in losing London she also lost the opportunity of coronation. The Empress Matilda was never to be truly Queen of England. With the defection of Bishop Henry she looked as if she might also lose Winchester.

Queen Matilda was now welcomed into London, probably with greater warmth than her namesake had been. A number of royalists began to creep out from under their stones. It looked after all as if everything were not lost in the king's cause. Among those she persuaded, was Henry of Winchester, who now again openly declared his allegiance to Stephen. Geoffrey de Mandeville, the castellan of the Tower of London, was another early convert back to the royal cause. All of the empress' three needs were now at risk: she had lost London, she was threatened with the loss of Winchester and of the church at the same time. The danger must be dealt with at once if her cause was to survive.

THE ROUT OF WINCHESTER

There were two castles in Winchester: the royal castle, which Matilda had already claimed, and the bishop's own stronghold, Wolvesey Castle, which has recently been reopened to public viewing. It was one of a series of magnificent buildings for which the bishop was responsible. Henry seems to have taken the first step in the conflict which was now to rage around his city, by besieging the royal castle, held for the empress. Then he waited to see her response. There was not long to

Henry of Blois, appointed Bishop of Winchester by Henry I in 1126. He carries his ring and staff, subject of much debate at the time as to whether they should be presented by the secular or the spiritual power. (BL MS Nero DVII, f. 87v)

wait. Matilda arrived with a besieging army on 31 July 1141. Bishop Henry, who had 'often turned over in his own mind how he could rescue his brother', had put his own castle into a position of defence in anticipation of a siege, and sent to Queen Matilda for aid.[36] He did not wait to be caught there, and escaped on a swift horse from one gate, as the empress entered by another.[37] But he left his men there to defy Matilda from within the town, while he, having gathered men from his own castles, joined the queen's forces outside.

Matilda was able to enter the town, relieve the royal castle, and besiege that of the bishop. But now she became caught in her own trap. In August a second force arrived outside Winchester. Queen Matilda and William of Ypres, having claimed London, had marched on in pursuit of the Angevins. Now they proceeded to blockade the town. So there was a double siege: Wolvesey besieged by the empress, and the town surrounded by the royalists. 'Everywhere outside the walls of Winchester the roads were being watched by the queen and the earls, to prevent provisions being brought in to the partisans of the empress.'[38] Only a few supplies could be smuggled through the lines from the west, and many of those trying to sneak through, were killed or captured and tortured. The royalists on the other hand were well supplied from London and the east, and could afford to take their time.

On 2 August Winchester was fired, thus denying Matilda both shelter and

Soldiers attacking a gate. Note the arms and armour depicted in this twelfth-century illustration. (Corpus Christi College, Cambridge, MS 2, f. 245v)

provisions. Henry of Blois himself is said to have ordered the burning, which was probably started by his men from within Wolvesey Castle.[39] Hyde Abbey and Saint Mary's nunnery within the city were destroyed by the flames. A great jewel-encrusted cross given to the abbey by Cnut was roasted by the heat, and 'began to sweat and grow black . . . and at the very moment of its catching fire a terrible crash of thunder cracked three times from the heavens'.[40] By September the Angevins were feeling the pinch of the blockade. They were probably also outnumbered, since the queen's army had been reinforced by volunteers from the city militia of London, as well as various barons who were returning to the royal allegiance, including Geoffrey de Mandeville, Earl of Essex.

The sequence of events during the siege of Winchester has been a matter of debate, since the chronicles are not entirely in agreement, but the main outline and outcome are not in doubt. As was common, the royalists began to seek control over surrounding strongpoints which might offer help.[41] Andover was fired. At some point an Angevin outpost established in the nearby abbey at Wherwell, which they had fortified, was attacked by the royalists, and also fired.

We have details of the event at Wherwell in the later poem about William the Marshal, but not an exact explanation of its role in the whole story.[42] Its garrison under John fitz Gilbert, William the Marshal's father, either set out from Wherwell in an attempt to force a diversion to help save the empress, or to break through the royalist blockade in order to relieve and supply the empress. The royalists decided to put Wherwell out of action, and set fire to it. The attackers threw burning torches inside the church where the Angevin garrison was taking shelter. Most emerged, singed, to surrender. William of Malmesbury, with his usual bias, condemns the 'impious' William of Ypres for setting fire to the nunnery, but not the Angevins for taking shelter within it and attempting to use it like a castle.[43] The nuns themselves were forced 'shrieking' from their home, as the flames spread. In the blaze, the lead roof fell in on top of John fitz Gilbert. He was lucky to escape with his life, but was blinded. Some of his men were captured and tied with thongs, while others managed to get him away to safety, but the outpost had fallen.

It is not clear whether the Wherwell incident was the cover for the imperial attempt to escape. At any rate the Angevins decided their only course was to break out and retreat. They packed their baggage in preparation for an escape bid. On Sunday 14 September, Robert of Gloucester made a feint attack to divert attention from Matilda's escape from the city, escorted by Brian fitz Count and Reginald, Earl of Cornwall. Once again a chronicler, this time the Worcester continuator, suggests that Bishop Henry was involved in some double dealing. The writer says that he arranged for the gate to be opened so that the empress could escape, which reminds one of his role at Arundel.[44] The same source says that the bishop then ordered his men to join the fray on the royal side. The *Anglo-Saxon Chronicle* seems to give support to this view, since it says that Bishop Henry, after the episode in London, had talks with Matilda and Earl Robert, promising never to support Stephen again, and to hand Winchester to the empress. One cannot easily dismiss the case against Bishop Henry, though there are some inconsistencies and some jealousies involved in the accusations. Most telling of all perhaps, with regard to his character, are the references shortly after this in some letters written by Brian fitz Count who said: 'he had a remarkable gift of discovering that duty pointed in the same direction as expediency', and wondered at the bishop's gall in accusing Brian, 'whose main offence consisted in refusing to change sides as often as himself'.[45]

The *Gesta Stephani* suggests that the companionship between Brian and Matilda during this escape gave rise to some, now lost, epic which celebrated their affection for each other, and which seems to be the source of the enduring tale about their relationship: 'But she and Brian gained by this a title to boundless fame, since as their affection for each other had before been unbroken, so even in adversity, great impediment though the danger was, they were in no way divided'.[46]

Matilda managed to get away, first riding on a horse, astride in male fashion, in days when ladies normally rode side-saddle. She found John fitz Gilbert's castle of Ludgershall, 'sorrowing and downcast'.[47] Next day her journey continued to the more distant safety of Devizes. She set out again riding 'in male fashion' but, not surprisingly, grew tired, and completed the journey 'nearly half dead', carried upon a litter. She was bound to the litter as if she were a corpse, and it was borne on to Gloucester upon horses.[48]

She escaped, and so did David, King of Scots, who was also with the empress. The King of Scots was taken three times, but each time he got away. Miles, Earl of Hereford, made his escape by discarding his armour so he would not be recognized, and managed to get through to his town of Gloucester, albeit 'half naked'.[49] But Earl Robert did not get away. He deliberately remained at the rear of the force, keeping his men in good order, determined to keep the royal forces from pursuing Matilda. But he was outnumbered, and the royalists were able to attack from all sides. He came into conflict with the enemy at Stockbridge on the road from Winchester to Salisbury. The earl had led a sortie from the city, sending Matilda on her way while he covered her retreat. Stockbridge was about 8 miles on the route to the west away from the city, where a bridge crossed the Trent. When he reached Winchester Hill, he was forced by the pursuing royalists under William of Ypres, to turn and fight. The rear section of the Angevin army was cut off from the rest. The empress' army was broken, knights knocked from their horses, horses running about loose. Some threw off their armour and ran for it. Some of these were captured by peasants and beaten up. Some hid wherever they could. Robert fought bravely, but was captured by the mercenaries of William of Warenne, Earl of Surrey, and sent back to be imprisoned in Rochester Castle under the guard of William of Ypres. The citizens of Winchester got little thanks for their part in helping the royalists. The London militia troops proceeded to sack the city which they now took over for the king. Homes and shops were wrecked and pillaged, as well as churches; spoils and captives were taken away.

The Rout of Winchester was as great a disaster for Matilda as Lincoln had been for Stephen. All her efforts to become queen, all her attempts to secure the necessary support, had come to nothing. During the months which followed it became clear to her, to the Angevin party, and thus to us, that her cause was hopeless without the support of Robert of Gloucester. The royalists tried to

Winchester Cathedral from the south.

persuade Earl Robert to change his allegiance, and offered him a position of power under the king, but his refusal meant there was no other escape for him except an exchange.[50] In the end the empress capitulated, and by the October 1141 Treaty of Winchester, agreed to 'a mutual exchange' of the major prisoners: Robert, Earl of Gloucester, for King Stephen.[51] On 1 November the king was released, to 'great rejoicings'.[52] The king emerged from his prison and rode out of Bristol, leaving behind his wife, his son and two magnates. Two days later he reached Winchester and Earl Robert was released, leaving his son behind. When Robert reached Bristol, the queen was set free, and when she got to Winchester, all parties were released.[53] It seemed like a return to square one, as one chronicler noted, they had returned 'to the earlier position of the civil war'. The king was met by a crowd of his friends, with much weeping and celebration, with 'cries of rejoicing and exultation that he was restored to them unharmed'. [54]

CHAPTER 6

The Castle War

The Battle of Lincoln was a key moment in the wars of Stephen's reign, and in the end, indirectly, decisive. It did not finish Stephen's career as king, as it might have done, but it effectively undermined his chances of complete success. Similarly, the Rout of Winchester was a key moment. It had not ended Matilda's hopes of eventual success, but it had dampened them considerably.

As the two sides dressed their wounds and contemplated the future at the end of 1141, they had new objectives. Stephen seems to have emerged from prison harder; more set on final success than before. He fought the war that ensued with great energy. The Angevins, however, seem to have accepted that they could, for the time being, do no better than fight to defend what they already had.

The harmful effects of Lincoln for the royalists had not been entirely removed by the release of Stephen. Not all the barons who deserted when he was in prison returned to the fold immediately; some did not return at all. Not all of the places taken over by the Angevins in 1141 had been given up, and some would not be given up at all. In the long run, the most disastrous thing that was left as a legacy from Lincoln, for the king, was the considerable loss sustained in Normandy. Because he became so embroiled in the war in England over the next years, and because his presence and effort were essential to that war, he was not able to go to Normandy again. The effect of that situation we shall observe in the next chapter.

CASTLES AT THE TIME OF STEPHEN AND MATILDA

The next episode in the war was fundamentally a castle war, a war of sieges, of attrition. The king had to be active in several regions, but it was in essence a static or at least slowly moving war, not unlike the trench war of 1914–18 in that respect. The boundaries were marked, moving beyond them was not easy. Both sides were naturally cautious of risking another battle after Lincoln and Winchester. Effort was mainly put into building, defending or attacking castles.

Little is known of the castles of this period. Some experts seem more or less to have decided that no castles at all were built in 'the Anarchy', though this is patently nonsense. One problem is that there are no pipe rolls for Stephen's reign, so the recording of royal expenditure on castles is not known. Reading Castle, which seems only to have stood from 1150 to 1153, was one of the few definite royal castles built in the period. Another problem is that the Latin phrases found in charters can usually be interpreted quite correctly to mean that either a castle was built, or it was rebuilt. By the twelfth century, when many castles had already been built, it is therefore probable that 'rebuilt' is often the correct meaning, but not always. The problem though is to distinguish the Stephen castles, since archaeologists have given little effort to define the features to be sought. In most cases, only observation of architectural features or archaeological investigation can show whether we have a castle from Stephen's reign. This, again, is less easy than it sounds. There are often few twelfth-century features to be observed, and since we have virtually no established Stephen models to go by, observers tend much more often to label unidentified castles as being Henry I or Henry II, than Stephen. And as for archaeology, stripping of castle sites is an extremely expensive and difficult operation, and not often undertaken. The kind of limited excavations which usually occur, often do not give the information which we are looking for at the moment. But that said, a trawl through archaeological reports on castles in local journals reveals literally hundreds of probable sites with evidence of use in this period. And enough can be shown from documentary remains to list castles which either originated or were added to in the period, which when checked archaeologically, will make a foundation for firmer historical work on this topic.

This book is not intended to be a work of research on Stephen's castles, though such a book could be written. We can, for the present, merely outline what is known on the subject, and make a few conjectures. Firstly, there is no doubt that several hundred castles existed at the time of this civil war. These may be listed from those mentioned in chronicle accounts, and in charters. Most of the castles in this war were already in existence before it began; what we can call old castles. The majority of these, built in the early Norman period, were of the earthwork motte and bailey type which we described in an earlier chapter. In most cases these were improved during the twelfth century, most commonly by having towers and walls rebuilt in stone. Other desirable improvements at the time were to widen the moat and to strengthen the gatehouse.

Because of the difficulty in identifying the castles of the reign, it is impossible to be categorical about the style favoured in the period. However, it is possible to suggest several dozen structures which were almost certainly new, and these provide enough evidence for a preliminary catalogue of their features. The first, as already noted in considering improvements, was the focus on stone fortification. New castles in this period were often built, from the first, in stone, certainly wherever a permanent fortification was intended, and where a wealthy builder such as a king or magnate was concerned. Bishops were also great castle builders, not least Roger of Salisbury and Henry of Blois. Each built impressive new stone castles, for example at Salisbury and Farnham.

But because of the critical situation, when fortification was again often a matter of emergency, some earthwork castles were constructed. Also, some castles which were never intended to be more than temporary, were erected. These were probably normally of a very simple type, though few have been identified or studied.

The work on Bentley in Hampshire is especially interesting, in showing what at least one of this type of temporary castle was like. It was suggested to have been a

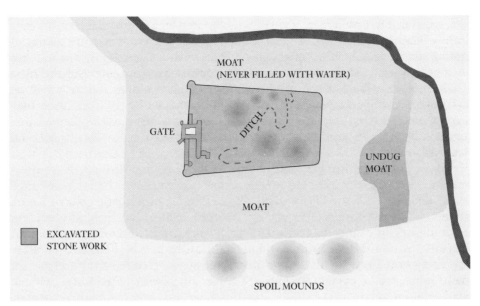

MOAT
(NEVER FILLED WITH WATER)

GATE

DITCH

UNDUG
MOAT

MOAT

EXCAVATED
STONE WORK

SPOIL MOUNDS

Plan of Burwell Castle, based on the plans from the excavation.

counter castle used against 'Lidelea', the latter identified as being Barley Pound Castle, a considerably larger structure. Bentley was thought to be merely a ringwork, but proved in fact, on archaeological examination, to be a motte and bailey castle of a moderate size, with a low motte inside a roughly circular enclosure.[1]

Another counter castle, in the previous reign, had been referred to by a chronicler as being nicknamed 'hare's form', from which one envisages a simple flattened enclosure, like a bailey, or what is sometimes called a ringwork, of an irregular shape.[2] Among others, counter castles were built during the civil war against Bristol, Dunster, Wallingford and Faringdon. However, at least one temporary castle, at Burwell in Cambridgeshire, was more elaborate. This was a royal castle, built against Geoffrey de Mandeville in 1143, and it was not known for how long it might be required. In the event it was never even finished. It therefore gives us a frozen image of one such castle, since it has been excavated.[3]

Burwell Castle was built in the shape of an almost regular rectangle, which had not been at all common before this period, and reminds one more of Roman forts than Norman castles. It was to have a very broad moat, 30 feet across and 9 feet deep, dug around this rectangular platform. The moat was never completed and therefore remained only as a great ditch, but the intention was clearly to lead in water from the nearby stream. From the recovered plan, it looks as if the intention was to build an interior tower as a keep. There was also the beginnings of a square-towered gateway. Both the gate and the surrounding curtain wall were begun in stone. So we know what was intended, even if the building was not complete. To our eyes it was quite a revolutionary design, and incorporated several of the features we have mentioned as desirable in new castles at this time.

Unfortunately, little of the castle is left to be seen above ground. Some 8 feet of wall which once stood was damaged when 'some ingenious person thought of testing the village fire hose against it', causing it to collapse.[4] Just a few stones may be seen now where they have been disturbed by tree roots. But the large grassy mounds still allow some idea of the depth and width of the moat and the height of the ramparts. Some mounds once thought of as siege works, now they have been excavated, have been shown to be spoil mounds made while the castle was still being built, and left in position once Burwell Castle was abandoned a year later.

We know that Stephen built other castles at the same time as Burwell as part of the same campaign. We should expect them to be similar to Burwell, but they have never been satisfactorily identified. The area around the Isle of Ely is absolutely littered with castle remains and other earthworks; there are over 300 moated sites in Cambridgeshire alone. But now that we know the shape of Burwell, we must be cautious about attributing rectangular moated sites invariably to the late Middle Ages. A study of plans of other earthworks, where these are available, suggests a number of apparently similar outlines, for example at Rampton, Caxton, Bassingbourn and Kirtling, but conjecture without excavation can take us no further.[5]

One feature of several castles built in this period, but not yet perhaps clearly acknowledged as being new and important, was that of 'buried towers'. The purpose of these is open to debate, but not their existence. This feature has been detected in castles which range from elaborate to relatively simple, from stone to

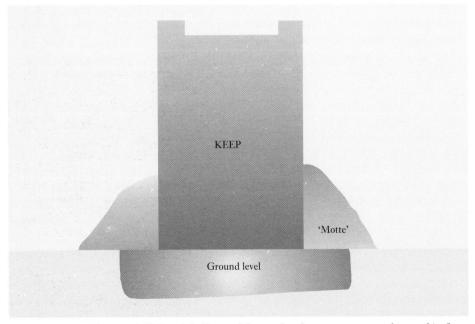

KEEP

'Motte'

Ground level

The buried keep. The stone-built keep is built on solid ground and a motte constructed around its foot.

timber keeps. The common design had a tower built on ground level, and a mound raised around the foot of it, so that it looked like a typical motte with a tower on top, but its structure was different. This could have been because by the mid-twelfth century, defenders recognized the usefulness of a motte to protect the foot of the tower, to make scaling, mining and attacking in general more difficult. A mound was desirable and so was a heavily built tower, but the two could not be combined unless there was a natural mound to use. In Norman motte and bailey castles, when the mound was new and artificial, the tower had to be a relatively light timber construction. Old Norman mounds were now settled enough to form the base for improved stone towers, but it was a different matter when it came to building a new castle. One answer was the buried tower, which gave the tower a firm ground foundation, with the 'motte' later built around its foot. It was also efficient in terms of space; instead of a useless large mound of earth, in these structures, the base of the tower was within the motte and gave additional space for storage.

One reason for the improvement in castles through stronger structures in stone, was the improvement in siege weapons. Throwing weapons of various kinds were commonly used in sieges, as they had been for centuries. In the twelfth century we begin to hear of them used more experimentally. Geoffrey of Anjou, in his own county if not elsewhere, used throwing engines to hurl Greek fire. The part of the Christian army for the Second Crusade which went to Lisbon is often

Geoffrey V besieged the original castle at Montreuil-Bellay, using Greek fire. He finally took the castle after a three year siege and then demolished it. The photograph shows a later reconstruction.

thought to have used trebuchets in the siege there.[6] This remains debatable, but the trebuchet does appear during this century, and the proposition is not impossible. It worked on a different principle from most throwing machines, by using a counterweight, and was able to hurl much greater stones and so do more damage.

The use of the castle in war was manifold: for offence, defence, shelter, control, and authority. It was also a symbol of power. No one could claim to have authority over an area unless they commanded its strongest castles. Lords naturally made their chief castle, their *caput*, the best built of their various strongholds, and it was therefore the most difficult to capture. In England, where castles had mushroomed during the century since the Conquest, control of an area meant control of its castles. Since they were constructed to be defensible, this control was not easily obtained. It might be gained by agreement, by recognition that although one person resided in the castle, another had superior claims upon it: the king over the castellan of a royal castle, an overlord over a feudal subordinate. But where the situation was one of civil war, usually nothing short of physical control of the castle would do, and this meant attacking it, besieging it, forcing its surrender, so that one could place it in the hands of a loyal garrison and thereafter use it for one's own purposes. In the areas which bordered the safe territories of Stephen and Matilda, or areas which were in dispute between them for other reasons, or areas where one side was seeking to extend its power, control of castles was usually the key point of the war. Hence the geographically confusing look of the war, with sieges here, there and everywhere. But they were not pointless and haphazard; they were examples of the leaders pursuing one of the major needs of this particular war.

Nor were our commanders simpletons. The theory of war was not unknown in the twelfth century. By this time manuals of the Roman writer Vegetius were available for those who wished to study methods of war. We know that Geoffrey, Count of Anjou held a copy of Vegetius in his hands in the final stages of the siege of Montreuil-Bellay in 1151, and that it gave him the inspiration which led to his success there. Several of our Anglo-Norman nobles we know to have been literate, such as Robert of Gloucester, and it would be unwise to believe they knew nothing of the current theories of war.

THE AFTERMATH OF WINCHESTER AND THE SIEGE OF OXFORD

Matilda had made Oxford her new base. This was a brave move and suggests that she had not entirely given up hopes of recovering from the disasters at London and Winchester. Oxford was part of the westerly salient in terms of Angevin safe territory, its only close partner being Wallingford. Oxford, therefore, became the first focus of the renewed warfare following the release of the chief protagonists. The Angevins made attempts to shore up their position, and a number of new castles were built, for example, at Woodstock, Radcot, Bampton and Cirencester; this showed the line they were trying to defend at their easterly most forward position near Oxford and Wallingford.

Stephen made use of a church council at Westminster, called by his brother, to

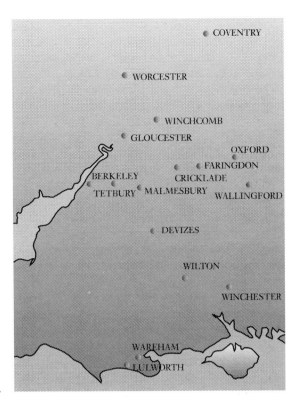

The Castle War in the west, 1141–5.

voice a protest about his capture and imprisonment. An earlier letter from the Pope was read out, which rebuked Bishop Henry for not doing more to gain his brother's release, presumably in order to demonstrate that the papal position was still firmly royalist. Bishop Henry felt the need at this point to justify his actions during his brother's captivity, and claimed that his agreement with Matilda had only been made 'of necessity'.[7] He also pointed out that she, and not he, had broken the agreement then made, by not giving the promised freedom to the church. He had used the same excuse for deserting first Stephen and then Matilda. He also accused Matilda of plotting against his life. He reaffirmed his brother's claims as an anointed king recognized by the papacy, and accused Stephen's enemies of being 'disturbers of the peace'.[8] A representative of the empress at the council reminded Henry that he had promised to give no more than twenty knights to aid his brother, and of his former encouragement of the empress' cause, including frequent letters to her in Normandy suggesting that she come to England, another interesting sidelight on the bishop's behaviour at Arundel. He also accused Henry of 'connivance' in the defeat and capture of his brother.[9]

Stephen was ill in the early part of 1142, probably a reaction to his imprisonment. Oddly enough, at about the same time, Matilda was also laid low; a reaction to the Rout of Winchester, she was 'worn out almost to the point of

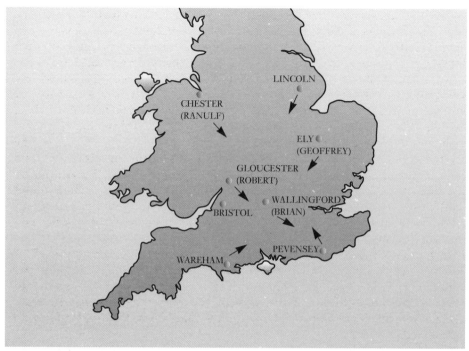

Angevin threats: the Castle War, 1141–5.

utter collapse'.[10] At Lent a truce was agreed, during which Matilda went to Devizes for a 'secret conference' with her supporters. Its conclusion shows that they were becoming anxious about their position, and decided to send to Geoffrey of Anjou for direct aid, 'it being his duty to maintain the inheritance of his wife and children in England'.[11] A delegation was sent off to him, which returned with little news to rejoice the empress. With what sounds like delaying tactics, Geoffrey had said he would only take note if Robert of Gloucester reported to him in person: 'it was merely a waste of time for anyone else to come and go'.[12]

At first Robert refused to go, saying that it was a hazardous journey through enemy territory in England and Normandy. He also feared to leave Matilda's cause in other hands. The weakness of the Angevin party at this juncture is made clear by his demands. He insisted on taking with him to Normandy, hostages for lords on the Angevin side, to ensure their continued loyalty. Not much trust was shown in that. Stephen was not the only one with loyalty problems among his followers.

Earl Robert finally agreed to go and petition Geoffrey. He set out for Wareham, which was now held by his eldest son, William of Gloucester. From there he sailed for Normandy, surviving a storm in mid-Channel. Only two ships kept going, including the one carrying Robert. He landed and made for his own town of Caen, from where he sent to Count Geoffrey, who now came to the earl. But again Geoffrey prevaricated, and said he could not think about coming to

England straight away, since there were numerous castles which he must first reduce in Normandy. The reluctant earl was dragged along in the company of Count Geoffrey's army to besiege various Norman strongholds. Altogether ten castles were captured, including Tinchebrai, Vire, Villers-Bocage and Mortain.

At the end of all this, after repeated requests to give his decision about coming to England, Count Geoffrey turned down the idea. Earl Robert must have felt extremely frustrated. Instead, the Count offered that he take back to England with him his son, the young Henry of Anjou, 'that on seeing him the nobles might be inspired to fight for the cause of the lawful heir'. Of course, the Angevins made the most of the boy's claims, for propaganda purposes, and with hindsight it looks like an important moment in our history. But at the time it must have been a terrible disappointment to the Angevin party in England. Count Geoffrey had made it only too obvious that his own priority was in Normandy, and he could spare neither his own time nor much of his resources to his wife's efforts in England.

During Easter, Stephen was at Northampton, and so ill that rumours of his death began to circulate. But after Whitsun, he began to recover, and the period of lull was over. He set about dealing with the new castles which the enemy had built. Cirencester was taken by surprise, with many of the garrison missing. It was fired and its rampart demolished. Bampton was taken by storm, and Radcot soon surrendered.

The king took advantage of Robert's absence in Normandy, and attacked Wareham. The town, within its roughly rectangular enclosure of walls, stood at a navigable point on the Frome, and still retains something of its old harbourside appearance. The motte and bailey castle was placed within its south-west corner. The castle remains are unfortunately not now open for public access, and the keep has been partially built over, but the motte can be viewed at an angle from the bridge over the river.[13] The garrison was inadequate, and the king fired and plundered the town, and captured the castle. This was quite a blow to the Angevins, lacking good south coast ports which linked to their own territories.

Stephen also attacked the empress in Oxford from 29 September 1142, 'seeking rather her surrender than that of the town'.[14] The castle then was thought to be very strong, defended by the deep river, and with 'a tower of great height'.[15] The Angevin garrison thought itself secure, and taunted the royalists from the safety of the walls, shooting arrows at the king's men over the river. Stephen took his force across the river by a ford, where the water was still deep enough to require swimming. Stephen dashed in and took the lead, himself swimming across. The enemy outside the gate were forced back in a fierce charge.

Stephen and his troops burst into the city and set fire to it, and then blockaded the castle. Matilda was trapped, and this time there was no offer of an escort to the west country. Stephen now believed 'he could easily put an end to the strife in the kingdom if he forcibly overcame her through whom it began to be at strife'.[16] Guards were posted all around the castle with orders to keep watch night and day, so that the empress and her garrison were pinned down. For three months the blockade continued, until the Angevins in the castle were weak with hunger. Siege engines were brought into play, and the plight of Matilda looked grim.

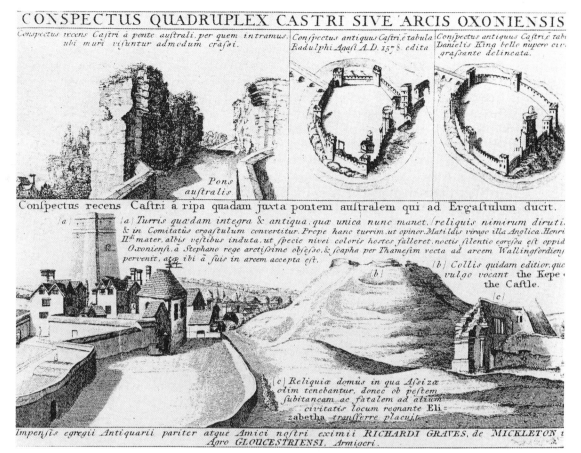

A nineteenth-century plan of Oxford Castle, by Joseph Skelton. Apart from the tower, little of the castle survives.

The Angevins, led by Brian fitz Count, assembled at nearby Wallingford to organize a rescue attempt. But they were not prepared to attack Stephen directly at Oxford, which suggests that they lacked the numbers to do it.[17] Robert of Gloucester brought the young Henry of Anjou back with him. They had 300 knights and 52 ships, which implies that Geoffrey had provided some cash for support after all. This time there were no storms, and the ships calmly followed in line across the sea, the waves 'gliding gently up to play against the shore'.[18]

Robert toyed with the idea of an attack on Southampton, encouraged by his seafaring supporters from the south, a family known as the Seals. But he chose in the end to return to Wareham, which he set about recovering. He soon occupied the landings stage, went on to recover the town, and then besieged the castle now with a royal garrison. Earl Robert set up throwing engines, and the threat was enough. An agreement was reached, of a type commonly employed in this period, that the garrison would be allowed to appeal to the king to come to their aid, but that if he did not come by a set date, the castle would surrender.

Oxford Castle, by Joseph Skelton. The main tower is depicted on the right of the drawing.

William of Malmesbury says Robert hoped the king would in fact be tempted to come in person, so that Matilda would be given relief in Oxford. But Stephen was not to be diverted this time. The garrison kept its word, and surrendered Wareham into Robert's hands, and the earl was now free to try and save Matilda. This, at any rate, is how William of Malmesbury presents his plans. But in fact Earl Robert did not make any attempt to go to Oxford immediately. First he took the Isle of Portland, with its castle, and then the castle of Lulworth from William of Glastonbury, a deserter from Matilda to Stephen. He then called an assembly of the Angevin supporters at Cirencester, which decided to make a bid to save Oxford. But on their way, they learned that Matilda had escaped, and being close to Christmas they now abandoned the idea of attacking the king.

Matilda's escape is a famous incident, and recorded in more than one chronicle. It was just before Christmas of 1142, and the weather was suitably wintry, with deep snow and ice. One account says she escaped down the walls by a rope at night, but the more likely version is that she slipped secretly out of a small postern gate.[19] She had decided on a risky venture, to escape with only a small escort of four knights, risking capture by the blockading troops.[20] They were not asleep, and as she slipped out, there was the sound of trumpets and men shouting, their voices carrying through the frosty air.

She managed to cross the frozen Thames, wrapped in a white cloak so as to escape notice against the background of snow. The ice was so solid that she did not even get her feet wet crossing the river. Matilda then had to struggle on foot

The surviving tower at Oxford Castle.

The motte at Wareham Castle, viewed from the bridge.

several miles to Abingdon, through ice and snow. There had just been a heavy fall, which probably helped the escape, but made the going difficult.

At Abingdon they obtained horses, and rode on to Wallingford and safety. This is the final incident described in William of Malmesbury's *Historia Novella*, so we lose another of our major sources at this point. William was heavily biased in favour of Robert of Gloucester, and sometimes distorted the truth or even invented, but he was a powerful writer, had good information, and could paint his pictures vividly. Though a monk, he was interested in politics and worldly events; he had a good brain and was well read, and could give shrewd and salty comment. We shall miss his assistance in the last part of our tale.

Matilda's escape is a well-remembered story, but it was hardly a triumph. The garrison left behind at Oxford did not hold out for long. Stephen accepted their surrender. The Angevins had to draw in their horns once more. Stephen was back on the warpath, and the key target of the fighting in 1142, Oxford, had finished up in the king's hands. The *Gesta Stephani* says that Stephen now 'exercised absolute authority over a very wide tract of country in that region'.[21] In this dispersed castle war, we must always bear in mind the chief outlines of events and the prime targets at given times, as contemporary chroniclers did.

After Oxford, Stephen made an attempt to recover Wareham, where Earl Robert had been strengthening the castle he had recently recaptured. It may be at this point that Stephen went to Wilton, though the chroniclers disagree over the chronology of the year. Henry of Huntingdon places at the beginning of his account of events in 1142, the episode at Wilton.[22] The king had built a castle here, to hinder Robert's activities. The royalist presence in the west country was feeble. The only lord of any consequence who was active on the king's behalf was Henry de Tracy. Wilton was to the royalists what Wallingford was to the Angevins, a salient in mainly enemy territory. It also became an assembly point for royal forces, including troops brought there by Henry, Bishop of Winchester.

But the Angevins came to besiege it. The pattern is remarkably like events at Lincoln, though in this case we are supplied with far fewer details. This time the king decided to make a sortie and break out, but almost failed to do so. The description in the *Gesta Stephani* suggests that Wilton was a pitched battle rather than simply a skirmish. Stephen arrayed his force with troops, probably cavalry, on each wing; Earl Robert divided his into three groups. The Angevins made a cavalry charge, and Stephen was forced to draw back. Stephen had to flee in order to escape. He was only saved by the selfless action of the royal steward, William Martel, one of his most loyal men, who sacrificed his own freedom to allow the king to escape. Stephen, at least, was a good lord to his loyal supporters, and agreed to hand over Sherborne Castle in order to obtain William Martel's release; it was a heavy price, and against Stephen's normal inclinations, which were to give the possession of castles very high priority. It was his only surrender of this kind, and shows how highly he regarded William Martel.

Wilton had come very close to being a second Lincoln. Stephen's escape on this occasion suggests how unwise he had been to fight on and be captured in the previous encounter. It also shows that he was outshone as a battle leader by Robert of Gloucester. At Lincoln, Stephen almost certainly had fewer troops, but

Wilton House.

The grounds of Wilton House, the site of the Battle of Wilton.

Sherborne Old Castle.

there is no reason to believe this of Wilton. Wilton itself suffered the consequences of the royal defeat, with burning torches thrown into houses, doors smashed down, and goods plundered. It seems as if the episode at Wilton also persuaded the hitherto loyal Henry de Tracy to make his peace with the Angevins for the time being.[23] The events of 1142 did not seem propitious for the king's future. If less disastrous than Lincoln, the Battle of Wilton was nevertheless a damaging defeat. Stephen had struggled to recover parity with the Angevins, but the situation was about to change.

GEOFFREY DE MANDEVILLE'S REBELLION

Again, there was much toing and froing in 1143, and the picture can become complicated and seem muddled, but one episode dominated the year – the rebellion of the Earl of Essex, Geoffrey de Mandeville. He has been the subject of much of the important study of this reign. John Horace Round, one of the most curmudgeonly, yet brilliant, historians ever, collected various pieces of research on the reign together in his *Geoffrey de Mandeville*. In Round's view, based on the evidence of the charters, Geoffrey was the outstanding example of the worst kind of selfish baron, out to better himself by constantly changing sides to obtain a higher offer, without holding any principles.[24]

R.H.C. Davis gave much of his life to a study of this reign, and is one of the most distinguished of recent medieval historians. Among other things, he showed that Geoffrey was no cynical turncoat, by redating the charters issued in his favour by the king and the empress. The conclusion of Davis' study, which has been debated but is accepted here, was to show that Geoffrey had not changed sides several times, each time bettering himself, but had only deserted the king when practically everybody else did, during Stephen's captivity after Lincoln. This makes Geoffrey no more than an average magnate looking to his own future. Indeed, he was one of the first barons to return to the king's allegiance once Queen Matilda offered hope of recovery, and had fought on the royal side at the Rout of Winchester.

Another leading modern historian, Professor Warren Hollister, has also given attention to this magnate. His study of the Mandeville family showed that its past history was not as had always been believed. Geoffrey's predecessor had been punished for allowing Rufus to escape from the Tower, and as a result the family's fortunes had declined. The revival had only come slowly, beginning under Henry I, but being most marked in the next reign with Stephen showing favour to Geoffrey.

Geoffrey had not recovered the Tower itself until well into Stephen's reign, not before 1137. Stephen's famous charter granting the Tower is not merely a confirmation of an earlier grant, but the actual record of restoration. In 1140 Geoffrey was also made Earl of Essex as part of the round of promotions by the king. Stephen had also pardoned his debts and made him sheriff of Essex, Hampshire, London and Middlesex. There could be little complaint against good lordship here.

Both these modern studies make the events of 1143 that much more puzzling. Geoffrey was not a recidivist turncoat, and he owed almost everything to the favour of Stephen. He had to some extent repaid that debt by joining the queen at Winchester after his brief desertion during the imprisonment. The puzzle would seem to be why he turned against Stephen in 1143. The answer is that he did not, at least not openly. It was the king who turned against him, but the reason for that is also puzzling. Historians have been able to do little more than speculate over the motives. Stephen certainly overplayed the move of arresting a potential enemy in order to gain key castles. We have already seen him doing it to obtain the bishops' castles in 1139, and his action in refusing Baldwin de Redvers' homage in 1136 and then demanding his castles was not far removed in concept.

In the case of Geoffrey de Mandeville too there is a hint of treason. Henry of Huntingdon says that if the king had not made the arrest, he would have lost his throne. And the *Gesta Stephani* records a rumour that Geoffrey had decided 'to bestow the kingdom on the Countess of Anjou', which other lords reported to the king. They then worked on Stephen to make the arrest, advice which he mulled over for some time before making a decision.[25] Stephen may have resented Geoffrey's actions after Lincoln, but it is difficult to see how he had any cause to resent them more than the actions of 90 per cent of his supporters.

Two possible answers present themselves. The first is that Stephen had an additional cause for resentment against Geoffrey which he had harboured for some time before the arrest. Geoffrey, as castellan of the Tower of London, had been host to Stephen's daughter-in-law, the French princess, Constance, who had married Eustace, while Stephen was imprisoned during 1141. And there are hints that in some way Geoffrey had insulted Constance, together with Queen Matilda, restraining their movements, perhaps even imprisoning them. He did return them to their freedom, though with reluctance. But this had happened several years previously.[26] If it was the main cause of the arrest, then Stephen's motives were personal and had been harboured rather a long time.

The other possibility is that the king's special cause for resenting Geoffrey's acceptance of Matilda, was simply its great significance. In granting him the restoration of his family lands, and then making him Earl of Essex, Stephen had entrusted Geoffrey with an absolutely key defensive position. Knowing that there was loyal resistance to the empress in nearby Kent, it must have been particularly disappointing that London was handed to the Angevins on a plate, particularly as the Londoners themselves showed loyalty to the king. This seems to be the most convincing explanation, and gives the king another motive. If he felt he could no longer fully trust Geoffrey, because he had been simply too willing to yield in 1141, then he needed to remove from Geoffrey's hands the major castles he held, not least the Tower of London, which was royal. If added to this, there was now the possibility of treason, we have at least an explanation of the king's action. Indeed, 'certain persons' now made an open accusation against the Earl of Essex of participating in 'a treasonable plot'.[27]

Even so, to arrest Geoffrey still appears as a rather underhanded act. He had been guilty of no immediate crime or offence. There is little doubt that this kind of action by Stephen began to erode magnate trust in him. It was underhanded and sly, not the sort of action one expected from a king, particularly one like Stephen, who seemed superficially open and accessible.

The arrest of Geoffrey de Mandeville was made in the royal court when the king was at Saint Alban's, and just as the bishops had offended by disturbing the peace of that court in 1139, so now Stephen offended perceptions of the protection which ought to be afforded to those who attended that court. Henry of Huntingdon, holding no particular brief for the earl, wrote that it was 'an act more fitting the earl's deserts than public right, more expedient than just'. The chronicler at Geoffrey's own foundation of Walden was more forthright, saying that Geoffrey was 'accused falsely and in secret of being a traitor to the king and betrayer of his country'. It was a fraudulent move, and 'unjust treatment'.[28]

Arresting individuals did at least prove to be an effective means of obtaining their castles. Geoffrey was not released until, under threat of hanging if he refused, he had agreed to hand over his main castles: the Tower of London, Saffron Walden, and Pleshey. As the *Gesta Stephani* points out, Geoffrey's castles were particularly important because of their strategic relationship to London: 'castles of impregnable strength built round the city'.[29]

Once released, the earl not surprisingly ignored the promises he had given, and set about trying to recover his property. This was the problem for Stephen throughout his reign. Whereas other kings might treat their magnates just as badly, and were perhaps less successful in gaining the castles of such men, in normal times a rebel baron had little hope of victory and nowhere much to hide. But in this time of civil war, there was always a ready-made refuge for any rebel against the king. So whenever Stephen made efforts to discipline his magnates, they were almost bound to join the ranks of his opponents and receive protection from them. It was this more than anything which undermined Stephen's position. It was not lack of firmness. Stephen has been criticized for releasing the men he arrested, but the furore against him had he not released them, or had he killed them during their captivity, would have been as great as that against John over the death of Arthur of Brittany half a century later. One often feels with this reign that Stephen did as well as was humanly possible in a virtually impossible situation. His only real failing was military; that he could never absolutely crush his enemies.

Yet if we move on from the puzzling question of motivation, the way in which Stephen triumphed over the rebel Geoffrey de Mandeville in his 'fenland campaign' was exemplary.[30] Geoffrey's rebellion again opened up a second front in the war, and again in East Anglia, and gave renewed hope to the Angevins, depressed by their failure to get much change out of the Count of Anjou.

Geoffrey de Mandeville chose to make a base not in his own territory, but in the geographically difficult lands of the Isle of Ely and its neighbourhood, probably with the connivance of Bishop Nigel. A number of areas of flat land, such as the Isle of Ely itself, stood above surrounding rivers, streams and marshes, and made an excellent refuge. Geoffrey arrived there by boat. The church did not long give him any sort of support, indeed Henry of Huntingdon says he was 'resolute in his ungodliness', and was soon roundly condemned on almost every side.

Geoffrey seized Ramsey Abbey and turned it into a castle. It was said that while it was used by him as a fortification, blood ran from its walls like tears, a phenomenon which Henry of Huntingdon claimed to have seen with his own eyes. The monks were unceremoniously turfed out and soldiers installed, 'turning the house of God into a den of thieves'.[31] Geoffrey probably had less compunction over this since the new abbot, Daniel, a favourite of the king, had been moved in to replace Abbot Walter. It was a reward for Daniel's aid to the king against Bishop Nigel. The violent events of 1143 are difficult to envisage in modern, peaceful Ramsey, where only part of the enormous church and the gatehouse survive from the twelfth-century monastery.

Geoffrey had suffered 'the deepest bitterness of heart', and vented his anger on royal supporters in the vicinity, attacking Cambridge with its royal castle. The town was pillaged, with a display of brutality and savagery. According to the Walden chronicler, Geoffrey behaved 'like a strong and unbridled horse not ceasing to tear in pieces with bites and kicks those whom he met'. Monasteries were attacked, church doors hacked down with axes, various places fired, goods seized. The Earl of Essex also used spies in disguise to make reconnaissance of places he intended to attack.[32] But his raids were not random; his main targets were the estates of the king and his supporters. He attacked 'the castles where the king's forces were', 'the manors, towns and other things pertaining to the king's property', and 'everything belonging to the adherents of the king's party'.[33]

Stephen made great efforts to deal with this rebellion, obviously recognizing its significance. He could not bring the earl to battle. The latter retreated into the safety of the fens, and then broke out to attack in another direction. Stephen had experience of the area from his earlier problems with Bishop Nigel.

Now Stephen built a number of castles against Geoffrey, 'in suitable places'.[34] Apart from Burwell, these castles have never been identified. The most likely candidates do not make a circle around the Isle of Ely, as historians seem to have assumed, but rather a screen between Ely and London, or between Ely and the castles of Geoffrey which the king had seized.[35] All Geoffrey's efforts in this campaign were aimed towards the south-west and his lost castles. Why did he choose particularly to attack Cambridge and Burwell? His former stronghold at Saffron Walden was only a dozen miles away from Cambridge. This was the whole focus of the fenland campaign: the attempted recovery of those confiscated castles by the earl, and the efforts to foil it by the king.

Geoffrey had the support of a number of his relatives, including William de Saye, his sister's second husband, and his own de Vere in-laws. Geoffrey's son, Ernulf, was also active on his behalf, and built a new castle at 'Walton'.[36] Geoffrey also made an alliance with the most powerful magnate in the region, Hugh Bigod, whose loyalty to the king had always been uncertain. Holding the two island castles of Ely and Aldreth, Geoffrey was in a strong defensive position. Ely Castle motte still stands in the park near the cathedral; Aldreth has never been identified, but may have been at the site called the Borough, where a track peters out at the edge of the island.[37]

Burwell Castle in Cambridgeshire was one of the new castles which provided additional cover to the existing royal castle at Cambridge. The king ordered part of the village of Burwell to be destroyed to make way for the construction of this emergency castle. The land used was in the possession of Ramsey Abbey.[38] A good deal of cash was put into it. A flat rectangular platform was prepared, as we have seen, with a broad moat around it. Work was started on the wall, the gatehouse and the keep.

Geoffrey de Mandeville was concerned about the royal preparations against him, and decided that attack was the best form of defence. He suddenly turned up with a force at Burwell and obviously intended to destroy the half-built castle. He surveyed it without a helmet on, removed because it was uncomfortable in the heat. A low-born crossbowman from the half-built walls sighted the earl, aimed at him, and shot him in the head. Geoffrey acted at first as though the wound was only slight, but in fact it proved fatal. He was taken away to nearby Mildenhall, probably seeking to reach the protection of Hugh Bigod at Thetford. A week later he died, on 26 September 1144, 'penitent to the bottom of his heart', according at least to the chronicle of his own foundation.[39] For Stephen the campaign had been a great triumph. The Earl of Essex was a powerful opponent. The opening up of an eastern war was a great threat. But before the Angevins could take any real part, the king had blocked off Geoffrey's activities, and now had brought about his death. And he had gained control of the earl's chief castles, which had been at the root of the initial conflict. But it is difficult to believe that the king had not lost something too. The ploy of arresting magnates and demanding their castles, on what appears to be increasingly flimsy evidence, must have left a legacy of distrust among the nobility who remained loyal to him.

The earl's body suffered various humiliations. Because he was excommunicated at the time of his death, he could not be buried in consecrated ground. However,

A physician tending a wounded man. (Trinity College, Cambridge, MS O.1.20, f. 248r)

he was taken away decently enough by the Templars, whom he had favoured and who covered him with a cloth on which was a red cross. One account says that he was thrown into a pit outside the Old Temple in London in a box; another that the body was wrapped in a lead shell and hanged from a crab–apple tree in the Temple orchard. Later on, his son managed to gain absolution for Geoffrey, so that the body could be given Christian burial, twenty years after the death.[40]

Geoffrey's son, Ernulf, retained control of Ramsey Abbey, but he was captured and sent into banishment. Ernulf's cavalry commander was thrown from his horse and died from the blow to his head. His commander of infantry, one Reiner, who had been employed in attacking churches, was crossing back to the continent with his wife, when the ship grounded. The sailors drew lots, and decided that the unfortunate Reiner was responsible, simply by being there, and so cast him adrift in a boat with his wife. The couple soon perished in the waves and the god of the waters was apparently appeased.[41] Militarily the events at Burwell had been a tremendous gain for the royalists. Stephen would now be able to concentrate on the war in the west. He seemed to be closing in again on his prey, just as in the period before Matilda's arrival. The death of Geoffrey had been a great boost to the morale of the royalists, and a blow to their opponents: 'a kind of darkness and dread filled all the king's enemies and those who had thought the king's efforts greatly weakened by the revolt.'[42]

Other Events of 1143–4

During the rebellion of Geoffrey de Mandeville, Stephen had seen the death of another major threat to his security. On Christmas Eve of 1143, Miles, Earl of Hereford, had gone on a hunting expedition. As commonly seemed to happen during these occasions, there was an accident, and the earl was hit in the chest by a stray arrow aimed badly at a stag, and died from the wound. He had been recently excommunicated by the Bishop of Hereford for his plundering of the local church, and his death seemed like another divine judgment.

Probably in 1143, there was a new threat to the royal position in Winchester, brought about by a quarrel between Bishop Henry and the treasurer, William de Pont de l'Arche. The latter appealed to the Angevins to take his part, and they were delighted to find a new ally in such a vital place. Therefore, they sent the mercenary captain, Robert fitz Hildebrand, to his assistance. He was one of that 'crowd of barbarians, who had swarmed to England in a body to serve as mercenaries . . . affected neither by the bowels of compassion nor by feelings of human pity'. Robert was a man of 'low birth', but with much military experience; he was also 'lustful, drunken and unchaste'.[43]

William de Pont de l'Arche held Portchester Castle, near Portsmouth, which he had obtained through marriage. Here came Robert fitz Hildebrand, acting with great swagger, coming in and out as he pleased, and seducing the unfortunate treasurer's wife. The pair decided to chain the husband up in his own castle while they enjoyed its comforts and his wealth. But all this did not avail the Angevins much, since the loose-living captain now decided to make his peace with Stephen and Bishop Henry. Of course, he could not be allowed to escape scot free after such disgraceful behaviour. The ecclesiastical chronicler who tells his story, relished his fate: 'a worm was born at the time when the traitorous corrupter lay in the unchaste bosom of the adulteress and crept through his vitals, slowly eating away his entrails till it gradually consumed the scoundrel, and at length, in the affliction of many complaints and the torment of many dreadful sufferings, it brought him to his end by a punishment he richly deserved.'[44]

In 1144 Stephen again besieged Lincoln Castle. Ranulf of Chester had recovered control of the place. Stephen began to make preparations for a prolonged siege. His men were preparing 'a work', presumably a siege tower, when it fell down and eighty of them were killed in the trench, suffocated, according to one source.[45] After the disaster Stephen abandoned the attempt.

Robert Marmion, who had fortified the church in Coventry, was killed when making a sortie from the place. Though in the middle of his men, and though no one else was killed, Marmion was hit. He fell into his own pit, fractured a thigh, and had his head cut off by a 'mean minion'. He had been excommunicated for his sins against the church and 'became subject to death everlasting'.[46]

The year 1144 seems to have been one of considerable destruction by various individuals, all making their own efforts to harm Stephen, including the sons of Robert of Gloucester in the southern part of England, and John the Marshal, 'that scion of hell and root of all evil', seeking revenge for his damaged sight sustained at Wherwell. The chronicler suggests that the Angevin intention was to draw a solid line of strength from the Bristol Channel to the south coast. But although the fighting obviously caused much harm, the Angevins had also established order within their own more carefully defined territory, where they 'imposed law and ordinances everywhere', even if in the chronicler's view this was not a completely legitimate authority.[47]

Another active Angevin was Stephen de Magneville, a supporter of Baldwin de Redvers, Earl of Devon. He, too, was consolidating the Angevin grip on a part of the west country. To this same end, Robert of Gloucester built three counter castles against the royal castle in Malmesbury. But Stephen made a sudden expedition and succeeded in relieving his garrison there.

Stephen went on to besiege Tetbury in Gloucestershire, taking the outer bailey and bringing up siege engines. Robert of Gloucester then hastily assembled a force, including Welsh infantry, to come to Tetbury's relief. Roger, Earl of Hereford, Miles' son and successor, joined him. There seemed to be the prospect of another pitched battle. But after Lincoln and Wilton, Stephen had learned his lesson. With a smallish force he did not wait for battle, but abandoned the siege and made for Winchcomb, a castle of Roger, Earl of Hereford. Some of the garrison fled on hearing of his approach. Stephen attacked the remaining force with determination, sending in flights of arrows, and ordering men to crawl up the motte to attack the keep. Winchcomb surrendered on terms. Again, the element of surprise had succeeded, where a prolonged siege had failed. There was no battle, but the expedition had given the king minor gains. Royalists built and held a number of additional castles within Gloucestershire, making 'deep inroads into the county'.[48]

Shortly afterwards, Stephen again exploited the advantage of surprise. Hugh Bigod had joined his enemies in the east, and thought himself safe with Stephen in the west country. But the king made a rapid cross-country march and struck against Bigod, capturing a number of his knights, wasting his lands, and ordering the construction of three castles in his territory.

Another notable Angevin supporter was William Peverel of Dover. He had been Robert of Gloucester's castellan at Dover, but had lost his castle to Stephen earlier in the reign. Now he set about establishing himself more safely within the territory under Angevin influence, and built a new castle at Cricklade in Wiltshire, protected by water and marshland. He assembled a force of mercenaries and archers and, using guerilla tactics, raided against the royalists along the Thames, with ambushes and night attacks. In one way or another, the focus of the war was becoming ever more concentrated on the Angevin home base.

FARINGDON

Again, in 1145, there was one major event – the taking of Faringdon Castle. Modern historians have been a little surprised at this, but contemporary chroniclers saw it as a major event. With a little thought the reason is clear. It was Robert of Gloucester who built the new castle there at the request of his son, Philip. It was a well-built castle, probably intended to become a permanent stronghold, and to control Malmesbury. It was on a naturally strong site, once a Celtic stronghold, on the mound known variously as Folly Hill, Faringdon Clump or Faringdon Hill, and seems to have had a timber keep, though some stonework is also reported.[49] It was a further attempt by the Angevins to revive their forward movement at the spearhead of their territories, close to Wallingford; 'to advance nearer to Oxford'.[50] It also seems that Robert had made great efforts to have the castle constructed, drawing in many of the Angevin supporters to help. The men put within to garrison it were the 'flower of their whole army'.[51]

Stephen appealed to his old allies the Londoners. He assembled a force at Oxford, and accompanied by a body of London militia, marched against the new castle. At Faringdon he built a counter castle to protect his own men. Earl Robert was hoping for reinforcements, and held back, waiting for them to arrive. But the royal attack was constant, daily, and effective. Engines were set up around the walls, hurling stones and missiles. A body of archers in formation was used so that a hail of arrows was shot into Faringdon Castle. Men were also sent to scale the rampart, despite its steepness. In the attack many of the besieged were killed. A secret deputation was sent to the king, and surrender terms agreed. Arms and booty in plenty were taken, and much profit resulted from the ransoms.

The chroniclers saw the capture of Faringdon as a turning point in the war, and so should we. The *Gesta Stephani* saw it as 'a splendid triumph', which disheartened his enemies. Another wrote that 'the king's fortune now at last began to change for the better and to be in the ascendant'. Many were led to make peace with the king.[52] Were the events after 1148 not known to us, it would seem as if the capture of Faringdon, like the death of Geoffrey de Mandeville, were major factors in turning the war the king's way.[53] One of the gains which swayed chroniclers' attitudes to the taking of Faringdon, was its effect upon the younger son of the Earl of Gloucester. Philip of Gloucester is described as a good soldier and, in the past two years, had been very active in the Angevin cause. He it was who had persuaded his father of the strategic gain from building Faringdon. Now he suddenly switched sides and joined the king. Perhaps he felt that his father had not given sufficient aid in defending Faringdon. He made an agreement with Stephen.

A relatively minor incident in 1145 involved the treachery of Turgeis of Avranches. Stephen had entrusted to him the castellanship of Saffron Walden after its seizure from Geoffrey de Mandeville. Turgeis seems to have seen himself as the possessor rather than the castellan, and refused the king entry to the place. It seems that Turgeis feared he was about to be replaced, for what reason we do not know. Stephen was naturally infuriated by the refusal of entry. The right of entrance to castles, or of render, was one of the king's hardest held policies. One day Turgeis went out hunting with hounds, and while pursuing a quarry, with horns sounding, was suddenly confronted by a party of knights with the king in their midst. Stephen threatened to hang Turgeis in chains at the entrance of the castle unless it was surrendered, and the castellan decided that discretion was the better part of valour. One significant lesson from the episode is the king's difficulty in finding anyone he could truly trust.

Even now, the war was not one-way traffic. In 1145 the Angevins had a minor victory in the west. Walter de Pinkeney had been made castellan of Malmesbury by Stephen. The castle had become a considerable problem to the Angevins in its forward position, and all their attempts against it had failed. But as at Saffron Walden, so here, troops roamed the surrounding countryside, and it was not safe for any man to travel without adequate protection. Walter de Pinkeney ventured outside the castle, and was caught by the men of William Peverel of Dover. Matilda tried alternately to cajole or threaten him into handing over Malmesbury, but he resisted. In any case Stephen, hearing of the capture, himself came to Malmesbury and reinforced the place, thus encouraging the garrison to resist surrender. The unfortunate Walter was tortured in a filthy dungeon on Matilda's orders. But in the main lines of the war, the years from 1143 to 1145 had seen a growing dominance by the royal forces.

THE END OF THE MATILDINE WAR

The events of 1146 less obviously favoured either side immediately. The major happening of the year was the breaking of relations between Stephen and Ranulf, Earl of Chester, who one chronicler reckoned held one third of the kingdom.[54] Probably inspired by the increasing success of royal arms, in 1146 Ranulf decided once again to make his peace with the king. His lands were suffering from Welsh raids, and he obviously believed that the king would give him more aid than the Angevins. Ranulf's Welsh interests were in the north, whereas most Angevin lords had territories further to the south. Ranulf also mentioned that if the name of the king was involved in an expedition against the Welsh, it would have more effect.[55] He approached Stephen at Stamford, accompanied only by a small retinue, and there a new pact of agreement was made, and the earl offered his services in the king's support.[56] He promised to contribute a considerable sum towards paying for a Welsh expedition, for troops and expenses. Together they recovered Bedford for the king. When Stephen once more attempted to capture Wallingford, Ranulf was with him again, bringing 300 horse, but thereafter relations soured.

Stephen had not fulfilled Ranulf's chief hope by undertaking a Welsh expedition. Royal counsellors advised against it, both because of the dangers of the Welsh country, and also because it would mean entering Ranulf's lands, and there were fears of treachery. Given the numerous examples of underhand ambushes and captures in recent times, such fears were quite understandable. They also pleaded that it would be unwise for the king to leave England in the present circumstances. A number of Stephen's more consistently loyal barons also resented the prominence of the unreliable Ranulf. It seems too as if he had been taking taxes in his own territories and not forwarding them to the royal exchequer, including those from former royal demesne.

Ranulf was obviously annoyed at the lukewarm royal response to his offers and assistance. An agreement had already been made, and he was not prepared to give any more. He therefore refused to give hostages for his conduct, when they were now demanded. 'Neither the king nor his chief counsellors had any confidence in the man's loyalty.'[57] Those close to Stephen accused the earl of plotting against the king, and suggested a repeat of the tactic used against Geoffrey de Mandeville – to demand the earl's castles, or else.

Stephen treated Ranulf much as he had treated Geoffrey de Mandeville, and probably for much the same reasons. Perhaps an even closer parallel is with the arrest of the bishops. Suddenly, at Northampton, Stephen arrested Ranulf and demanded major castles from him, including Lincoln, before he would release him. The earl was chained up and imprisoned at Northampton, despite his denial of treachery. Of all Stephen's arrests, this was the one for which least cause had been given, and which in the end was probably most damaging. It was condemned by chroniclers. He 'forgot his royal dignity and honour'; it was 'an infamous deed'.[58] The evidence does not suggest that Ranulf had done anything to break his new allegiance. It would hardly have been in his interests to do so. It is difficult to believe that his surrender to Stephen had been anything but genuine. Ranulf had not been a particularly good friend to Stephen over the years, but he had not been an enthusiastic Angevin either. At once his own men in his broad territories began to operate against the king, demanding the earl be set free. The arrests of Geoffrey de Mandeville and Ranulf of Chester seem to have grown out of previous similar arrests, but whereas we have argued that for those earlier events Stephen had reasonably good cause, he had less cause with regard to Geoffrey, and very little indeed in the case of Ranulf.

Once released, Ranulf's reaction was to join with the Angevin forces. This arrest was a greater error than any of the others. Stephen had always gained key castles from his arrest of magnates, and he did so now. But the Angevin cause had reached its nadir in England, and the switch of allegiance by Ranulf revived it. Stephen had no doubt recognized his enemies' weakness, and intended by the arrest to show his new power. He meant to crush his opponents, to kick them while they were down. But it misfired. Ranulf acted with 'the tyranny of a Herod and the savagery of a Nero', says the author of the *Gesta Stephani*, capturing a number of royal castles, and building new ones of his own.[59]

It is true that when Ranulf brought men with him and tried to achieve a rapid recovery of Lincoln, he failed, and many of his men were killed in the attempt. They tried to break in through the north gate of the city, and could not force their way in. Ranulf's chief lieutenant was slain in the fighting. The Earl of Chester also tried to recover the castle at Coventry, building a counter castle there. Stephen came to relieve his new garrison, and was wounded in fighting outside the town. But the king soon recovered and again attacked the earl, winning a victory against Ranulf, who took to flight.

Once Ranulf had openly rebelled, Stephen had seized as a hostage, Gilbert fitz Richard. Gilbert had been a royalist, made Earl of Hertford by the king in the promotions at the beginning of the reign. But he was also Earl Ranulf's nephew, and presumably his loyalty was now in question. His castles also were demanded. The ploy of demanding castles under menaces was moving dangerously near to becoming an obsession. The king threatened Gilbert with exile and banishment; his castles were surrendered. The result was that Gilbert immediately joined in his uncle's rebellion. Stephen then went quickly in pursuit of Earl Gilbert, prepared to fight a pitched battle against him if necessary. But Gilbert disguised himself and escaped. Several of Gilbert's castles were taken over, but that at Pevensey resisted and Stephen had to be content with leaving a besieging force on the Sussex coast. We do not know the outcome, but probably the castle was taken eventually.

Philip of Gloucester, who had changed sides in the previous year, proved an active campaigner for his new overlord, Stephen. He had been well rewarded by the king, though he had to give hostages, which is a sign that his loyalty was not altogether trusted. But Philip put all his efforts into impressing the king. He fought even against his own father. Among his successes in 1146, was the capture of Robert Musard, a Gloucester baron. Robert was yet another example of someone who ventured outside his castle without taking sufficient precautions, and was made prisoner. Philip of Gloucester ambushed him and put a halter round the man's neck, threatening to hang him unless his castle was surrendered. The surrender was arranged and effected.[60]

Even more dramatic was the capture of Reginald, Earl of Cornwall, made by his erstwhile ally, Philip of Gloucester. There appears to have been some trickery involved here, since Reginald was apparently at the time in negotiation with the king over peace terms while the earl was under a safe conduct. As a result, after protests, the earl was released, though the two sides failed to agree any settlement.

Also in Gloucestershire there was an episode involving the brothers Caldret, Henry and Ralph, who were Flemish mercenaries apparently employed by the Angevins. The *Gesta Stephani*, which covers the event, does not say on which side they fought, and none of our main historians of the period attempts to do so either, but the context of the narrative suggests that it would be more likely they were defending Angevin strongholds. Both had been castellans, and both lost their strongholds; one was hanged before his own castle, and the other, having lost his castle, left England in poverty. Even if the suggestion that they were Angevin is incorrect, we are still left with the knowledge that in 1146 Stephen was carrying the war into the heart of imperial territory.

There was another incident at Berkeley in Gloucester, a major castle. The unfortunate Roger of Berkeley was also captured outside his stronghold by Walter of Hereford, brother of the earl, and with his brother's approval. So far as we can see this was an incident which did not involve royalists, since we are told Roger had made a compact with the earl, and was related to him. Roger was captured by a trick and then stripped of his clothes and strung up before his own castle in chains to encourage the garrison to surrender. He was not actually killed; it was merely a show to get his men to surrender, though he nearly died, and on the third attempt to hang him, he was allowed to fall unceremoniously to the ground. He was taken off half dead, 'a faint breath of life fluttering within his tortured frame', and imprisoned in a dungeon. But his castle had not surrendered.

This story shows that all was far from well within pro-Angevin circles, and that sometimes within their territories the normal code of decent conduct was breaking down. It is probable that Roger had changed sides, because we know that his niece married Philip of Gloucester, and we are told that Philip had made himself responsible for Roger's protection. In which case, again, we see royal inroads into previously firm Angevin territory.[61] Philip of Gloucester retaliated by

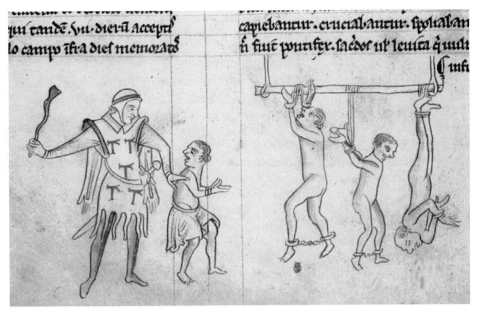

Prisoners being tortured. (Corpus Christi College, Cambridge, MS 16, f. 48v)

ravaging the lands around. But then he was taken ill, and during the illness vowed to go on pilgrimage to the Holy Land.

Stephen's dominance in England from 1145 to 1148 was undoubted. He could still not crush his enemies completely, but he recovered virtually all the territory lost during his captivity and made gain after gain. In 1148 he attacked Worcester, which he took and burned, though he did not manage to capture the castle. In the following year he made another attempt, and built two counter castles against it, leaving a force to blockade the place. However, the Angevins destroyed the counter castles and relieved Worcester. According to Henry of Huntingdon, the castle was held by Waleran of Meulan, given it by Stephen himself, and his brother, Robert of Leicester, aided the destruction of the counter castles. In which case Stephen had lost a major magnate. From other sources we only know that Robert, Earl of Leicester, joined Henry of Anjou at the last gasp in the reign, in 1153, but Henry of Huntingdon's suggestion of an earlier defection may well be true, and gives the earl some motivation for his move.[62]

Stephen still held far more of England than his enemies. The deaths of Miles of Gloucester and Geoffrey de Mandeville had greatly strengthened his position. There was a general discontent with continuing war: 'they wearied of lengthy conflict and their efforts slackened'.[63] The arrest of Ranulf had not yet worked to its climax, but by 1147 the fighting seemed to have died down. Ranulf was licking his wounds, but had been unable to recover his main castles lost in 1146. At Christmas 1146 Stephen had emphasized his recovery of Lincoln Castle by a crown-wearing in the city, despite a superstition against kings entering the place.[64]

The king had advanced the focus of the war into the west country, and the Angevins were on the defensive. In the two following years his dominance seemed only further underlined. In 1147 Robert of Gloucester died. He had been the main warrior of the Angevin opposition. Without him, in 1141, they had been unable to contemplate continuation of the war, even with Stephen in prison. He was still actively planning further efforts when he died suddenly at Bristol on 31 October. His eldest son, William, succeeded but was never to be the force his father had been, being 'effeminate and a lover of bedchambers more than of war'; the Angevin cause was undoubtedly weakened by Robert's death.[65]

There was still sporadic fighting, and a visit of Henry of Anjou to England, but it was such a failure that it could give his party little cause for hope. It is not accurate to claim that the empress stood down in favour of her son, whose hopes in 1148 were close to being forlorn. When in 1148 Matilda retired to Normandy, it has the look of resignation to defeat. She was not to die for nineteen years, but she would never return to England. Her own war for her own succession had come to an end. Her cause in 1148 was at a low point. Her husband still showed no inclination to give any aid, despite his success in Normandy.

Everything pointed towards Stephen's victory in the Matildine war. During the previous five years, several of Matilda's strongest or most powerful supporters had died: Miles of Hereford in 1143, Geoffrey de Mandeville in 1144, Robert of Gloucester in 1147. In 1148 she gave up her struggle for the throne. She did not entirely retire from an active life, but she left the struggle in England for others to resolve. She settled in Rouen, and her efforts there to add to the work of rebuilding begun by her husband, resulted in a monument to her name in the Pont Mathilde over the Seine.[66] Her political life was not over, but her personal struggle for the English throne was.

CHAPTER 7

The Henrician War

There is little doubt that by about 1147 Stephen had come out of the conflict better than his opponents. The deaths of Miles of Gloucester, Earl of Hereford, in a hunting accident on Christmas Eve 1143, and of Geoffrey de Mandeville in 1144, the taking of Faringdon in 1145, the death of Robert of Gloucester in 1147, and the retreat of Matilda to Normandy by early March of 1148, all point in the direction of a royal victory.

But Stephen's victory was not complete. His series of arrests had given him control of a number of vital castles, but had also succeeded in alienating a succession of key figures in the realm. Such victories were Pyrrhic. Because of the diminishing level of chronicle sources as the reign continues, our knowledge of the details of these events is increasingly slight, and analysis of motivation progressively difficult. Even the fullest source for the reign becomes less full at this point.

The *Gesta Stephani* was thought to end in 1147. The part of the chronicle which covers the years from 1147 to 1154 was only found by Professor R.A.B. Mynors quite recently, in time to be included in the 1955 edition of the work by K.R. Potter.[1] The Valenciennes manuscript is a very valuable addition to the relatively scanty sources for the later reign. This is not the place to argue the matter in full, but it may be that the previous editors were incorrect in seeing it merely as a lost section of the work of one author. There are several glaring differences between the later part of the work and the earlier, though the division begins before the end of the known section. That is to say, that two authors may have written the original work, and it was the last part of the work of the second writer which formed the lost section.

We must remember that only copies survive. The chapters become much shorter and more laconic, and the attitude of the writer becomes pro-Angevin rather than pro-royalist, seeing Henry of Anjou as 'the lawful heir', no longer scorning David, King of Scots, when taking flight from York. Whereas Earl Ranulf of Chester's arrest in the first section is called prudent and wisely counselled, now it becomes an arrest which broke a safe conduct. The first writer approves of Walter de Pinkeney, the commander of Malmesbury for the king in 1145, 'a man of resolution and very well approved', but the second writer thinks him a man of 'cruelty and wickedness'.[2] There is a *prima facie* case for believing that the lost section is part of a continuation by a different hand, whose work commences at the end of 1147.

Part of this second work was retained in the known section, and that part with the whole of the continuation had been added before the lost part went missing.

A scribe writing. (Trinity College, Cambridge, MS O.9.34, f. 22)

The writer of either section is unknown, and there is no autograph manuscript.[3] The copies which survive also have missing sections in the middle.

Davis argued for the authorship of the Bishop of Bath, Robert of Lewes, and made an interesting but not conclusive case.[4] One problem would be that the first writer is hostile to Henry of Blois, whereas the Bishop of Bath had been close to Henry and employed by him for work in his own abbey. The second author shows more interest in the north than the first writer, whose interests are predominantly west country. Nor is it clear why the sections end in 1147 and 1154, when the bishop lived on until 1166. Davis argued that the differences in viewpoint came from a change of attitude, rather as if a modern politician changed from Conservative to Labour. This is not unknown, now, and not impossible, but is not the only possible solution or even the most likely. Hundreds, probably a majority, of medieval narrative sources are the work of more than one person; continuing an existing work was a normal process. We conclude that the differences before and after 1147 in the *Gesta Stephani* are more likely to represent the work of two men with differing views than the work of a single individual who changed his mind. Certainly after 1147 the source becomes hostile to Stephen and supportive of Henry of Anjou, which it had not been previously.

We now need to examine the events which led up to Henry of Anjou's bid for the throne. There was some sporadic fighting in the period after 1145, but it went

The seal of Robert, Bishop of Bath, 1136–66.
(BL Harley Charter 75.A.30)

largely in Stephen's favour: the episode with Ranulf of Chester, the rebellion in Kent which saw Stephen capture three castles from Gilbert fitz Richard of Clare, Earl of Hertford; the loss but then recapture of Henry of Blois' castle of Downton from Earl Patrick in 1148.

But it is equally clear that although it was a sort of victory for Stephen, it was not a complete one. Matilda's young son Henry was growing to manhood and seemed intent on claiming his mother's rights; in place of the older generation which had been divided against itself in the Matildine war, was emerging a new generation of sons, not always with quite the same allegiances as their fathers. Parts of England, though restricted in area, which had been consistently pro-Angevin, were still not under the authority of the king, and had been added to by the desertions from the king since 1145. This was the situation in England, but in Normandy Stephen had lost the war against the Angevins, and the outcome there seemed more thoroughly settled than in England.

HENRY OF ANJOU'S EARLY VISITS TO ENGLAND

With the Henrician episode of the civil war in England, it is even less clear who was the military victor. Some historians, following the pro-Angevin chroniclers, who were nearly all writing after the outcome was known and when Henry was king, have seen Henry's final expedition in 1153 as a triumph. Politically it was, but not militarily. Henry had been to England before 1153, and his experiences had been largely humiliating. Henry probably visited England four times during Stephen's reign, and before 1153 he made little impact.

His first visit was with Robert of Gloucester as a boy from 1142, when he may have stayed for several years. His second visit was in response to the urgent requests for aid from the desperate Angevins in England. What they wanted was intervention and cash from Geoffrey of Anjou; all they got was the teenage Henry. In 1147 Henry brought with him only a few mercenaries, whom he could not even afford to pay.

At first a rumour spread that he had come with an enormous army and much treasure, which created a stir, and disheartened the royalists. When it proved that neither point was true, interest waned. He had only a few knights, and only promises of money to come. According to the *Gesta Stephani*, he had arrived without forethought or judgment, a mistakenly premature expedition. At Cricklade, in Wiltshire, which Henry attacked, his force was put to flight, and at Purton in the same county, his force fled in panic. Stephen 'had the upper hand over them in the kingdom'.[5]

Those knights who had come with him, left him, and he could not afford to pay off his mercenaries. Neither his uncle, Robert of Gloucester, 'brooding like a miser over his moneybags, [who] preferred to meet his own needs only', nor his mother, the empress, was prepared to underwrite Henry's costs.[6] Only a desperate and secret appeal to Stephen as a relative, provided enough cash to pay off the mercenaries and allow Henry himself to return to Normandy. This act of the king's has been seen then and since as another foolish piece of chivalry, 'even childish', but is perfectly justifiable.[7] As things stood in 1147, Stephen could afford to be generous. The presence of Henry, ineffective as it had been, was about the only hope left to the Angevins at that time, so a little cash in order to see him off the premises must have seemed a good investment.

Henry of Anjou came to England again in 1149, a little older and wiser, but not much stronger. His apparent motive was to receive knighting at the hands of his great uncle, David, King of Scots. Probably it was also an attempt to feel out the chances of reviving the struggle in England under his own banner. If so it could not have been very encouraging, though he did reach Carlisle safely, and was knighted by David on 22 May 1149.

There he also made contact with the newly amenable Ranulf de Gernons, fourth Earl of Chester, who has been called one of the 'major troublemakers' of the reign, and who gave hope to the Henrician phase of the war in the same way that Robert of Gloucester did to the first phase.[8] Ranulf was indeed Robert of Gloucester's son-in-law, married to his daughter Matilda, and a very powerful magnate with lands stretching from the Welsh border, across the midlands into the north and Lincolnshire. He had been an obstruction against all Stephen's attempts at peace ever since causing the Battle of Lincoln by seizing the castle in 1141, but he had not been a very staunch Angevin either. Round was not far wrong in believing that 'the real springs of his policy are found in Carlisle and Lincoln'.[9] In 1146, as we have seen, he actually deserted back to Stephen, in the hope that the king would be more likely to assist him in Wales than the Angevins. According to the *Anglo-Saxon Chronicle*, Ranulf was arrested on 'bad counsel', and released 'on worse counsel', when he 'flew to arms'. He was not to be dealt with as easily as Geoffrey de Mandeville had been.[10] He failed to take Coventry or to recover Lincoln in 1146, but he became a powerful new aid to the failing Angevin cause, prepared even to give up Carlisle to the Scots. When Stephen went against Coventry, he was wounded, which one might say was the first small victory for Ranulf's secession to the Angevins.

Another development of the 1140s was the rise of Stephen's eldest son, Eustace. He began to take part in the war on his father's behalf, and though at times showing a certain rashness, seemed a worthy warrior with 'soldierly qualities', and a proper heir to his father. He was already showing abilities as a knight though his beard had hardly begun to grow.[11] He also shared some of the better traits of his father, being gentle, courteous, and generous.

Since Stephen was the properly anointed king, and his coronation had been confirmed by the papacy afterwards, there is no doubt that in any normal concept of heredity, then or now, Eustace was the 'lawful heir'. Only a convinced supporter of Henry of Anjou, persuaded by Angevin propaganda, could really believe otherwise. There would be no legal or ecclesiastical case for Henry. Of course, he posed as the lawful heir to give his claim some validity. Stephen groomed his eldest son to succeed him, knighting him in 1147, giving him lands and his own retinue, and passing to him Queen Matilda's rights, and his own, to make Eustace Count of Boulogne.

However, let us pursue the 1149 visit of Henry. Henry had reached an age when he was ready to be knighted, and chose to go to his great uncle, David, King of Scots, for this purpose. Roger, Earl of Hereford, and a number of young noble Angevin supporters, went with him to the north. Henry was also clearly feeling out the position in England. He sent messengers on ahead to prepare King David for his coming, and then set out. The King of Scots welcomed him, and agreed to bestow knighthood upon him at Carlisle.

David and Henry also made a pact of mutual aid, which included the promise of alliance from Ranulf, Earl of Chester, who had joined the party. It would appear as if in 1149, the new Angevin party was formed after the retirement of its former leader, the empress, in the previous year. Having made some contact with his potential allies, including Ranulf, the hopes of the visit soon fell apart. The allies planned an attack on York, but Stephen was warned of events, and received an appeal for aid from yet another city which showed its sympathy to him rather than his opponents. The king turned up with an army in the north, before expected, and the coalition simply broke up and made a run for it, each to his own base.

Henry had to dodge about to avoid a series of attempted ambushes, travelling well to the west by 'lonely and devious' ways to escape attention, a sign of royalist strength throughout the country.[12] Traps were laid first by Stephen and then by his son Eustace. Henry's supporters made diversionary moves – Ranulf against Lincoln, Payn Beauchamp at Bedford, and Hugh Bigod in East Anglia – none with much success. But Henry got to Hereford safely, and then moved on south.

Almost nowhere, though, was entirely safe. Eustace, in particular, set traps for him, even in Gloucestershire. Henry evaded the ambushes, at Dursley having to leave in the middle of the night in order to do so. From a base at Oxford, Eustace raided around Bristol, in Gloucestershire, against Marlborough, Devizes and Salisbury in Wiltshire. It is clear from the placing of these attacks that the Angevins were entirely on the defensive now. Meanwhile, Stephen was busy in the north, going to York; another sign of his spreading power. Then he joined Eustace in the south once more. Soon he was off again, to Lincoln, where Ranulf was keeping his part of the bargain made at Carlisle, by trying to take the castle which he would never abandon hope of recovering. But Stephen saw him off, and built a new castle which restricted Ranulf's activities.

Once back in Angevin territory, Henry did make one or two aggressive moves, including the capture of Bridport, whose castellan had earlier surrendered it to the king. He also raided the lands of Stephen's western supporter, Henry de Tracy. But Henry withdrew his men into his castles, and Henry of Anjou achieved little against him.

At Devizes, Eustace made a sudden attack, which almost succeeded, breaking into the outer part of the castle. Devizes stood on a spur with steeply descending slopes, jutting out over the level of the land, and was a powerfully built castle with a deep ditch, the work of Roger, Bishop of Salisbury.[13] As we have seen, it

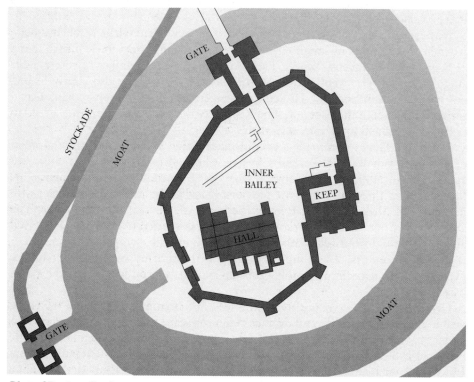

Plan of Devizes Castle.

had experienced a good deal of action through the war, and had changed hands several times. In the end Henry saved Devizes, which was important, but hardly a great military triumph.

In effect the 1149 visit produced little for his supporters to crow about. It had, as Warren said, been little more than 'a private escapade'.[14] It was clear that most of England was still firmly in Stephen's hands, and that Henry's very life was in danger if he ventured beyond the safe Angevin territories. According to Henry of Huntingdon, writing about 1149, Stephen was now 'holding the upper hand everywhere'. The *Gesta Stephani* says much the same, and in the 1150s saw Stephen 'successful all over England'. In fact, his advisers suggested that Henry return to Normandy to try and persuade his father, yet again, to send the help which his party so sorely needed in England. They saw little hope otherwise in the current position.[15]

The pro-Angevin leaders, Reginald of Cornwall and Roger of Hereford, soon appealed to Henry to come back to England, because they were 'in sore distress'. They had been 'weakened by the king's superior might'. They sent to Henry to tell him that his own supporters 'had all bound themselves to him [the king] by pledge of peace and friendship', and those who remained loyal (to Henry), like Brian, found their castles besieged and battered, and their lands stripped bare by royal pillagers.[16] Henry spent four years out of England after 1149, a period of some difficulty for his supporters, with Stephen in the ascendant, taking Newbury in 1152, and besieging Wallingford. They appealed to him to take urgent action, not only if he wanted to save his claim, but also if he had any regard for his supporters. He promised to come, but there was a very long delay before he kept the promise, and some began to despair of him ever doing so.

THE CONQUEST OF NORMANDY

The greatest irony of Stephen's reign, is that although he was, on the whole, militarily successful in England, events elsewhere, in the end, determined the fate of his kingdom. It would have been possible for the kingdom of England and the duchy of Normandy to go their own separate ways again, England under the Blesevins and Normandy under the Angevins. But the strong tendency of the age was for the nobles, many of whose families had acquired lands on both sides of the Channel, to favour one ruler over both regions and thus avoid almost inevitable conflicts of interest with a concomitant risk of losing lands. That tendency had worked in favour of Stephen against the chances of his brother Theobald in 1135; it worked against him now.

Geoffrey V, Count of Anjou, although he was never even to visit England, played a very great part in its fate. He was born in 1113, the son of Fulk V, Count of Anjou, the later King of Jerusalem (1131–43). Fulk V had been a considerable threat to the stability of Henry I's Normandy, defeating that king at Alençon in 1118, and participating in the 1119 invasion of the duchy. He was the first Angevin count to rule directly over the county of Maine, which had formerly been possessed by the Norman dukes. Geoffrey V's marriage to the Empress Matilda had sealed a peace with Henry I which that king had been seeking for some time in order to counter the menace of William Clito. In 1129 Fulk V had said farewell to his family, and left his young son Geoffrey, at the age of sixteen, to rule in his place while he went off to seek his fortune in the Holy Land.

Although the marriage to Matilda had begun rather stormily, with her leaving him to return to her father for a while, it produced children, including three sons: Henry in 1133, Geoffrey in 1134, from whose birth Matilda nearly died, and William in 1136. Geoffrey felt that Henry I had not fulfilled the promises made at the time of the marriage. Certain castles on the southern border of Normandy had been promised, but Henry had retained control of them, and 'the proud youth took umbrage'.[17] In the end Geoffrey had sought to recover them by force in 1134. Henry was also annoyed that Geoffrey had dealt summarily with Roscelin, the Viscount of Maine, without reference to himself, though Roscelin was married to his illegitimate daughter Constance.

The war over these castles between Geoffrey and his father-in-law was still in progress in 1135 when Henry I died. Geoffrey seems to have made no move either on his own, or on his wife's or son's behalf, to claim either England or Normandy in 1135, but he did seize the disputed castles. There is no doubt that in 1135 the Norman nobility had no wish to accept a claim from Geoffrey. An assembly in the duchy made its views clear by selecting first Theobald of Blois, and then his brother Stephen. The old prejudices against Anjou must still have had force, as witnessed by the hostility shown to the Angevins as invaders over the next few years.

But there had been some nobles who had been at odds with Henry I, and who welcomed Geoffrey's opposition to that king. One of these was William Talvas, son of the disgraced Robert of Bellême. Henry had recently taken back Alençon from William, who was one of the first allies of the Angevins in their efforts to win Normandy. Robert of Torigny says William also surrendered his castles into the count's hands, probably meaning that he offered him the use of them with his homage. In any case he received them back.[18]

Geoffrey knew the weight of opposition against him, but he was a shrewd and effective operator. He did not bite off more than he could chew. He was always cautious about overreaching himself. Thus, he never weakened his own forces and resources in any significant degree in order to assist either Matilda's or Henry's efforts in England. England he felt could look after itself. Nor did he expect to conquer all Normandy at a blow. He knew that here, as in England, in the end, it was solid control of the strong points, especially the castles, which would ensure that a conquest was permanent.

Geoffrey's first efforts had secured only a handful of castles on the central southern Norman border: Argentan, Exmes and Domfront, handed over by Guigan Algason, but they were the ones most easily supplied from his own territories. He also took control of a number of castles on the border with Brittany, namely Ambrières, Goron and Châtillon-sur-Colmont, which were given to Juhel de Mayenne to hold, in return for his aid in Normandy. The southern castles were strengthened, supplied and garrisoned, and they were never lost to his enemies. Geoffrey's conquest was one of gradual expansion outwards from his home territory.

Domfront Castle, Normandy.

Geoffrey's allies in Normandy had also been active. William Talvas had defeated Gilbert of Clare and captured Henry de Ferrières. Roger of Tosny, in conflict with the Beaumont twins at this time, had probably also allied himself with Geoffrey. Roger was involved in fighting against Stephen's brother, Theobald, and was another who had opposed Henry I late in the reign. Another probable ally for Geoffrey, given his name, was Robert Poard of Bellême, who defeated Richer of Laigle near La Ferrière. What we are suggesting is that, as in England, the 1138–9 rebellions were not haphazard and coincidental risings but a concerted effort to support Robert of Gloucester's defiance, so in Normandy the examples of disturbers of the peace given by Orderic and others were really acting in alliance with the Angevin count: William Talvas, Roger de Tosny, and Robert Poard of Bellême among them.

Geoffrey's difficulties should not be minimized; expeditions into hostile territory were far from easy. In 1135 the local people of Normandy had themselves halted the Angevin advance. Geoffrey's invasion of Normandy in 1136 was a disaster, and lasted only thirteen days.

The state of his men, and of Geoffrey himself, meant that on the next day the whole expedition had to be abandoned. 'Plagued by diarrhoea, they left a trail of filth behind and many were barely capable of dragging themselves back home'. Waleran of Meulan added to the Angevin defeat by capturing their ally, Roger of Tosny. On the journey there were even further problems, and the count's baggage, with his robes and precious vessels, was stolen. But even this campaign with its disgusting

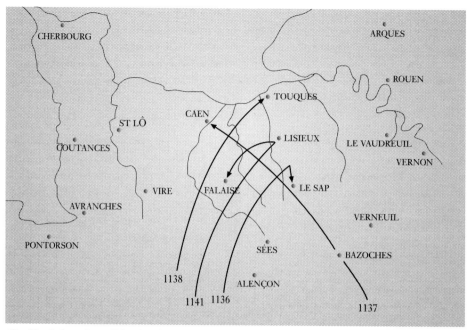

Geoffrey's invasion of Normandy, I: 1136–41.

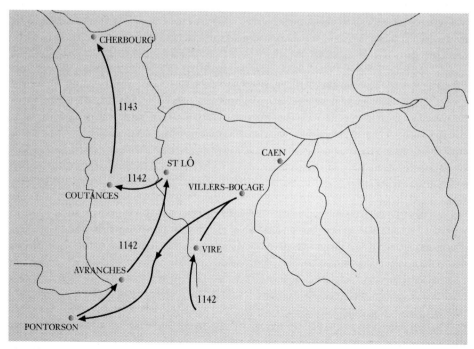

Geoffrey's invasion of Normandy, II, the west: 1142–3.

conclusion, had not been an entire write-off. Geoffrey was unable to keep all that he had taken, but he did retain territory to the north of Sées.

In 1137, as stated earlier, Stephen had mounted his own personal campaign in Normandy. Stephen's arrival in March caused a postponement of Geoffrey's plans. Geoffrey invaded Normandy in that year, as he had every year since 1134. Orderic says he was acting as his wife's 'mercenary commander', but this was an unwarranted sneer, and tells us more about Orderic's attitude to the Angevin count than it does about Geoffrey's role in the conquest.[19] He attacked the Hiémois, burned Bazoches-au-Houlme and subjugated a number of monasteries.

Stephen had made his peace, both with his brother Theobald, and with the King of France, incidentally denying their possible aid to Geoffrey. He had also made efforts to deal with the problems of law and order in the duchy, successfully reducing the castles of several troublemakers. Stephen had planned a head-on attack against Geoffrey at Argentan, but then had occurred the problems with his own troops. There had been the obscure attempt against Robert of Gloucester which may have impelled that noble into the enemy camp, or encouraged him in a direction already taken. There had been the quarrel between Stephen's Flemish mercenaries and his Norman troops, possibly also involving Robert of Gloucester against William of Ypres, and leading to the desertion of many of the Norman nobles. Stephen had meant to approach Argentan, or even go beyond Normandy, with the intention of bringing Geoffrey to battle, but the whole project had to be abandoned at Livarot because of the disagreement among his own troops.[20]

Nevertheless, Geoffrey had still been willing enough to make peace with Stephen, and had agreed a truce in return for an annual pension of 2,000 marks out of the English revenues, beginning in the present year. It is also noticeable that Stephen's activities had been almost entirely confined to the eastern part of the duchy, which proved throughout his rule there, to be his most secure base.

The peace did not last long, its existence quickly threatened by Robert of Gloucester's defiance. Geoffrey also gained other adherents, including Reginald of Dunstanville, later to become Matilda's Earl of Cornwall. At this moment, Reginald's lands in the Cotentin were a useful addition to the territorial control of the Angevins. It is clear that what is presented by Orderic as an extremely chaotic situation, with virtually everyone at war with everyone else without reason, was really much more akin to the English Civil War.

In Normandy most of the fighting was a war between Stephen and those who were loyal to him against the Angevins and their supporters. Reginald and his friends were resolutely opposed by Roger the viscount for Stephen. But then Roger was ambushed by unnamed enemies, and his throat was slit. However, Engelran de Saye won a victory for the king against Reginald, Baldwin de Redvers and others. In these early years the king's party more than held its own.

June of 1138 saw a new Angevin invasion of Normandy. Through Robert of Gloucester, Geoffrey was promised a number of major western Norman strongholds, including Bayeux and Caen. But when Waleran and William of Ypres put an army into the field, the Angevins decided to abandon their expedition, and it seems that even Caen refused to surrender itself, Robert keeping quiet inside.

However, by the time the Count of Anjou besieged Falaise on 1 October, it was in company with Robert of Gloucester. The captain of the garrison was Richard de Lucy, who every day opened the gates and taunted the besiegers to come in if they could. The garrison was well provisioned and well armed and felt secure. The Angevins stayed nearly three weeks, until 19 October, and then abandoned the attempt. Orderic says the Angevins fled suddenly, leaving behind tents, food, wine, weapons and clothes, but does not say why. One would guess news, perhaps false news, of an approaching army. Ten days later Geoffrey returned and recovered some of his abandoned possessions.

The expedition ended with another disaster, this time at Touques. The Angevins arrived there in November, which at least meant that they had broken right through central Normandy to the sea. Geoffrey intended to use the town as a base for an attack on the nearby castle of Bonneville-sur-Touques. Many of the citizens fled, and the invaders found empty houses well stocked with food and drink. Others were still at home and were taken prisoner as they sat in their chairs. The Angevins prepared feasts in celebration.

William Trussebot, the castellan of the nearby castle, had heard of the arrival of the enemy. He contacted the citizens of Touques and arranged a plan. Boys and women were sent quietly back to start no less than forty-six fires in every part of the town. Chaos followed. The relaxing Angevins were taken by surprise. Outside the town Trussebot waited with his men, but there was so much confusion that no real conflict took place. The Angevins panicked and fled, both sides confused by the billowing smoke. Count Geoffrey found himself sheltering in a cemetery. At dawn he decided to abandon Touques and rode for Argentan, 'not without disgrace'.[21]

By 1141, Geoffrey had made a little steady progress, but was far from certain of complete or even partial success. Stephen's appointed deputies, at first William of Roumare and Roger the viscount, later Waleran of Meulan and William of Ypres, defended the duchy effectively. From the little that Orderic has to say about the period, one would suspect that Normandy was relatively peaceful from 1139 to 1141, though Geoffrey did make one or two further incursions, including a revenge attack on Robert Marmion for holding Falaise against him.[22] This involved besieging and then taking Robert's castle of Fontenay-le-Marmion, near Exmes, on the right bank of the Orne, which was then destroyed.

The Battle of Lincoln had a dramatic effect upon the Norman situation. As in England, most magnates believed that Stephen's reign was ended and that Matilda would take over in the kingdom and perhaps in the duchy. At any rate, the sensible thing to do was seek terms with the man on the spot, and save one's estates. Orderic says 'when Geoffrey, Count of Anjou, heard that his wife had won the day, he came at once into Normandy, sent out envoys to the magnates and commanded them as of right to hand over their castles to him'.[23]

Geoffrey's power was soon established as far as the Seine, and opposition to him began to look a very risky choice. As in England in 1141 most nobles came to terms with Matilda, so in Normandy they did with her husband. Even some of Stephen's chief supporters at that time, now did the prudent thing, including Waleran, Count of Meulan, one of Stephen's main representatives in defending the duchy against Geoffrey, who was 'superior to all the rest of the Norman nobles in castles, wealth and the number of his connections'.[24] Rotrou, Count of Mortagne, and John, Bishop of Lisieux, head of the administration of Normandy for Stephen, and who had resisted Geoffrey's previous attempts to take his city, both joined Geoffrey.

Waleran of Meulan's desertion was perhaps reluctant. So far as is known he never opposed Stephen directly in arms after his move, and at the end of the reign, after going on the Second Crusade, was helping the king again indirectly through a second change of allegiance to the King of France.[25] But it was a serious loss to Stephen's power in Normandy in 1141.

One must remember that Robert of Gloucester was also a major Norman landholder, so that Geoffrey's position in the duchy was now transformed. Geoffrey's conquest would undoubtedly have progressed faster, had he not at the same time been reinforcing comital power at home. He had to subdue two major rebellions in Anjou during the decade which saw the conquest of the duchy. By the end of that decade his authority was firmly established in both areas.

The Norman nobility held an assembly at Mortagne to debate the situation with Stephen in prison, and decided once again to offer the rule of the duchy to Stephen's brother, Theobald of Blois. Theobald not only refused, but actually suggested that they should offer it to Geoffrey, on condition that Geoffrey recognize his right to Tours, release Stephen, and restore him. Geoffrey was not likely to fulfil these conditions, but Theobald seems now to have lost any desire to rule Normandy in person. The outcome of all this was that the Normans accepted Geoffrey, and 'many who had previously resisted the Angevins had now

The city walls at Caen.

given way to them . . . [and] recognized the lordship of Count Geoffrey and Matilda'.[26]

Geoffrey's steady accumulation of castles continued. One recalls that the visit of Robert of Gloucester in 1142 to seek aid in England merely resulted in Robert being dragged along in the count's wake as he captured some ten castles, including Aulnay and Mortain. It was the beginning of Geoffrey's westwards push, and was obviously encouraged by the assistance of a major landholder in that region, Robert himself.

The Rout of Winchester and the release of Stephen had reversed the direction of events in England in 1142 for over a decade. Most of the former supporters of the king rejoined his ranks. But Normandy did not follow the same pattern. This was probably because, during the year's interval, Geoffrey had made a better job of securing the duchy than Matilda had of the kingdom, and the events of 1142 in England seemed less immediate across the sea.

But though Geoffrey's position was now far more secure, he still persevered with the gently, gently, approach of solid castle gains. He also proceeded in a logical manner to reduce the duchy by sections, with a strategic plan. His first aim had always been to move forward from his southern Norman base and keep that secure. His next drive, which took several years, was to divide the duchy in two by moving forward to the coast so that he would hold the whole of central Normandy.

From 1142, with this objective achieved, he then turned to the isolated western block of the duchy, much weakened after the change of allegiance by Robert of Gloucester. He mopped up resisting strongholds across the Orne. He then attacked each major stronghold in turn in the Cotentin, capturing Avranches and Coutances, then St-Lô and Cherbourg after short sieges. With western Normandy taken, only the vital eastern area around Rouen remained.

Geoffrey turned his attention eastwards at the same time as he was finishing off operations in the west, in 1143, taking Verneuil, and making the Seine his frontier. By January 1144 Geoffrey was able to concentrate all his efforts on eastern Normandy. He crossed the Seine at Vernon accompanied by Waleran of Meulan who had considerable influence in the eastern part of the duchy, and they besieged the Norman capital, Rouen. The Count of Anjou camped on a hill overlooking the city, at La Trinité-du-Mont. Trees were felled, throwing engines set up, and the walls given a hammering.

The town soon surrendered, though Geoffrey's attack had dealt a fair amount of damage in the meantime, as did a strong wind on the very day he entered Rouen. Then Rouen's castle, known as the Tower, was besieged, which still held out under the Earl of Warenne. One side of it collapsed under the weight of stones hurled against it. The siege was a dramatic climax to the conquest of Normandy, and it was three long months before the castle finally capitulated in 1144, when running short of supplies. Other places then quickly capitulated.

Normandy had changed hands, and Geoffrey began to style himself duke. One last stronghold remained to be taken in the far north-west of the duchy, Arques. It was defended by William the Monk, a Flemish renegade from religion, now a mercenary captain in Stephen's pay. When William the Monk was accidentally killed by an arrow during the following summer, the siege came to a quick end. There was no resistance left. By 1145 Normandy had been added to the great swathe of Angevin territories. The conquest had been a remarkable achievement, not least in that it had been achieved without a single battle throughout a whole decade of warfare. It had been accomplished by unremitting effort, by sieges and diplomacy; 'those he subdued, he won over to himself more by clemency than by force'.[27]

Geoffrey ruled Normandy as duke, issuing over forty charters which have survived, and making decisions in his own name, not in either that of his wife Matilda or his son Henry. Nor is it likely that he in some way abdicated before his death, though historians frequently suggest this to be the case. What he almost certainly did do, was to begin to associate his eldest son, Henry, in the government of Normandy, with himself. This was a relatively common practice, and was grooming Henry for the succession, but does not mean that Geoffrey stood aside. Geoffrey's rule brought peace to Normandy, and was regarded there much as his son's rule in England. Under the previous regime, the chroniclers like Orderic had described much disorder, the duchy 'cruelly harassed by its own sons', who 'gnawed themselves with their own teeth'.[28] John of Marmoutier wrote that now 'the land was quiet under the watchful count for about ten years'.[29] The main problems remaining were to establish internal government, and fend off external attacks. Louis VII and Eustace made attempts to overthrow Geoffrey, but the latter arranged a peace with the king and foiled the efforts of Eustace.

It is necessary to pause a moment and consider the value of the work by John of Marmoutier, especially the *History of Geoffrey, Duke of the Normans and Count of the Angevins*. It is an unusual work, placed somewhere between a chronicle and an epic poem. It is partly biographical, following the exploits of Geoffrey, but is not strictly chronological, preferring generally to pursue a theme around one aspect of the count's character or exploits. It is written in prose, but often in poetic style. I have suggested elsewhere that it may have been based upon a verse work now lost.[30] It also repeats several well-known topoi and adapts them to fit its own hero. John himself admits a debt to several earlier writers, the most obvious one being Thomas of Loches, since many of the stories in the *History* are placed in and around Loches. He also, unusually for a medieval chronicler, names the men who have been his sources of information and who brought him new tales every day, including Renard Ruffus. He says he has 'worked in the long watches of the night on this little product of my labour, searched out evidence in many places, and condensed it all', in order to bring it to his reader.

The *History* was written later, well into the reign of Henry II, so as well as being poetic in style it is also not contemporary. For these sort of reasons it has been largely ignored or dismissed by historians. But the English and Norman chroniclers give us little information about Geoffrey, and that generally hostile, so the *History* is a useful antidote, and also is often detailed. Clearly we need to have some care in using it, but better that, than excluding its information.

The author identifies himself in the prologue as 'Brother John, the most humble of the monks of Marmoutier, himself a cleric', and he dedicated the work to the Bishop of Le Mans. Others he said had travelled far to tell stories of foreign lands, but 'we undertake in our compilation only to describe the facts closest at hand, the domestic deeds of an exceptional man, Geoffrey, Duke of the Normans and Count of the Angevins'.[31] He gives us a description of Geoffrey: 'tall in body, handsome and ruddy in appearance, lean and taut, with sparkling eyes . . . grown strong through nature and through exercise . . . gentle, charming and generous of spirit.'[32]

Geoffrey's was no passive rule. He had long experience by now of rule in Anjou. In a story told by John of Marmoutier, the count was lost during a hunting expedition.[33] He met up with a soot-covered peasant, who did not recognize him. 'Tell me, good fellow,' he asked, 'what do men say about our count?' The peasant replied that Count Geoffrey was a lover of the law, a guardian of peace, a conqueror of his enemies and a helper of the oppressed, but also went on to point out the abuses by some of his officials, of which the count was ignorant. Humbly, the peasant said he had better stop 'in case by jabbering on in my rustic fashion, I offend your elegant ears'. Geoffrey assured him that nothing was better than speaking the truth.

As the man finished his complaints they entered in through the city gates of Loches. Then, of course, Geoffrey put right the abuses, and rewarded the peasant for his honesty. He ordered his local castellan to provide 500 shillings from the revenues kept within the castle to be given to the peasant, 'in case the work he has lost for my sake should seem to be lost in vain'. He freed him from all exactions, and from his serfdom. He then investigated complaints from other subjects and corrected them, and punished those whose guilt had been revealed by the peasant's remarks. He threatened to execute any who did not now confess to the abuses they had committed in his name. The author gives the count's philosophy in a quotation: 'value justice, you who have jurisdiction over the land'.[34]

It was a considerable compliment that the man who was seen with such contempt before the conquest by Orderic, became to another Norman chronicler 'a man of great worth and energy'.[35] It should not be forgotten that Geoffrey was the literate count, 'well read', good at debate, 'not least when it came to a knowledge of antiquity', who could benefit from reading Vegetius, and who was a lover of music, an intelligent and cultured man, 'dedicated to liberal studies'.[36]

In Normandy, Duke Geoffrey developed an organized chancery, and under him Norman charters were streamlined by his chancellor, Thomas of Loches. Every year for the rest of his life Geoffrey spent some time in the duchy, and his son was educated there. The damage done to Rouen during the siege was repaired, including the bridge over the river and the stonework of the Tower. Geoffrey, in the government of Normandy, brought in some of his own people, such as Jocelyn de Tours, but he also employed Normans such as Robert de Neubourg, who became his steward. It has been suggested that Geoffrey was the first to introduce seneschals into Norman government.[37] He used itinerant justices and the sworn inquest, and introduced the supervisory local *baillage* – all of which were probably inspirations for the government of Henry II. In Normandy Geoffrey had done much to produce a stable duchy for his son to rule, and it became the launching point for the successful attack upon England.

THE 1153 EXPEDITION

Only in comparison to his earlier efforts was the 1153 campaign a success for Henry of Anjou. In practice, even in 1153, Henry won only a few new strongholds, and made little military impact on the steadily royal regions. At best, militarily, he had reopened a war which had seemed dead – but this was perhaps the kernel of his overall victory.

Henry, now Duke of Normandy, arrived in England again on 6 January 1153, braving rough seas in a winter crossing. Even now he could not afford a large force. He brought a mere 140 knights, with 3,000 infantry, in 36 ships. The mercenaries he brought proved unpopular, and his friends persuaded him to send them back to Normandy. Many of them in fact drowned on their return journey. Henry's hope was to raise forces in England. News of his arrival spread through the land, 'like a quivering bed of reeds swept by the blasts of the wind'. But again there was disappointment that his force was not larger.[38]

Henry was certainly a person of greater standing in 1153 than he had been in 1149. He had become sole Duke of Normandy as well as Count of Anjou on his father's death in 1151. Henry also acquired at least a claim to Aquitaine through his marriage to Eleanor in 1152, 'unlooked-for good fortune'. Eleanor was the heiress to the great duchy of Aquitaine in southern France. She had been married to Louis VII, King of France, but it had been a troubled match. She had gone with her husband on the Second Crusade, and dallied with her attractive uncle, Raymond of Tripoli. She said that being married to Louis was more like being

Eleanor of Aquitaine, on the left, with the young Isabella of Angoulême, 1200.

wed to a monk than a king. She bore him daughters, but no son, and Louis decided upon a divorce.

Henry of Anjou and his father had been in Paris to make their peace with Louis, and probably met Eleanor during that period. By the time her divorce was arranged on 21 March, Geoffrey was dead and she left her husband's court, evaded a number of hopeful suitors and sought out the young Henry of Anjou. The attractions of the lady, and perhaps even more of her inheritance of Aquitaine, soon won over Henry, and they were promptly married on 18 May.[39] But the marriage incensed Eleanor's former husband, Louis VII of France, who now joined with Stephen and Eustace to try and dislodge the Angevins from Normandy.

Henry held off attacks on the duchy by Louis VII in alliance with Eustace, but it would still be taking a very considerable risk to come to England in 1153. Waleran of Meulan, for one, took advantage of his absence to cause trouble in the duchy. But Eustace, like his father, gave his priority to the English war, and followed Henry across the Channel.

The 1153 campaign was seen by Leedom as a triumph, Henry showing himself to be 'a brilliant military commander'. He claimed that Henry 'won impressive victories over King Stephen in that year'.[40] But this view has been queried. Henry had some success, but also some failure, for example at Bedford and Crowmarsh. In the early pipe rolls of Henry II's reign, the burgesses of Bedford were

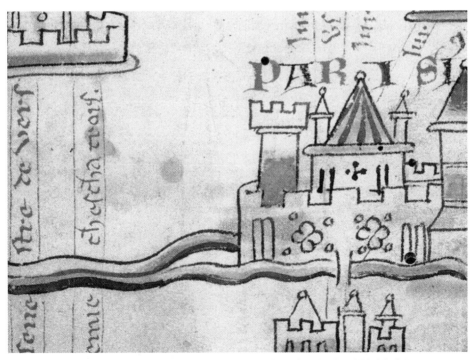

Paris, showing the wall and tower. (Corpus Christi College, Cambridge, MS 26, f. i.v)

compensated for the harm they suffered against Stephen, presumably partly at least those inflicted on this occasion. The rival armies twice confronted each other, but there was to be no battle, and on at least one of these occasions it was Henry rather than Stephen who refused a fight.

The delicacy of Henry's position is clear. In the poetic lines of Henry of Huntingdon:

> Before thee, Stephen's countless hosts advance,
> Behind thee, low'rs the might pow'r of France.[41]

Henry knew that he could not be absent from Normandy for long. Robert of Torigny says that the Normans had believed, when Louis VII invaded, that Henry would lose all his possessions. There had also been rebellion in Aquitaine. Torigny told an obscure tale about a man who had been advised in a dream that he ought to cut off his hands and feet in order to be saved, did so, and then expired. It seems like a heavy hint that Henry had to beware. There were some significant desertions from Stephen, but in truth only a few men of standing came over to him. Robert, Earl of Leicester, was Henry's main new acquisition, possibly driven by the need to defend the family position, threatened by Waleran's problems in France and the conflict over Waleran's previous holding at Worcester. As we have suggested earlier, Robert's desertion may have occurred before 1153.

However, the recent support Henry was receiving from such as Ranulf of Chester and Hugh Bigod, could not be greatly relied on, and was bought dear. Ranulf was promised the honor of Peverel of Nottingham, a promise which antagonized Robert de Ferrers, Earl of Derby. Robert of Leicester was promised the restoration of the family honor of Breteuil in Normandy for his son, and was himself made steward to Henry in England and Normandy.

Henry attacked Malmesbury Castle, but Stephen's castellan, Jordan, fought more stoutly than expected, and the citizens of the town showed their loyalty to the king by lining the walls. Henry ordered archers to shoot against those manning the walls, and began a mining operation. His men used ladders to scale the wall and broke into the town, taking over a church which sheltered some monks. Priests and monks were killed in the attack, and even the altar was robbed.[42] It was the ruthless behaviour of Henry's mercenaries at Malmesbury which led to his English supporters requesting that the foreign troops be sent home. The town was taken and now Henry besieged the castle.

The castellan, Jordan, escaped and himself went to Stephen with an appeal for help. The king brought an army to relieve the place: 'as though he meant to fight a pitched battle'. The two armies faced each other over the Avon, Stephen to the north, his banners glittering gold. Stephen sought battle; Henry with a smaller army refused it.[43] But Stephen gained nothing because of the heavy rain and storm, which blew against his force 'in the faces of the king and his troops, so that they could hardly support their armour or handle their spears, soaked with rain'. It also proved impossible to cross the river, so the king tamely gave up and returned to London.[44] It seems that he was also persuaded to this action by the knowledge of how difficult it would be to maintain his force in the field in a hard

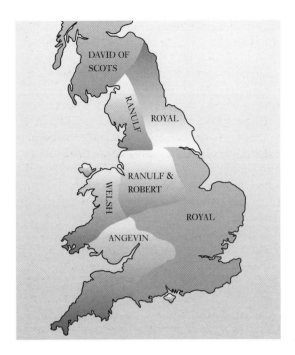

Approximate areas of control, 1153.

winter and with a famine in the region. 'It seemed as if God Himself were fighting for the duke.'[45]

Stephen also knew that some of his men were in negotiation with Henry and were planning to desert him, though how far we should see him as Stephen's man by 1153 is open to doubt. It has been suggested that Robert, Earl of Leicester, may have been one of these. The whole business left Stephen feeling depressed, gloomy and downcast. Both leaders were reluctant, but both agreed a truce. The castellan, Jordan, who was supposed to destroy the castle, then surrendered it to Henry, another man apparently disillusioned by the actions of his master. Henry of Anjou had reason to feel 'more cheerful than usual' after Malmesbury than for many a year.[46] This was the turning point in the Henrician war, and it was the attitude of the English barons, rather than any military action, which had given Henry cause for hope.

Henry had other successes in the midlands, marching through Worcestershire, Warwickshire, Northamptonshire and Bedfordshire, successes which included the taking of Tutbury and the surrender of Warwick to him. The latter was handed over by the Countess of Warwick, in May or June of 1153, though her husband was with Stephen at the time, and is said to have died of shame over his wife's action. The countess was half sister to Robert of Leicester and seems to have made the decision on her own behalf, managing somehow to take control of the castle from the royal soldiers who were there. The castle was taken by 'tricking the royal garrison' rather than by assault.[47]

One of Henry's successes in 1153 was brought upon him by his favours to Ranulf of Chester, when he was forced to deal with the dissident Robert, Earl of

Derby. Henry attacked, and the earl's castle at Tutbury surrendered to him. Robert, Earl of Leicester, had made the decision to abandon Stephen, and joined Henry at this siege.[48] The Earl of Derby then made an agreement with Henry, but it was a reluctant submission rather than a desertion, since Henry held his son as a hostage.

The Angevin position in the midlands was much improved in 1153, but rather because he now had the support and territories of Ranulf of Chester and Robert of Leicester, than because of military gains. He captured a few castles, including Tutbury, but he failed to take Bedford. Bedford had also come within the Beaumont territories since it had been given to Hugh the Poor by Stephen. It had passed through the marriage of his daughter, to the Beauchamp family. Henry arrived suddenly, using the sort of tactics which had served Stephen so well through the castle war. But although he set fire to the town and plundered it, he was not able to capture the castle and went away again.

By the time Henry confronted Stephen at Wallingford, according to David Crouch, he 'had achieved little' from his military efforts. Stephen made Wallingford his chief target in 1153, having built two counter castles against it in 1152, which were described as elaborate of their type, and set up a permanent blockade.[49] Several times in the past he had besieged and attacked this constant thorn in his flesh, but always he had failed. Wallingford was a powerfully built castle on a good natural site. It was also the Angevins' flagship castle, more easterly than any of their permanent strongholds. And it was held by that devoted and reliable friend of the Angevins, Brian fitz Count. But by 1153 the Angevin garrison was in sore straits from lack of food.

This time Stephen's most trusty allies, the Londoners, provided a force to assist him against Wallingford, and other lords came in as well. Stephen was reaching the climax of his war. The king took the bridge over the Thames which led to the town. Roger of Hereford had joined Brian inside the castle, and they made a strong sortie, but could not break through the king's blockade.

Roger of Hereford's loyalty to the Angevin cause was less firm than that of his father, Miles. Probably disheartened by the blockade of Wallingford, and not hopeful for Henry's success, he sent secretly to Stephen to suggest a deal. He would surrender to the king, on condition that Stephen assist him in gaining Worcester. The latter place was held for Waleran of Beaumont, formerly Stephen's leading magnate, but now in the other camp, whose men had captured the rival Angevin magnate seeking to hold Worcester, William Beauchamp, and imprisoned him. William was on good terms with Roger of Hereford, and it must have seemed like a good opportunity for the king, who had little to lose, since his own influence in the town had virtually vanished. It was another opportunity offered to Stephen because of division within the Angevin ranks. Indeed, Stephen was convinced, and raised a force to besiege Worcester. This was to prove an abortive hope for Stephen. Because he was worried about other events, in the end he left Roger to continue the siege alone, though some royal troops also stayed. When Roger eventually won back Worcester, he then immediately abandoned Stephen once more. Of the cynical baronial moves during the reign, of which there were probably fewer than have been imagined, this was surely one of the most barefaced.

The bridge over the Thames at Wallingford, leading to the castle on the right, and to Crowmarsh on the left.

Henry now approached Wallingford and besieged the counter castle at Crowmarsh, which was on a high mound and guarding the bridge, with Wallingford just over the river. This indecisive meeting was to prove the last major conflict of the war. According to Gervase of Canterbury, the counter castle at Crowmarsh possessed a wooden tower.[50] Henry arrived there suddenly, his men clambering up the slopes and entering the outer enclosure. But he had been outmanoeuvred, and hidden royal forces suddenly appeared and set upon the Angevin troops. Henry did not give up his attempt, and 'erected a strong earthwork encircling both the king's castle and his own army'. He also managed to get in some supplies to the garrison of Wallingford. Henry succeeded in capturing a wooden tower, possibly a siege tower or belfry is meant, with a garrison of twenty men. He also captured and beheaded sixty royal archers. So Henry had some success at Wallingford, but the royal army was not defeated.

The king had seen the significance of the conflict over Wallingford, and sent a considerable force of 300 knights to nearby Oxford, with orders to them and to royalists of the region, to harass the Angevin army.[51] Then the king assembled an 'inexpressibly large' force of his own, and accompanied by Eustace and other nobles, approached Wallingford. The armies again faced each other across a river, and again recoiled from a battle. They 'shrank on both sides from a conflict'.[52] Stephen was thrown from his horse no less than three times, when it kept rearing, which left him shaken, and may have affected his attitude so that he was ready to settle for a truce.[53]

The path to the top of Wallingford motte.

The nobles, nay rather the traitors of England, arose and discussed terms of peace among themselves. They loved indeed nothing better than discord, but were unwilling to commit themselves to war; for they wanted to raise up neither one nor the other of the claimants to the crown, lest by humbling the one they might become entirely subject to the other.

The chronicler adds that both leaders were 'aware of the treachery of their followers, and were reluctantly compelled to make a truce'. During their private conference, when the two leaders had conferred alone across a stream, 'both complained bitterly of the disloyalty of their nobles'.[54] One wonders what was Stephen's impression of his young rival; was it the occasion when he was swayed towards his eventual decision over the succession? Certainly, afterwards, Eustace rode off in a very bad temper.

Although Stephen was not defeated on either occasion, his loss of Malmesbury, and now his agreement of a truce at Wallingford which allowed the destruction of his counter castle at Crowmarsh, shows that in the negotiations at least, Henry was gaining the upper hand, and given their relative strengths, this is itself a curious fact.

The truce in any case did not halt the fighting for long. But after Wallingford, there were only minor operations by either side. Henry went on to drive a small royalist force back into Oxford, capturing twenty prisoners, and then to attack Stamford. He broke into the town, but had to besiege the castle. Because Stephen

The Great Hall at Winchester.

was unable to come to its aid, diverted by Hugh Bigod, Stamford surrendered on terms on 31 August.

At Nottingham, Henry again suffered a military reverse. Ranulf of Chester had an interest here, since he had an enduring hatred of its constable, William Peverel of Nottingham. It was said that the latter, when Earl Ranulf was his guest, had tried to kill him and his men with poisoned wine. Three men died, but Earl Ranulf, after suffering agonizingly, recovered because he had drunk less than the others. This is one of those stories which is impossible to verify.[55] Henry took the town, but the castle resisted, and when the garrison itself fired the town, he was forced to move out.

At Winchester the armies approached each other again, but this time a more lasting peace was agreed. The civil war, in fact, was over, though possibly few realized it at first. The fighting of 1153 was neither very dramatic nor decisive. Henry's position was stronger than it had ever been, but mainly because a number of people had switched their allegiance to him. The main feeling that comes from studying the warfare of 1153, is its desultory nature, as if men on both sides were simply fed up with war.

CHAPTER 8

The Peace

The civil war of Stephen's reign is an unusual war. The general rule of war is to the winner, the spoils, but in this case, King Stephen seems to have won the war but lost the peace. Stephen, as we have seen, was neither overthrown by Matilda in England by 1148, when the empress retired from the conflict, nor militarily defeated by Henry of Anjou during the 1153 campaign. The peace was a compromise, by which Stephen kept his throne for life, but had to agree to yield the rights of his son to succeed him as king. Since the war had in essence been one of succession, the agreement cannot be viewed as anything but an eventual defeat for Stephen. The major puzzle is why, if he did not lose the war, he agreed to losing the peace.

THE NEGOTIATIONS

Further to clarify the situation, we need to re-examine the settlement of 1153. There has been much historical debate around this settlement in recent years, but we are left still with some uncertainties, and even perhaps some inaccuracies. It is now clear that the settlement was the result of several meetings and prolonged negotiations. These were pressed upon the contestants by churchmen, as was often the case.

There were a series of meetings between the two sides during 1153, and clearly much negotiation. Twice battle was avoided, when the two armies faced each other across rivers and seemed prepared to test the issue by conflict. At several points, truces were agreed and discussions about peace held. While Matilda was still in the field, peace discussions had been held, though they came to nothing.

Throughout the war churchmen sought to bring the sides together. To some extent the ambivalent attitude of Henry of Blois, as demonstrated at Arundel and later, stemmed from a genuine wish to follow the teachings of the church and prevent Christians from fighting each other. As was usual in the period, clerics took on the role of negotiators for peace. And often men who might have been expected to have attachments to one side, seem truly to have acted as mediators; thus Henry of Blois argued for Matilda's release from the trap at Arundel, and thus Theobald of Canterbury, despite being refused permission to attend a church council and disobeying that refusal, still argued with the Pope against Stephen being penalized.

The armies of Henry and Stephen faced each other at Malmesbury, when a battle was avoided and a truce agreed, whereby Stephen was to demolish his

King Stephen, with a falcon, from a fourteenth-century manuscript. (BL MS Royal 20 AII, f. 7)

castle there. In the event it was not demolished, but handed to Henry and the war continued. After this, a number of royalist barons 'sent envoys by stealth and made a compact with the duke'.[1] The two sides met again at Wallingford in August 1153, when both armies still wanted to avoid a battle.

The nobility 'had no inclination for war', and pressed the truce upon their respective leaders. Henry of Huntingdon suggests it was because they were traitors and enjoyed the division of power in the country, but more likely they were tired of war and wanted greater stability. Churchmen approached both leaders, seeking a halt to the conflict.[2] There were discussions regarding peace, and a short truce was arranged. Neither leader could trust his troops for a battle. This was the occasion when Stephen and Henry had a 'private discussion' about peace, and complained to each other about the loyalty of their own men. Henry of Huntingdon specifically says that there was a beginning of the peace negotiation, but it was decided to postpone its completion to another occasion.[3] The *Gesta Stephani* says that Stephen wished to continue the conflict, but his brother,

The remains of Wallingford Castle.

Bishop Henry, 'made himself a mediator between the duke and the king for the establishment of peace'. Henry of Huntingdon adds that Theobald of Canterbury was also seeking to persuade Stephen to agree a peace, and was also in touch with Henry. Theobald had frequent meetings with the king 'in which he urged him to come to terms with the duke'.[4]

The peace was finally made at Winchester in November. There were further meetings, at Westminster, and in 1154 the two leaders came together several times: at Oxford, where the royalist magnates did homage to Henry, saving only their allegiance to the king; at Dunstable in January, and later at Canterbury and Dover.

But however much discussion there was before and after, the settlement was reached in its essentials late in the year 1153 at Winchester. Here, according to Gervase of Canterbury, in a 'public assembly' (*conventu publico*), the agreement was made. He says this 'concord' was later confirmed. One chronicler saw this as the key moment; 'what a happy day'.[5] The chroniclers describe this event, but the main evidence of the detailed agreement survives in a charter issued later in the year by Stephen at Westminster. It would seem that in this charter, some of the more controversial declarations at Winchester were quietly omitted, including the treatment of castles, and the restoration of lands to those holding under Henry I. Such things in the end had to be dealt with on individual merits, not by broad policy.

It has been argued that the terms were made early in 1153, before the meeting at Winchester, and that Eustace reacted against them after Wallingford. Leedom claimed that Eustace's death 'came after peace had already been made'. However, the evidence does not show this. Eustace reacted against a peace negotiation between his father and Henry at Wallingford. He reacted angrily, which suggests he did not like what was happening, but this does not prove what terms, if any, had been agreed. The *Gesta Stephani* says he raged 'because the war, in his opinion, had reached no proper conclusion'; that is, against a truce rather than against peace. He went off in a fury, took to arms, and did his best to break up the peace, ravaging Cambridgeshire, but then suddenly died on 17 August 1153.

Before the death of Eustace there had been negotiations but no settlement; the sides were still at odds, the truce at Wallingford which had caused Eustace's anger was only for five days. Both sides continued the war afterwards, albeit somewhat desultorily. Both leaders rejected peace at this stage, Henry besieging Stamford where he took the town, but the castle resisting for a time, and Stephen capturing Ipswich from Hugh Bigod. The agreement at Wallingford was only a truce, and Eustace's death was a major step towards resolving the conflict.[6] It was only at Winchester that we hear of concrete terms agreed by Stephen, and it seems wiser to revert to an earlier view of these events, which sees the death of Eustace as vital in the process. William of Newburgh clearly states that the death of Eustace 'offered a great opportunity of creating peace', a peace which had been impossible during his lifetime because of his 'youthful aggression'.[7] Only after Winchester in November 1153 was peace established, and it was 'firmly settled that arms should be finally laid down'.[8]

THE SETTLEMENT: THE TREATY OF WINCHESTER, 1153

The peace made at Winchester was confirmed by Stephen's well known charter issued at Westminster. But it must be stressed that the formal peace had already been made at Winchester, which Stephen marked by leading the duke in a procession through the streets, as he would later do also in London.[9] It is from chroniclers' descriptions of Winchester, and from Stephen's Westminster charter, that we know what was agreed. The charter was a document for action to those who must enforce the new arrangements; it was not a formal treaty at all. It was a confirmation of what had already been agreed. There is no 'treaty' of Westminster. The tone of the charter is of agreement made in the past, that is, at Winchester.[10]

It was settled that both sides should lay down their arms. The main agreement was that Henry should become Stephen's adopted son and heir, and therefore succeed him on the throne. Henry of Huntingdon says that he 'adopted' Henry. Robert of Torigny makes a point, which could well have been significant had things turned out differently, that Henry would succeed Stephen to the throne 'if he were the survivor'.[11] Stephen was recognized as king for life by all, including Henry, who had never done so before. Recently built castles were to be demolished. Those holders of land who had been disinherited since the time of Henry I were to have their estates reinstated. Law and order was to be restored at a national level, with 'laws and enactments made binding on all according to the old custom'. Mercenary troops, who were seen as a plague, were to be sent home, and according to William of Newburgh, they 'slid off'.[12]

The agreement was repeated in Stephen's charter issued at Westminster, probably in December of 1153.[13] This is an official document, as opposed to the descriptions given above by various chroniclers. It has also moved us on a month or so, and one or two of the more contentious issues agreed at Winchester have been quietly dropped, perhaps because they could not be administered in a cut and dried manner, including the demolition of recently built castles and the restoration of lands to those disinherited. But otherwise, we have here the details of the peace.

In the charter, Stephen recognizes Henry as 'successor to the kingdom of England and my heir by hereditary right, and thus to him and to his heirs I have given the kingdom of England, and confirmed it'. As a result, in return, Henry has done him homage and made an oath as guarantee to keep the 'agreements [*conventiones*] made between us, which are contained in this charter'. It says that William of Blois, Stephen's son, has done homage to Henry and recognizes that William will be able to hold the personal lands that Stephen now holds or has held, in England and Normandy, and those gained by his marriage to the Warenne heiress. William is also to have the castle of Norwich, much desired by Hugh Bigod, Earl of Norfolk. All the magnates, of either party, will both recognize Stephen as king and Henry as his successor. Certain key castles will be held by named individuals, who guarantee to hand them over to Henry at his accession, namely the Tower of London, Windsor, Oxford, Lincoln, Winchester and Southampton. The leading churchmen would also take an oath to recognize Henry. In the conduct of his government, Stephen promised to take the advice of Henry. He also declared that from now on he would do justice in all parts of the realm, royalist and Angevin. These were the terms on which the civil war came to an end.

The feeling of relief throughout the country was great. Late in 1153 Osbert of Clare, prior of Westminster, wrote to Theobald, Archbishop of Canterbury, congratulating him for his part in making the peace: 'you have restored order to our distracted country'. He wrote also to Henry of Anjou, calling him 'the new light . . . a leader given to us by God . . . [who] shall found a new Jerusalem'.[14]

WHY THE PEACE WAS MADE

Again, in order to understand the outcome, we must look at the results of the peace for those who had been engaged in the war. The peace mattered to the church, to citizens, to peasants, to traders, but politically it was its effect on the nobles concerned, which most dictated the settlement.

If we review those who lost lands or position, it is a fairly short list. In the remaining year of Stephen's life, and in the first few years of the new reign, very few great figures actually lost their lands and positions through royal action. This was partly because Henry was not vindictive. Those who submitted to him were usually not hounded. They might be penalized, and some certainly received less than they hoped for, but in most cases the key family lands were retained.

Henry abided by certain principles in the settlement: that there should be a return to the position as under Henry I, and that those who had been unlawfully dispossessed should be repossessed. He also claimed that adulterine, or at least recently built, castles, should be demolished. William of Newburgh rather glibly says they 'melted away like wax before a flame', but in practice none of these three principles was pursued consistently or with vigour.[15]

Many developments which had occurred under Stephen were allowed to remain undisturbed. Few men who had gained from Stephen were dispossessed; few castles of any kind were actually destroyed. Robert of Torigny's figure of 1,115 castles has been widely quoted as the number destroyed by Henry II, but this has never been substantiated by research. His figure in another manuscript of 126 sounds more probable, and is still a greater number than any which have been shown to have been demolished. Robert of Torigny also gives a figure of 375 castles, a figure erased from one of the manuscripts.[16] These widely differing estimates, even by one chronicler, suggest much uncertainty in the minds of contemporaries over this matter. Undoubtedly, some new castles had been built during the anarchy, and often defensible buildings had been employed in emergencies. In some cases, the military purpose no longer existed, and clearly once there was peace, no one would maintain a church as a castle. Equally, castles with only a temporary purpose, such as a counter castle, would be abandoned. In this sense, with study, one might accumulate a number of 'castles' which disappeared, but these were not all demolished. Of useful and used castles, very few were actually permanently dismantled.

In a careful and localized study, Emilie Amt showed how few castles were destroyed, for example in Gloucestershire (Angevin) or Oxfordshire (divided). Even in Essex, where a large number of new castles had been built, only a handful were demolished, and those mainly belonging to Geoffrey de Mandeville. As Amt has pointed out, allowing the castles to stand proved a useful form of patronage. As the pendulum of opinion swings on this issue, it has even been suggested recently, that Stephen may have been more successful in demolishing castles than Henry. William of Newburgh suggests the true picture when he remarks that those new castles which were 'conveniently located', were to be kept by '[Henry] himself or his partisans for the defence of the kingdom'.[17]

After the initial revolts caused by the royal efforts to recover castles from his own followers, Roger of Hereford (Gloucester and Hereford), Hugh Mortimer (Bridgnorth, Wigmore, and Cleobury –the latter was destroyed), Henry used his discretion and let the matter drop. The truth is that almost no one was a loser, at least in any comprehensive way.

Few leading royalists of the civil war lost everything in the new reign. Some even recovered their positions. Stephen kept the throne, and his son, William of Blois, retained all the family lands, and even the broad estates gained from his marriage to the Warenne heiress. He became the wealthiest magnate in England. Henry seems to have treated him with caution at first, holding fire over remitting his Danegeld payments.[18] Henry demanded that he hand over a number of castles, and backed down on his generosity of 1153. But William remained loyal to Henry II, and was knighted by him in 1158. William of Blois was to die in 1159 on the return journey from Henry II's Toulouse expedition, on which he had fought for the king. William, as a younger son, had not expected the throne while his brother

Eustace lived, and so far as we know made no effort to gain it thereafter. The settlement excluded him from the throne, but he was much better off after 1153 than he had been before. We have no evidence that he ever expressed any regret over the agreement. It may be that not everyone wishes to be a king.

It is not always easy to categorize magnates as being 'royalist' or 'Angevin'. Many had changed sides during the course of the war, others had not seemed to have a very strong attachment to either side. Nevertheless, it is worthwhile attempting to make some distinction between the lords on either side, and how they fare in the peace that was now made. The main question in our minds must be whether the royalists were greatly penalized as a result of their commitment.

Let us first consider a group of royalists, who stayed with the king at least until 1153. William of Blois may well be considered as a member of this group. One consistent supporter of Stephen had been Simon de Senlis, made Earl of Northampton by the king. Like many of the main contestants, he died before the end of the reign, in 1153. But we should include such men, by considering whether or not their allegiance affected the inheritance of their heirs. Simon was seen at the time as Henry's most determined enemy, along with Eustace. Yet his son was not a loser, since Henry split the old earldom of Huntingdon and gave him part of it with the title Earl of Northampton. This was not a loss, since although Simon had maintained a claim to the earldom of Huntingdon, Stephen had given that earldom to the son of the King of Scots. Henry II maintained that situation.

William of Aumale had been made Earl of York by Stephen in 1138. He did not relish Henry II's policy of taking back royal castles into his own hands, and rebelled at the beginning of the new reign. William was forced to submit and had to give up Scarborough. But this should be seen as a punishment for his rebellion after the new rule had begun, not as punishment for his previous allegiance. Henry II's policy with regard to royal castles was applied just as rigorously to pro-Angevin magnates, and it must be said, with similar results.

Alan of Penthièvre (Alan II, the Black) had been a consistent supporter of Stephen, becoming Earl of Richmond, and dying in 1146. He had also been made Earl of Cornwall by Stephen, in opposition to the Angevin Earl Reginald, but had not been able to win the conflict. Alan's son, Conan, did not of course get the earldom of Cornwall, but he was recognized by Henry as Earl of Richmond, the only position which his father had held in practice. Henry's toleration towards his former opponents did not in this case pay off. When Conan pursued his claims in Brittany, he took over the county of Nantes in defiance of Henry, and as Duke of Brittany (1156–70) acted largely in opposition to the king.

William Peverel of Nottingham, the father-in-law of the Earl of Derby, had been a supporter of Stephen, and was an enemy of Ranulf, Earl of Chester. Indeed, he was one of the few barons forced out of England after the change of dynasty, but again, not as a result of his activities in the war, but because he was accused of poisoning or trying to poison (accounts vary) Ranulf of Chester. The exile seems to have been his own choice in the first place, and was not in any case the consequence of any action of Henry II because of William's allegiance in the civil war.

William de Chesney was a lesser lord, but an interesting example for our purposes, being one of Stephen's favoured followers. Gilbert Foliot was his nephew, and holding a different political persuasion, Bishop Gilbert tried to encourage William to good works, warning his uncle that when he died he would have to leave his castles behind him, but that his sins would follow him to heaven.[19] It is not clear that the bishop's exhortations had any effect. In the last year of the reign, anticipating losses for William from the settlement, Stephen compensated him with new grants.[20] He did not lose those lands in the new reign, nor was his castle at Deddington demolished. In fact he received grants from Henry II and Danegeld exemptions, even for Deddington, after a delay, in 1157. William's niece and heiress was married to a royal chamberlain, Henry fitz Gerold, which might be taken as a sign of favour to her, as well as to the chamberlain.[21] Other Stephen supporters were generally treated well. Hugh de Lacy, for example, had Pontefract restored to him. Henry dealt with the disputes and problems empirically. He had made some general declarations about his policy, but none of them were adhered to strictly. The policy, never declared, which seems to have been most consistently followed, was to leave things as they were in 1153, whenever possible.

Henry of Essex is an interesting example of a lord below the very top rank. He was a significant figure in the county for Stephen, holding the castle of Rayleigh, which he himself had rebuilt, but if anything, Henry of Essex bettered himself under the new king, becoming sheriff of Hertfordshire, and later of Buckinghamshire and Bedfordshire. Even in Essex, which had been a mainly royalist county, no major landholders were disinherited. Henry of Essex even became royal standard bearer, but apparently fulfilled his duty poorly during the first of Henry's Welsh wars. In a minor battle in Wales in 1157, when there was a rumour that the king had been killed, Henry of Essex is said to have thrown away the standard and fled, leaving the Welsh to believe that the English were cowards.[22] Even then Henry II took no action against him, and Henry of Essex was taken with the king on the Toulouse campaign. It was only a private accusation over his actions in Wales, made by Robert de Montfort in 1163, leading to a judicial duel between them, which made public Henry's alleged cowardice. Henry of Essex was defeated in the duel, which was equivalent to a verdict of being guilty of cowardice, and he was left for dead on the jousting field. His lands and his castle at Rayleigh were declared forfeit, though the castle was not demolished. The monks of Reading Abbey picked up the wounded man, and saved his life. He lost his lands and retired into the abbey as a monk. Henry of Essex ended as a loser, but not because of his support of Stephen, or even through any action of Henry II.

William of Ypres was one of the few losers by the settlement. His had been a torrid career. He was an illegitimate descendant of the Counts of Flanders, and during the political crisis in that county, which saw the fall of one dynasty and the rise of another, he had twice sought to win Flanders for himself, and twice failed. He had then gone into exile and become a mercenary captain in the employ of King Stephen, soon recognized as his main military lieutenant. William of Ypres received rich rewards, including estates in England; virtually the whole of Kent. He was Earl of Kent in all but name.

William of Ypres was the scapegoat of Henry II's promises; a mercenary, a Fleming, the military commander in chief under the king throughout the Matildine war, a dedicated opponent. But he was also, by 1154, something of a back number, not having been active for some time. William had been seriously ill, and by the end of the reign had for some time been blind. He had not been a witness in charters for Stephen since 1148, and had played no part in the Henrician phase of the war. Rough treatment by the new king against the now enfeebled and largely friendless William of Ypres was not likely to have any serious repercussions.

Henry could afford to be tough, and had no mercy on William, confiscating his lands. Even then, Henry did not press for immediate possession – the lands in Kent were not repossessed for two years. William had never been made earl, so there was no title to lose. In fact we are not clear about the details of his removal from England, which might even have been voluntary, with the death of his long-time master, Stephen. In any event, William of Ypres left England to go to Loo, that is to return to retirement in the castle of Loo in Flanders. There he gave alms to the poor, restored churches, and made pious foundations before his death, which was probably in 1162.[23]

Faramus of Boulogne is an interesting counter to the tale of William of Ypres, if we assume the latter lost out under Henry because he had been a foreign mercenary loyal to Stephen. William was a loser and a scapegoat, but Faramus was in a similar position, a continental mercenary who had been very valuable to Stephen, particularly militarily. He was descended from an illegitimate line of the comital family of Boulogne, and was probably closely attached to Stephen's queen. He had been castellan for Stephen of the key castle at Dover. The difference was that in 1153 he was still active, and serving William of Blois. The new king treated Faramus much more cautiously than he had William of Ypres. Henry took over Dover Castle for himself, but early in his reign granted lands to Faramus in compensation, including estates to the value of £60 in Buckinghamshire. Faramus held these lands to his death in about 1183, when they passed to his heir. So, apart from William of Ypres, even Stephen's foreign mercenaries did not all lose in the new set-up.

An understanding of Henry's attitude to those who had been engaged against him and his mother in the civil war, may be found by examining his actions over royal demesne lands. Although Henry was generally prepared to let all and sundry keep their family lands, and rarely disinherited anyone completely, he was less generous with former demesne lands. It was certainly a sign of favour that men such as Richard de Lucy and Richard de Camville were permitted to keep such lands.

Whenever opportunity offered, Henry recovered former demesne, for example from royalists like William of Blois and William of Ypres. But it was not a purely anti-royalist policy, since Angevin supporters such as Earls Patrick of Salisbury and Roger of Hereford were also subject to demands of the same kind. To demonstrate the impartiality of this policy, it should be noted that some former royalists benefited from the few grants from demesne that were made, including Faramus of Boulogne. The overall policy of Henry II was one of recovering royal demesne rather than of punishing former enemies. Incidentally, he followed the same policy in Normandy, by reclaiming ducal demesne.[24]

Lower down the ranks there were some changes, but certainly at first Henry 'made shift with such sheriffs as were already in place'.[25] There was a purge of sheriffs in 1155, but those then introduced were often men with experience from the previous reign. The replacement sheriff in Essex, even in 1157, was still Maurice de Tilty, who had been a sheriff under Stephen. Ralph Picot had been Stephen's sheriff for Kent, and took over for Henry there in 1154, and also in Sussex in 1157. Very few of the early sheriffs for Henry II were new men. Most of Henry's early sheriffs were either inherited from Stephen, or had experience of administration under that king. Richard de Camville had been a Stephen supporter, but was used by Henry as sheriff of Berkshire in 1156 and 1157. He kept his own holdings, kept his castle at Middleton Stoney – which passed on to his son – and received exemptions from Danegeld and taxation.

Not surprisingly, in administration, Henry introduced some of his own servants. Some of Stephen's men were dropped, including William Martel as chief steward and Baldric de Sigillo as keeper of the seal, though William continued till 1155 as sheriff of Surrey, which suggests that Henry was seeking a loyal man in the administrative office, rather than intending to punish a royalist.[26] Only one of Stephen's scribes has been identified as continuing under Henry (perhaps incorrectly), but then by the end of the reign there were few operating anyway. And in practice, Henry did make heavy use of men with experience of administration under Stephen, including most notably, Richard de Lucy.

The above examination of royalist magnates, and leading figures, does not suggest that many suffered in the change of 1154. With very few exceptions they had kept their family lands. Those few who suffered serious losses nearly all did so for reasons other than their wartime allegiance. Let us now consider a group of less committed men, those who had stood apart or changed over to the Angevin side late in the war. How were they treated by Henry II?

Geoffrey II de Mandeville had hardly been a fervent Angevin. It was Stephen who had allowed him to recover the family's fortunes and improve upon them. He had gone over to Matilda only briefly, during the period when it was prudent to do so, with Stephen in prison. He had been brought down by his own king, Stephen, perhaps for reasons other than those which divided England, and had never really fought for the Angevin cause. In fact, the Mandeville family recovered much under Henry II. His son Ernulf is now known to have been illegitimate, and so was not disinherited as used to be thought.[27] The legitimate sons, Geoffrey III and William II, in turn succeeded as Earls of Essex, the latter later becoming a royal justiciar.

Aubrey II de Vere was a lesser magnate with lands in Essex. He had died in 1141. His son, Aubrey III, had become an earl through defecting to Matilda in 1141, but had returned to Stephen's court and had never been very active in the civil war. He paid Henry to take up his father's office, and seems to have continued in virtually the same position.

Richard de Lucy was a long-time supporter of Stephen who only deserted to Henry in the last year of the reign. Like Robert of Leicester, he received his rewards at the time of desertion. Henry was more generous during the uncertain times of 1153, when he needed to win over men to his cause, than he ever was after he became king. Richard's rise had depended on Stephen's favour, and on his usefulness as an administrator. He became equally useful to Henry, and was quickly trusted, holding the Tower and Windsor to guarantee their passing to Henry on the accession. He shared the leading role under the king in the new regime, along with Robert of Leicester. Richard was also made sheriff of Essex and Hertfordshire and farmed several royal manors.

Another family with a mixed history of allegiance during the war, was that of the Beaumonts. Waleran of Meulan is difficult to categorize; he had early been an enthusiastic pro-Stephen lord, and at the end of the reign had deserted his new friends, the Angevins, for the King of France. The hesitancy and illness of Louis VII undermined the attack on Normandy, and Waleran lost his grip in Normandy. In 1153 he was captured by his nephew, Robert de Montfort, and from then on his former authority was gone. Waleran was at any rate a loser in Normandy, and in England his earldom of Worcester was retained by the crown. But thanks to the timely desertion to Henry of his twin brother, Robert of Leicester by 1153, the family fortunes did not suffer drastically. Waleran was pardoned for his activities against Henry in Normandy when in alliance with France by 1162, and lived quietly until his death in 1166, becoming at the last a monk at Préaux.

His brother Robert, Earl of Leicester, became a figure of great importance during the early years of the new reign, apparently trusted and given high office, no doubt partly in recognition of his abilities, but also perhaps as a reassurance that there was some continuity, and that the new ruler would not destroy all that had been of value in the old regime. It has also been suggested recently that Robert of Leicester, along with William of Albini, had been the chief lay figures responsible for making the 1153 peace.[28] Henry II showed that he would be more generous to new recruits to his side than Stephen had been. Robert was to act as justiciar for the new king until his death in 1168, when he became an Augustinian.

What was the consequence of the peace for the committed Angevin supporters? One might expect them to make considerable gains. But unless Henry was to confiscate vast estates from his former opponents, there would not be a great deal to grant out, especially by a king who was very careful about letting go royal demesne land. In the event, not all the pro-Angevins of the war period gained enormously from its outcome.

Of the leading figures during the Matildine war, many had died before the new reign, including of course Robert, Earl of Gloucester, in 1147, but also Miles, Earl of Hereford, in 1143, and Brian fitz Count in about 1151, and Roger, Earl of Warwick, in 1153, Baldwin de Redvers (1155) and Gilbert de Gant (1156) early in the new reign.[29] Ranulf of Chester saved Henry much anxiety by dying in December of 1153, allowing him to think again about the over-generous grants made to win his support. The roll call of deaths eased Henry II's problems very considerably. He had made some very extravagant promises in 1153, which thanks to the number of deaths of expected beneficiaries, did not have to be kept in 1154. The heirs of these newly deceased Angevins did not receive the larger grants promised in 1153. The Angevin supporters often had more cause for disappointment or resentment over the settlement than their royalist counterparts.

The seal of Robert de Beaumont, Earl of Leicester (1118–68). (BL Harley Charter 84.H.19)

Robert of Gloucester had been the prime supporter of Matilda, 'the chief of the king's enemies'.[30] His younger son, Philip, had deserted to Stephen late in the war, 'in rather mysterious circumstances', making a pact of peace and concord with the king, which muddies a little the picture of allegiance.[31] But the elder son and heir, William of Gloucester, had remained with the Angevins, and inherited the earldom of Gloucester.[32] He also married the daughter of Robert of Leicester, one of those marital connections which greatly helped to heal old wounds and restore a more harmonious feeling among the Henrician aristocracy. Earl William's daughter married Richard of Clare, Earl of Hertford, and thus into another previous royalist family. Two recently discovered charters show Henry granting favours to William and also to his son, Robert, in 1153 and 1154. It may be that Henry, in his early years as king, showed some 'reservations' over Earl William of Gloucester, delaying the pardons over tax and Danegeld which he might have expected, but William kept the earldom.[33] The king's reservations may have arisen from the activities of William's brother, Richard, who had rebelled against Henry in Normandy in 1154.

David, King of Scots, had been the most consistent of all the Angevin supporters, of both Matilda and Henry. It was King David who had been by Matilda's side at Winchester, who had knighted Henry and helped to keep the Angevin cause alive during its period of greatest weakness. Both David and his son might be seen as English magnates through their holdings in the north and in

Huntingdon, though the northern territories were treated as Scottish. Like Ranulf, David had been generously rewarded by Henry while still duke. Like Ranulf, he also died conveniently before the promises had to be fulfilled.

David died on 24 May 1153. His son, Henry of Scots, had already died in 1152, and therefore David's grandson succeeded as Malcolm IV (The Maiden). He was only eleven years old, and Henry had little compunction in reneging on these promises too. The old earldom of Huntingdon was broken in two, though Malcolm did retain the title. The other half went to the son of Simon de Senlis. Malcolm proved no match for Henry II. His nickname seems to have derived from his mother's unsuccessful efforts to make him a man. She sent a nubile maiden to his room, but rather than bed her, Malcolm chose to spend the night sleeping alone on the floor. Whatever the truth of this story, he was forced to acquiesce in the loss of much that his grandfather had gained in the north of England. Later, this led to a return to the traditional attitude of hostility between the Scottish and English kings, and the invasion of England by William the Lion. William was then defeated in 1174 and the Scottish losses confirmed. Allegiance to the Angevin cause during the civil war of Stephen's reign had not brought much gain to the Scots.

Miles of Gloucester had become Earl of Hereford, and his son Roger inherited the earldom. Roger may be seen largely as pro-Angevin, but was less devoted to the cause than his father had been. Roger's allegiance had been in doubt in 1152, when he made approaches to Stephen 'to enter upon a pact of inviolable peace and friendship' in order to recover Worcester, but he had earlier accompanied

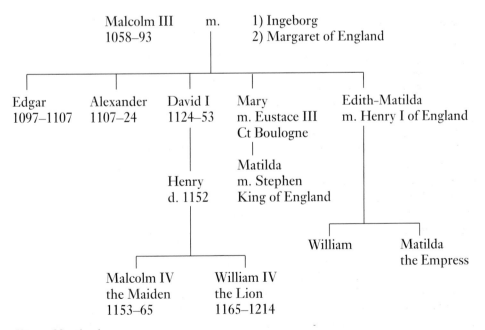

Kings of Scotland.

Henry for his knighting, and became perhaps his main supporter in 1153–4.[34] Roger rebelled against Henry II, when Henry went back on his early promises and demanded the handing over of Gloucester and Hereford Castles. Roger rebelled but was persuaded to submit by his relative, Gilbert Foliot. He was reconciled to the king, but could never become one of his most trusted men, and on his death the earldom was not continued.

The reduction of earldoms, like the recovery of royal castles, was not aimed against previous supporters of Stephen; it was pursued where chance allowed against friend and foe alike. When Earl Roger himself died in 1155, Henry took the opportunity of taking back the acquisitions, and did not renew the earldom for his heir, Walter.[35]

The last of the trio of original Angevin supporters of 1139, Brian fitz Count, had died during Stephen's reign, probably in 1151. He had died without heir, and the fate of his honor of Wallingford is not entirely clear, but it seems to have been taken into the hands of Henry II. Another of the early Angevin partisans, Reginald, Earl of Cornwall, was Henry II's uncle. He was trusted with protecting Henry's interests during the vital period between the making of the peace and his nephew's accession. Thereafter, he was a trusted man at the centre of affairs; his earldom of Cornwall was even excused the normal payments to the exchequer right up until his death in 1175.[36]

Ranulf, Earl of Chester, had spent more time in the later years of the reign as an opponent than a friend of the king.[37] Stephen's arrest and seizure of his castles had forced him back into the Angevin camp, whereupon he became 'the enduring enemy of the king'.[38] Ranulf had even swallowed his pride over Carlisle in order to make his peace with Henry, probably with little option, and yielded his rights in it to the Scots, receiving the honor of Lancaster with Lancashire north of the Ribble, in exchange. But in the words of Gervase of Canterbury: 'he did little for the duke unless it fitted in with his own designs'. After 1146, the Angevins can have placed little trust in Ranulf, but he was useful during 1153. He died at the end of that year, on 16 December.[39] No one was allowed to inherit his vast power. His son, Hugh, retained the lands held in 1135 and the earldom, but again the larger promises of 1153 were revoked.

Hugh Bigod, Earl of Norfolk, had been a constant trouble to Stephen, and was not all that easy an ally for Henry. Matilda had given him his earldom, which included Suffolk. At several points in the later part of Stephen's reign he had provided welcome relief for the Angevins by his troublemaking in East Anglia. Stephen's very last military success was to wrest Ipswich from Bigod after the truce at Wallingford had ended. In 1155 Henry had issued a charter confirming Hugh's earldom and his possessions, but William of Blois kept Norwich, the natural *caput* for an earldom of Norfolk. Henry demanded castles from him, and Bigod remained a discontented and difficult magnate until his death at the ripe age of eighty-three in 1177. Like many other pro-Angevins, he had not gained a great deal by the change, and had lost one of his major strongholds.

Some other Angevin supporters were also to be disillusioned. Not all would get what they hoped. In Essex, a largely royalist county, William de Helion had sacrificed the family possessions in order to support Matilda, going with her to

Normandy, and accompanying Henry from 1151, but he gained nothing at all in England, and died a disappointed man in 1156.[40]

But many lesser Angevin supporters either retained what they had recently gained, or made some gains from the new king. One example was the family of Eustace fitz John, who had gone over to Matilda in 1138. He had been associated with Ranulf, and had made considerable territorial gains after 1141. His son did homage to Henry, and the gains were confirmed.[41] Henry insisted on the need to confirm all gains made during the previous reign, but he did not reverse many of them. Emilie Amt's recent study of three regions in detail, shows that changes were generally few, whether the area be royalist or Angevin. She concluded that below the level of the magnates, holdings remained stable: 'the *tempus werre* had left the tenurial geography essentially unchanged'.[42]

R.H.C. Davis has written: 'one of the most puzzling features of Stephen's reign is the way in which it came to an end'. The main question is why did Stephen give up so much in the 1153 settlement? The answer is not because he had been militarily defeated. He had won the war against Matilda, or at least had come out of it stronger than she did. He was not defeated by Henry, and in terms of military force and land in England, was always stronger than Henry. What then is the explanation of his apparently feeble acceptance of defeat in the peace?

Why did he agree to his descendants losing the English throne? Of course, he might not have believed this would happen. No one knew in 1153 how long Stephen would live or what events might intervene to change affairs. It might have been Henry who died; indeed he became seriously ill in 1154. Everyone knew that Henry had serious problems on the continent: hostility from France, a potential difficulty with his brother, Geoffrey, a lack of experience in England where many great men had still remained loyal to Stephen.[43] The acquisition of all the lands which we know as the Angevin Empire was by no means inevitable.

But if we accept that Stephen was prepared to see through the agreement, is there an explanation for his acceptance of it? There are in fact many explanations, and history shows that is the way of the world. There were many pressures upon the king, and upon his nobles. Stephen had suffered personal tragedy, and no one can be completely unaffected by such things. He was ageing – fifty-seven in 1153 – his wife, Queen Matilda, had died on 3 May 1152, his eldest son, Eustace, had died on 17 August 1153, when Stephen 'grieved beyond measure'.[44] Stephen himself had been wounded towards the end of the war, and had been ill on more than one occasion; he also had to endure the aggravation of piles. His surviving son, William, suffered a serious accident when riding his horse too fast, 'as young people do', and had broken his leg at the thigh, news of which had badly upset his father.[45] Such events may have pushed Stephen towards despair.

Perhaps he reflected upon the constant barrage of criticism about how he had gained the throne, by breaking a solemn oath, an act condemned by many churchmen. Perhaps Stephen pondered upon this and his misfortunes, as old age crept upon him and death approached. One sometimes questions the significance of the religious element in decisions, but oaths and beliefs did matter in the twelfth century. One only needs to consider the number of magnates, however worldly their careers, who chose to end their days in religion: Robert of Leicester as an Augustinian, his brother Waleran as a monk at Préaux, Henry of Essex as a Benedictine at Reading. The monasteries were truly the last refuges of every rogue of the day. It may seem to us an unworthy kind of Christianity, even a form of superstition, which allowed a life of bloodshed and political trickery, so long as the last moments were spent after penance under the protection of a monastic life, but it does demonstrate that such men believed in the afterlife and thought that such practices mattered. The family deaths and constant misfortunes were seen by others as judgments of God upon the king, perhaps even by the monarch himself. Henry's constant claim to be the lawful heir might have had some effect upon Stephen; it certainly seems to have persuaded the chroniclers.

The church had become quite uncooperative with Stephen over recent years; there had been a number of difficult disputes over elections to positions in England. When Stephen sought for the recognition of Eustace's rights as his heir, the church had refused the sort of confirmation which it had agreed to for other rulers in the past. This was partly misfortune. Briefly there was greater papal cooperation, but the early death of the more amenable Lucius II in 1145, was followed by the election of the Cistercian Eugenius III, and a hardening of attitude towards Stephen. The matter of Stephen's oath-breaking in order to gain the throne was raised again. Certainly chroniclers often saw such deaths as that of Eustace as a judgment of God. But for all the pressures, Stephen had clearly wanted his son Eustace to succeed him, and briefly, in fury, imprisoned all the bishops concerned in the refusal to associate him in the kingship in 1152, confiscating their possessions.

One point which seems to have been neglected is the attitude of Stephen's brother, Henry of Blois. Henry has generally been seen as tougher and shrewder than his brother. Davis says he 'had the qualities his brother lacked', and was 'the real grandson of the Conqueror'. Henry, however, had been largely responsible for one of the oddest decisions Stephen ever made: to escort Matilda in safety from Arundel to the west country in 1139, and thus lose an excellent chance of nipping the civil war in the bud. The bishop's actions during the war speak more of self interest than loyalty. He had condemned Stephen's arrest of the bishops in 1139 at a church council, and had joined the empress' side when his brother was in prison.

Now in 1153, Bishop Henry was largely responsible, with Theobald of Canterbury, for the peace negotiations, and hence for the settlement, and has been credited with it. But he was Stephen's brother, and so he too was accepting the loss of the English crown to his family, and was more enthusiastic than Stephen for the peace, by all accounts. Henry of Huntingdon says that it was the bishop who suggested the terms. The *Gesta Stephani* says that Stephen 'yielded to the advice of the Bishop of Winchester'. The Hexham chronicler even says that Henry 'exerted himself to promote the interests of Duke Henry'.[46] There is no certain answer as to why both Stephen and Henry were prepared to give up the succession, though Henry of Huntingdon says that Henry repented of helping Stephen to get the crown in the first place.[47]

The position of the house of Blois in France would seem to be relevant. In addition to the personal losses of Stephen, already mentioned, one might add that his older brother, Theobald IV, Count of Blois and Champagne, had died in 1152.

*The four Norman kings. Clockwise from top left: William I, William II, Stephen, Henry I.
(BL MS Royal 14 CVII, f. 8v)*

On his death Blois and Champagne were separated in the hands of two of his sons: Theobald V and Henry the Liberal. These two brothers made spectacular matches to two sisters, Mary and Alice, none other than the daughters of Louis VII and Eleanor of Aquitaine. Eleanor, therefore, became their mother-in-law, and she was now the wife of Henry of Anjou. The need for the house of Blois to have a personal representative on the English throne was rather less than it once had been. Indeed, to support the candidature of the unenthusiastic William of Blois, would obviously have antagonized Eleanor and Henry. There was at least some reason for the house of Blois to accept what almost everyone now seemed to desire – the succession of Henry II to the throne of England. Henry himself was eager at the time to have the acceptance of his succession by the French crown, and that seemed to require the acceptance by the house of Blois and its four powerful brothers: Theobald V, Henry the Liberal, William, Archbishop of Reims, and Stephen, Count of Sancerre. The sister of these brothers, Adela, became Louis VII's new queen, and indeed the mother of his only son, Philip Augustus. Compromise was on the cards, not war and battle. The Bishop of Winchester gained little by his part in the peacemaking, at any rate immediately. He chose to go into exile, back to his old abbey at Cluny, but without the king's permission, giving Henry the opportunity to demolish some of his castles. A reconciliation was eventually made.

Yet for all the personal reasons and all the pressures, Stephen had continued to show signs of resistance up till the last moment; he had made Eustace, Count of Boulogne in 1147, had attempted to get him associated in the kingship in 1152, and clearly, therefore, wanted his son to succeed him. Stephen had attacked and taken Ipswich after the peace negotiations at Wallingford in 1153. Even after Winchester, he could annoy Henry by apparently treating the recently built castles in a partisan fashion. And during his last year, Stephen exercised his new authority with energy, dealing promptly with trouble at Drax. He was not acting like a man ready to give up his own, or his family's, claims.

One of the most notable developments was in the standing of Henry of Anjou. Within three years, he had moved from being simply a youth with no wealth and some expectations, to being a man of wealth and power. He had been associated in the government of Normandy by his father, Geoffrey. On his father's death in 1151, Henry had taken over not only the duchy of Normandy, but also his father's other possessions in greater Anjou – giving him a solid block of territory in north-western France. Then, when Eleanor of Aquitaine had been divorced by Louis VII in 1152, 'a dislike having sprung up between them', she had turned to Henry – perhaps by prior agreement, 'either suddenly or deliberately', according to Robert of Torigny.[48] They married, and through her, he laid claim to Aquitaine. Virtually all of western France had dropped into his hands. Nor had this happened simply by accident. Henry had been forced to struggle and fight for his rights. He had shown himself to have courage and good sense. Men now knew that he was a person of weight, a ruler to be reckoned with. He also showed a streak of adventure and opportunism; he was ambitious.

Among those who watched these developments were the barons of England. What were their thoughts? Suppose now they were to fight against Henry. They

Henry II and Eleanor of Aquitaine on board ship. Through their marriage, Henry laid claim to Aquitaine. (BL MS Royal 14 CVII, f. 134v)

knew that he might become King of England. They would, therefore, be risking their own futures. And no one in this period lightly wanted to take the field against their own ruler.[49] It was not only Stephen who avoided a fight. Henry himself on several occasions showed that he respected authority and allegiance. He insisted that his overlord, the King of France, should have the superior accommodation in 1158; he refused to fight against the King of France in Toulouse, and he was violently angry when his own rights were ignored and his son's supporters tried to kill him. Even if Stephen was a usurper, he was, nevertheless, the anointed king. Beyond that Henry could not be sure of any military outcome. King Stephen had the greater resources, the greater territorial area from which to draw feudal forces, the greater access to mercenary forces, and the greater support from urban militias – including that from London.

Henry had been able to raise only a tiny force from the continent for his expeditions, even in 1153, hardly big enough to talk in terms of invasion. It is true that some of Stephen's men, even some of his greatest and most trusted, had deserted to Henry, which certainly helped to alter the balance. But in 1153 no really major magnate had left the fold, except perhaps Robert, Earl of Leicester, who had probably in fact already changed his allegiance. Henry could not be sure of victory. There were many pressures towards making a settlement rather than fighting it out. Henry also had to worry about his French territories, where his marriage to Eleanor on 18 May 1152 had for once roused Louis VII to anger. Henry had left Normandy in a state of some tension. Robert of Torigny reported that many there 'thought that Duke Henry would rapidly lose all of his possessions'.[50]

The general feeling of economic malaise in the 1150s could not have helped. Writing of 1150, Robert of Torigny spoke of four hard winters in a row, and of famine and pestilence. Even the grape harvest failed in 1151, and according to Robert, the French were reduced to consuming a beverage other than wine: 'even in France, there sprang up taverns for the sale of beer and mead'. The *Walden Chronicle* speaks of 'days of grief and want' in England. There were several bad harvests, droughts, floods, and famine, as well as the results of the 'devastation of almost the whole of the country' by war.[51] There had also been a Norse invasion by Eystein Haraldson in 1151, which Stephen had beaten off, but which had done damage to Whitby and elsewhere. In 1153 the *Gesta Stephani* speaks of a hard winter which had brought 'severe famine'. The high figures for waste in the early years of Henry II's reign, though surely made more acute by it, need not all have been caused by war. Henry of Huntingdon described the misery, in verse:

> Gaunt famine following wars, wastes away
> Whom murder spares, with slow decay.

Accepting the return to the view that waste generally meant what it said, then the high figures for certain areas such as the midlands and Yorkshire may speak of economic difficulties in the early part of Henry II's reign, as well as destruction by war.[52]

Much recent work has also been done on the agreements made between magnates in England during the later years of Stephen's reign; the concords or private treaties. These show that the magnates of England were prepared to make peace, desirous of keeping stability in their own territories. The details of what they agreed in the concords say a good deal about their attitude to war. William of Newburgh wrote that the struggle subsided as they 'wearied of lengthy conflict and their efforts slackened'.[53] The magnates were, it might be said, already practised in arranging their own peace-keeping. An overall national peace would be well in line with such desires. The concords which had been made, also meant that those we see as opponents in the civil war, had in fact already been learning to live with each other.

The chronicles suggest that it was not so much the two commanders, as their troops, who insisted on peace rather than battle. The concords became almost commonplace, both between allies and between enemies, between laymen and between laymen and ecclesiastics. An early example was that between Robert of Gloucester and Miles of Hereford, perhaps in 1142: a *confederatio amoris*; they agreed not to do separate deals with their enemies, and Miles put his son in Robert's care as a hostage.[54] Their sons, William of Gloucester and Roger of Hereford, made a similar agreement in about 1149.

Such agreements were also made by other lords, for example, between Ranulf of Chester and Robert of Leicester, as a 'final peace and concord'.[55] Ranulf granted the castle of Mountsorrel to his fellow magnate. The two earls promised not to use more than twenty knights against each other if forced into hostilities through their respective liege lords. They made detailed arrangements to restrict hostility between each other, should they become embroiled in struggles through allies. They promised not to erect new castles in sensitive areas which lay between their respective territories. They pledged themselves to keep the agreement to the Bishop of Lincoln, giving him and the Bishop of Chester, the power to put right any breach of the concord.

There were treaties also between the earls of Derby and Chester, Chester and Leicester, Leicester and Northampton, Leicester and Hereford, Gloucester and Hereford, and others, making what Davis called the 'Magnates' Peace'.[56] This method of assuring peace did not end with Winchester, and there are examples of similar agreements in the early part of Henry's reign, for example between Reginald of Cornwall and Richard de Lucy.

Not many great lords went over to Henry in the key period at the end of the reign, but those who did were important and influential, including Robert of Leicester and Richard de Lucy. It must have undermined support for Stephen. One significant factor was the knowledge that unless one went over to Henry, family lands in Normandy would be lost, now that Henry's grip on the duchy seemed firm.

It must also be said that if Stephen was never able to crush his opponents completely, then neither was Henry an out and out victor in the peace. He too had to compromise; he suffered losses. He had submitted to the King of France as predecessors never had, going to Paris to give homage, promising vital lands in the Vexin to France. To gain the support of English magnates he had made promises which would have been very hard to keep had most of them not conveniently died before the bets were called in. It was his good fortune that some of the greatest beneficiaries from his generosity died and so released him from his potentially most damaging promises. Henry had also recognized Stephen as the properly anointed king, and agreed to his rule for life, and this too was a gamble which paid off, but which could have turned out otherwise. In fact, in October 1154, some doubts must have arisen in people's minds when Henry fell ill of a 'dangerous sickness', only shortly before the death of Stephen.[57]

It was indeed what has been called 'a precarious peace'.[58] For a year, Henry was in a dubious position. Given Stephen's previous record over promises, Henry could have had few moments of certainty that all would be his, that given half a chance Stephen would not renege on the Treaty of Winchester. At Dunstable in 1154, Henry had already complained about Stephen's failure to implement the agreement on castles, and then, when Stephen showed himself less than pleased about the complaint, had to drop the matter for fear 'lest it should disturb their concord'.

Already it seemed that the Count of Flanders was involved in some conspiracy with Stephen against Henry.[59] The chronicler says that some sought to sew seeds of discord between king and duke while the latter was out of the country, 'and some thought he was already yielding to them'. Meanwhile, Stephen was taking full advantage of the peace to recover his position; he 'enjoyed very powerful royal authority'; he 'had taken the whole kingdom into his hand'.[60] In March 1154 Henry returned to Normandy, but could hardly have been easy in his mind about the future in England.

On 25 October 1154, Stephen died. He was buried at his own foundation, Faversham Abbey, alongside his wife, Matilda, and his son, Eustace. It was again fortunate for Henry that the death came so soon after the agreement of 1153. The actions of the king since the agreement do not suggest that he was tired of ruling. He had demolished castles, perhaps too many Angevin ones, rather than too few royal ones, for Henry's liking. He organized a recoinage, and 'enjoyed very powerful royal authority'.[61]

Because of the short space of time between the Treaty of Winchester and Stephen's death, the peace arrangements were still dominant in the thoughts of all those who mattered in England. There had been no major development to alter that agreement, and no one who seemed to prefer any other settlement. William of Blois made no attempt to gain the throne. There can be no doubt that in England there was a general desire to escape from war, and says William of Newburgh, 'the people hoped for better things from the new monarch'.[62] Henry did not come to England for some time, largely because the weather prevented him sailing, and he was again fortunate that there was no opposition to his succession. He sailed on 7 December from Barfleur, and was crowned at Westminster on 19 December. His reception, with crowds shouting 'long live the king', sounds remarkably like a modern celebration.[63]

The conclusion must be that events, rather than planning, dominated the final outcome. Stephen had not wished to lose the throne or to disinherit his sons. He had been gradually forced into giving away more than he wished by the pressure of a growing support of Henry, and the hostility to war of the English barons. Personal tragedy and the approach of death no doubt helped him to yield, but it had been with reluctance. Henry had sought the throne, had failed to win it by force, but used the opportunities of negotiation, and the wishes of the barons and the church, to further his own ends.

Henry had not won a war, but he had survived one, and was there for all to contemplate – a young ambitious, energetic man contrasted with the ageing monarch. The prospect was of the Matildine war all over again, unless some settlement could be reached. By backing down from war, Henry no doubt won much gratitude and respect from the barons and the church. In the end it was enough to bring him the throne; it was a gamble which paid off.

The reason the pressure against battle was so great soon became clear. It is now a commonplace to point out that medieval commanders normally tried to avoid battle, largely because of the potentially enormous penalties of defeat. It must be said that medieval lieutenants and subordinates had much the same fears. The barons who had pressured Henry and Stephen into avoiding battle reaped the rewards of their policy. There were very few losers. Most of the great men of Stephen's reign who survived into the new reign kept their lands and their position. Where those great men had died, their sons normally kept the family lands. Where families did lose, it was usually through natural wastage rather than vindictive royal policy, or as a result of new opposition to the crown which brought its own punishment. Few men could have regretted that Henry's accession came about peacefully and through a settlement rather than through another military conflict.

The warfare of Stephen's reign had, in the end, been indecisive. It was not inevitable that the peace settlement turned out as it did. The Treaty of Winchester, and the concomitant individual baronial agreements with Henry, were made for the mutual benefit of practically all. The royalist barons had sought a settlement without fighting in Henry's favour, and he kept the gentleman's agreement by not turning his success into a punishment for losers. The civil war of Stephen's reign had an outcome more in line with that of the commoner conflicts of medieval war, the sieges, than with the usually more drastic outcome of battles. The war was settled by agreement, so that suffering was moderated and both sides had some compensation. The pro-Angevin barons do not seem to have gained much in the way of territories, but they had gained the stability desired by all of their class, and were apparently satisfied that it be so.

ANARCHY?

As we look back over the years of struggle, we must to some extent share the chroniclers' regrets at nineteen years which had seen so much damage done to the country. They described famine, burning, death, torture, atrocities. We cannot doubt that these occurred. Henry of Huntingdon thought that the new reign was like dawn coming after 'a night of misery'.[64] Since that age men have read the chronicle accounts and believed that this was one of the worst periods in our history, and they dubbed it 'The Anarchy', the only period in our whole history to be given the title. Was it, therefore, worse than any other period, and was it truly a time of anarchy?

The west country writer of the first section of the *Gesta Stephani* paints a bleak picture of the effects of the war in his region. Everywhere, he wrote, was in a turmoil, and 'reduced to a desert'. Some chose to go into exile abroad rather than remain. Some built new shacks near the churches so they could flee into them for protection when necessary. Food was short: 'a terrible famine prevailed all over England.' Men were forced to eat dogs and horses, or raw herbs and roots. People died in droves from famine; fields and villages were empty, 'the peasants of both sexes and all ages were dead, fields whitening with a magnificent harvest . . . but their cultivators taken away through the devastating famine'. Mercenaries pillaged the poor, while lords imposed 'forced levies and taxes'. Churches were robbed and clerics abused and beaten up or flogged.[65]

William of Malmesbury, another west country writer, described soldiers

A depiction of Hell, from the Winchester Psalter. A queen, possibly Matilda, is shown in the upper part, a king in the lower part. The illustration was perhaps inspired by the disorders of the civil war. (BL MS Cotton Nero CIV, f. 39)

A king enthroned, surrounded by soldiers killing children. This illustration made at Canetrbury in c. 1140 is not intended to depict a contemporary scene, but was no doubt inspired by contemporary events. (detail from BL Add 37472, f. 1)

disturbing graveyards, presumably when they built castles in churchyards, seizing herds and flocks, bringing devastation to the countryside. Clearly the needs of campaigning armies had a harmful, sometimes disastrous effect upon ordinary folk. William also speaks of tenants and peasants being tortured or ransomed in order to get their wealth.[66]

During the Scottish invasions, those on the northern border had suffered even worse atrocities, and again we have a band of writers from the region: Ailred of Rievaulx, and the Hexham chroniclers. The Scots were accused of being barbarians, who 'ripped open pregnant women, [and] tossed children on the points of their spears'.[67] Mercenaries in general were viewed in England as wolves who brought nothing but death and destruction, who were merciless to the ordinary population of the land, who often in the course of the wars destroyed crops and homes.

The East Anglian chroniclers, Henry of Huntingdon and the author of the *Anglo-Saxon Chronicle*, give an equally depressing view of the reign. The Peterborough chronicler describes the oppression perpetrated by those holding castles: they confiscated men's goods, they destroyed, they captured and tortured:

[they] put them in prison and tortured them with indescribable torture to extort gold and silver. . . . They were hung by the thumbs or by the head, and chains were hung on their feet. Knotted ropes were put round their heads

and twisted till they penetrated to the brains. They put them in prisons where there were adders and snakes and toads, and killed them like that. Some they put in a torture chamber, that is in a chest which was short, narrow and not deep, and they put sharp stones in it and pressed the man in it so that he had all his limbs broken. . . . [There were chains] fastened to a beam, and they used to put a sharp iron around a man's throat and neck so that he could not sit or lie or sleep in any direction.[68]

The writer claimed that thousands were starved to death. He also described the way taxes were levied illicitly upon villages in the form of protection money. There was collection of the arbitrary tax of *taille* by local lords, and demands for a food and money rent, known as *tenserie*.[69] He spoke of deserted villages, land not tilled. He said that food became expensive because of the shortages: corn, meat, butter and cheese. Many had to turn to begging. 'There had never been greater misery in the country.' In a famous passage the anonymous monk wrote: 'men said openly that Christ and his saints were asleep . . . we suffered nineteen years for our sins'.

A letter in *The Book of Ely* also mentions *tenserie* being collected in that area in 1144, and Gilbert Foliot condemns the 'tyrannical exactions' made by William Beauchamp.[70] *Taille* and *tenserie* also appear at Sherborne, and Miles of Gloucester was excommunicated for his tax collecting. One notes, though, that some of these complaints were against Angevin lords, who no doubt had to improvise in order to maintain some revenues. And one suspects in East Anglia that the causes of complaint were more likely to be Geoffrey de Mandeville and Hugh Bigod, than the king.

We cannot doubt that at times and in some places the situation was truly awful. But we can receive an exaggerated picture if we do not approach our evidence with a certain number of questions. One would expect damage from the nature of twelfth-century war, but how widespread was the war and the damage? It so happens that nearly all the major writers who provide us with our information were based in areas at the centre of the troubles: Peterborough, Malmesbury, the west country, Worcester, the Scottish border. Inevitably they described the damage which they knew about, perhaps even were inspired to write because they were in the middle of such dramatic events.

But elsewhere, many places saw little of the fighting; some counties may have escaped altogether, others saw at the worst, intermittent conflict. H.W.C. Davis wrote that as for Surrey, it enjoyed 'uninterrupted peace'.[71] The amount of waste in several of Stephen's firmly held counties was very low, only 0.4 per cent in Kent.[72] As we have seen, the nature of the war was largely one of royal offensives against Angevin strongholds, so naturally those strongholds were at the centre of the worst damage. It is interesting that the pipe rolls of the reign of Henry II show that the areas where there was most waste, and which might have suffered worst, were not in the west country or East Anglia, but in the midlands. This is not difficult to explain, and may be highly significant. In the first place, much of the very last campaign of the war had been fought in the midlands, by Henry of Anjou, and the pipe rolls no doubt reflect this. It also suggests that damage elsewhere caused by the war, may have been less long lasting than is sometimes assumed, otherwise surely counties like Wiltshire, Oxfordshire and Cambridgeshire would have been at the top of the list.

There is other evidence that the war may not have been as damaging as some have assumed. We have the baronial concords which make it clear that the magnates were making considerable efforts to restrict fighting within their own territories. We also have some facts and figures about damage done to churches and monasteries. Not only was this less than might be expected, but it was far from being the whole story. A good deal was already provided during Stephen's reign for repairs, apart from what was given under Henry II, and there was in fact a steady process of new church building and extensions to existing churches through Stephen's reign.

Ten per cent of the monasteries suffered some harm, though the wealthiest were more likely to suffer, than the humbler houses.[73] It has been calculated that of fifty known damaged churches, some 44 per cent were given compensation. Even at Peterborough, the home of the writer of the *Anglo-Saxon Chronicle*, who painted such a damning picture of conditions, the abbey itself seems to have prospered, and a new vineyard was built there. Over a hundred new houses for religious orders were begun. The artistic and architectural achievements of Stephen's reign are a useful antidote to the belief that all was chaos and destruction.

And what do we really mean by anarchy? The word literally implies that there was no government. The evidence is clear and growing that this was simply not the case under Stephen. There are no exchequer records, no pipe rolls, but then only a single one exists for all the period before Henry II, so it is almost certainly an accident of survival, rather than evidence that none were produced or that no exchequer existed. How did Stephen raise the money to pay his mercenaries?[74] And how did the exchequer get going again so quickly in the new reign, when pipe rolls survive from the second year of the reign onwards? The exchequer buildings needed some repair, but only of a minor nature.[75] Clearly there was an exchequer operating under Stephen and he was able to draw upon the revenues it produced. He also had a large personal income from his own estates. One notes that when Henry of Anjou could not find the money to pay his own mercenaries, and neither Robert of Gloucester or Matilda seemed able to fund him, it was Stephen who provided the cash.

More positive are the records of a writing office. For the whole Anglo-Norman period the major evidence of governmental activity rests on the surviving charters. These were mainly letters sent by the king with instructions for action to be taken, or to confirm action which had already been undertaken. Stephen lost control of certain areas of England to the Angevins, so there would be little point in him sending charters to such areas. One would, therefore, expect a reduction in the number of charters issued during his reign, against what had gone before. But what is the case? If one divides the number of charters per reign by the number of years in the reign, one finds that more charters survive *per annum* for Stephen's rule than for any previous reign.[76] Of course, this is partly from a better survival rate, but it is our chief evidence, and it does not speak of a

A coin minted during Stephen's imprisonment in 1141. The coin shows the king and his queen.

completely inactive or ineffective government. Not only were charters issued, but their form developed and improved during the reign.[77]

The answer is that not only was there not anarchy, but there was a properly organized and operating government able even to make improvements on the methods of its predecessors. Indeed, some of Henry II's 'innovations' were preceded by methods of Stephen's, for example in the use of the writ for *mort d'ancestor*, and in bringing cases from local baronial jurisdiction to royal.[78] Stephen had certainly been careful over keeping his own rights and lands, and had alienated less crown land in his region than did Matilda in hers.[79] Therefore, one cannot believe there was anarchy in the areas which Stephen firmly ruled.

There is also coinage evidence, which has received much attention in recent times, and which suggests, from the placing of royal mints, areas in which royal government was operating: around London, in the south-east, Canterbury, Bedford, Colchester, Ipswich, Norwich, and that despite the trouble from Hugh Bigod. Henry II's much vaunted work on the coinage is now seen as 'only continuing what Stephen had begun'.[80] Some coins once thought to be Angevin products are now less certainly so, and the view of a restricted Angevin territory is confirmed. The same conclusion comes from consideration of the allegiance of the great prelates and the bishops, the great majority of whom remained loyal to Stephen. The same is true if one considers the allegiance of the great towns and ports.

But what of the areas held by his opponents, or by more or less independent magnates like Ranulf of Chester? The Angevin areas were taken almost entirely out of royal control, in particular the country west of say Malmesbury, to the Welsh border. But there was no more anarchy in Angevin areas than in royal areas. The magnates there, especially Robert of Gloucester, treated Matilda as their ruler, themselves took on certain normally royal functions, and maintained a governmental system. They issued charters, they collected revenues, they maintained order, even issued coins. In the north a similar situation prevailed. Once David of Scots' position had been worked out, after the Standard and Lincoln, David ruled the far north of England as if it were part of his own realm.[81]

More difficult to assess is the position in the territories of the great magnates who deserted the king but were not firmly attached to the Angevins. The main example of these men must be Ranulf, Earl of Chester. The concords give an insight to the situation here, and again the answer is not anarchy. Ranulf ruled his own lands, and was not a man to be easily crossed within them. But he sought to keep them as orderly and peaceful as possible. Hence the numerous agreements with bordering magnates and prelates, restricting the degree of warfare, giving guarantees where royal protection was failing. The number of prelates involved in these concords, demonstrates that the church gave its approval to this method of peace-keeping. One could mention the agreements between Jocelyn, Bishop of Salisbury, with the Earls of Cornwall, Devon and Gloucester, or of the Bishop of Chichester with his local earl. The great magnates involved in the war, whose lands were in danger of suffering, made agreements with their neighbours in order to reduce the risk. They were intent on keeping order within their own territories. And, as the concords show, and their role in making the 1153 peace, they preferred peace to war, order to anarchy.

The answer to the question of what system of government, if any, prevailed in England during the civil war, has been given by a number of historians in recent times, none of whom any longer care to use the word 'anarchy' loosely. Dr Chibnall, for example, has written: 'if the situation is to be described as anarchy, it is a modified anarchy; a type of regionalism more characteristic of France at a slightly earlier date.'[82] The conclusion of H.W.C. Davis retains much validity; the anarchy for him was 'organised government which broke down for short periods in particular places'.[83] We cannot escape from the popular historical label of 'The Anarchy' for the period, but we are becoming clearer all the time that it was not truly a period without government or one of utter chaos. It was a period when the area in the grip of central government was reduced, but what remained were a number of more or less separate governments: English royal, Scottish royal, Angevin, and magnate. It was not an ideal situation, but then neither is civil war. In a condition of civil war, it is impossible for one government to rule a whole country, as in the seventeenth-century English Civil War, or in the American Civil War; separate governments emerge for each participating power in the struggle. The wars of Stephen, Matilda, and Henry, were on a par with these struggles in regard to the form of government which was forced upon the country: divided but not neglected, and certainly not non-existent. There was no anarchy in The Anarchy.

THE EFFECTS OF THE CIVIL WAR

It may be true that anarchy did not take over, but there was certainly much disturbance and disruption of the normal state of affairs. Government, the economy, the rural and urban populations, the church, all suffered to some degree. The recorded waste in the pipe rolls of Henry II, however interpreted, leaves a clear impression of a damaged nation and economy.

But the damage was temporary. Henry II benefited from the fear of war which the civil war had engendered. He did face one major rebellion in 1173–4, led by his sons and encouraged by his wife, but the fear of new civil wars was a major contributory factor in giving him victory. He was able to restore law and order in England and elsewhere, and is indeed remembered as one of our great monarchs in this respect. He may not have destroyed all the newly built castles, but he greatly lessened any threat to the monarchy from them. His court became a symbol of the new stability, with its contribution to the cultural achievement of the twelfth-century renaissance. Henry was a patron of poets, historians, and political thinkers, men of the calibre of John of Salisbury.

The outcome of the war had given the throne to Henry, already Duke of Normandy, Count of Anjou and claimant to the duchy of Aquitaine. His success marked the formation of the Angevin Empire. It was never so called in its time,

Henry II's Angevin Empire.

and it may never have been governed entirely as a political unit, but it was a remarkable accumulation of territories all under the control of an individual ruler, whether it be as king, duke or count, and it made Henry II one of the most powerful men in the Europe of his day. It also gave England a new place in Europe, with connections not only to Normandy but to all of western France. The melding of English and Angevin cultures was one of the glories of the period of the twelfth-century renaissance. During the so-called Anarchy, there were developments in art, manuscript illumination, sculpture, architecture, the growth of towns and of the new monastic orders; a firm foundation for further achievements under Henry II.

The less positive effect of the civil war, in the long run, was the new threat which this growth of power under one man, posed for the kingdom of France. The French and English royal families were very closely connected and inter-related, and this did not end at once. But the powers of the French monarchy were also expanding at this time, and would do so more obviously after the accession of Philip Augustus in 1180. The clash between France and the Angevin Empire was inevitable, and it marked the history of England for a century. At the end of it, the English kings had lost virtually all their French territories, which Henry III accepted by the Treaty of Paris of 1258. The clashes of that century did not heal easily, and left wounds which were eventually reopened in a new major struggle between the monarchies in the Hundred Years War. In a sense, therefore, the outcome of the civil war of Stephen's reign led to a lengthy conflict with France which scratched a bloody gash across the whole Middle Ages. Had Stephen won the war more convincingly and left the throne to his son, to rule England alone, who can say what would have happened in Europe?

Abbreviations

ANS	*Anglo-Norman Studies*
BN	Bibliothèque National
BL	British Library
BM	British Museum
CG	*Château-Gaillard, Études de Castellologie Medievale*
EHD	*English Historical Documents*
EHR	*English Historical Review*
EHS	English Historical Society
HSJ	*Haskins Society Journal*
Howlett	*Chronicles of the Reigns of Stephen, Henry II and Richard I*, ed. R. Howlett, 4 vols, RS no. 82, London, 1884–9
IPMK	*The Ideals and Practice of Medieval Knighthood*
JMH	*Journal of Medieval History*
King	E. King (ed.), *The Anarchy of Stephen's Reign*, Oxford, 1994
Orderic	Orderic Vitalis, *The Ecclesiastical History*, ed. and trans. M. Chibnall, 6 vols, Oxford, 1968–80
PP	*Past and Present*
PR	Pipe Roll, Great Rolls of the Pipe, published by the Pipe Roll Society, 1884 etc.
RAB	*Studies in Medieval History presented to R. Allen Brown*, eds. C. Harper-Bill, C. Holdsworth, J.L. Nelson, Woodbridge, 1989
RHF	*Recueil des Historiens des Gaules et de la France*, eds. M. Bouquet and L. Delisle, 24 vols, Paris, 1869–1904
RRAN	*Regesta Regum Anglo-Normannorum*, 1066–1154, ed. C. Johnson and others, 4 vols, Oxford, 1913–69, vol iii unless stated otherwise
RS	Rolls Series
ser.	series
Stevenson	*The Church Historians of England*, ed. J. Stevenson, 5 vols, London, 1853–8
TRHS	*Transactions of the Royal Historical Society*
VCH	*Victoria County History*

Notes

1. The Causes of the Civil War

1. Orderic Vitalis, *The Ecclesiastical History*, ed. and trans. M. Chibnall, 6 vols, Oxford, 1968–80, vi, pp. 295–307, gives a detailed account of the disaster.
2. Henry of Huntingdon, *Chronicle*, ed. and trans. T. Forester, 1853, p. 249; Henry of Huntingdon, *Historia Anglorum*, ed. T. Arnold, RS no. 74, 1879, p. 242: *'fere omnes sodomitica labe dicebantur'*.
3. Orderic, vi, p. 303.
4. William of Malmesbury, *De Gestis Regum Anglorum*, ed. W. Stubbs, 2 vols, RS no. 90, 1887–9, ii, p. 488.
5. J. Bradbury, 'Geoffrey V of Anjou, Count and Knight', *IPMK*, iii, 1988, eds. C. Harper-Bill and R. Harvey, pp. 21–38.
6. John of Marmoutier, 'Historia Gaufredi Ducis' in *Chroniques des Comtes d'Anjou et des Seigneurs d'Amboise*, eds. L. Halphen and R. Poupardin, Paris, 1913, p. 176, 178–9; Bradbury, 'Geoffrey V', p. 37.
7. J. Chartrou, *L'Anjou de 1109 à 1151*, Paris, 1928, pp. 83–5; J. Bradbury, 'Fulk le Réchin and the Origin of the Plantagenets', *RAB*, pp. 27–41.
8. John of Marmoutier, pp. 179, 181–3. A translation appears in Bradbury, 'Geoffrey V', pp. 32–3.
9. John of Marmoutier, pp. 180–1.
10. C.W. Hollister and T.K. Keefe, 'The Making of the Angevin Empire', *Journal of British Studies*, xii, 1973, pp. 1–25.
11. John of Worcester, *Chronicle*, ed. J.R. Weaver, Anecdota Oxoniensia, Oxford, 1908, pp. 22–3, 26–7; William of Malmesbury, pp. 3–5; Roger of Howden, *Chronica*, ed. W. Stubbs, 4 vols, RS no. 51, 1868–71, i, pp. 186–7.
12. Orderic, vi, pp. 466, 468, 472: 'guiribecci' and 'hilibecci'.
13. M. Chibnall, *The Empress Matilda*, Oxford, 1991, p. 57, thinks Geoffrey at least as much to blame for the split as Matilda; others have considered the age difference and Matilda's personality to be at fault.
14. William of Malmesbury, *Historia Novella*, ed. K.R. Potter, Edinburgh, 1955, p. 12.
15. Henry of Huntingdon, ed. Forester, p. 259; Henry of Huntingdon, ed. Arnold, p. 254: *'comedit carnes murenarum quae semper ei nocebant'*.
16. Orderic, vi, p. 453.
17. *Gesta Stephani*, ed. and trans. K.R. Potter, notes by R.H.C. Davis, Oxford, 1976, p. 5.
18. R.H.C. Davis, *King Stephen*, 3rd edn, Harlow, 1990, pp. 12–14.
19. *Gesta Stephani*, pp. 8–9.
20. Ibid., pp. 6–7.
21. Henry of Huntingdon, ed. Forester, p. 262; Henry of Huntingdon, ed. Arnold, p. 256: *'vir magnae strenuitatis et audaciae'*.
22. J. Bradbury, 'The early years of the Reign of Stephen, 1135–39', in *England in the Twelfth Century*, Harlaxton Proceedings 1988, ed. D. Williams, Woodbridge, 1990, pp. 17–30.
23. *Gesta Stephani*, p. 7.
24. Ibid., pp. 4–5, calls London queen of the whole kingdom, *'ipsam totius regionis reginam metropolim'*; it also, pp. 8–9, refers to Winchester as 'the second place in the kingdom'.
25. Ibid., p. 8–9: *'in communi breui colloquio'*, a phrase similar to that used for London.
26. William of Malmesbury, p. 15.
27. Bradbury, 'Early Years', p. 22.
28. *Gesta Stephani*, pp. 10–11.
29. John of Salisbury, Historia Pontificalis, ed. and trans M. Chibnall, Edinburgh, 1956, p. 84.

30. Ibid.
31. William of Malmesbury, p. 13.
32. Henry of Huntingdon, ed. Forester, p. 259; Henry of Huntingdon, ed. Arnold, p. 254: '*artibus scilicet filiae suae*'.
33. Bradbury, 'Early Years', p. 20.
34. Gervase of Canterbury, *Opera*, ed. W. Stubbs, 2 vols, RS no. 73, London, 1879–80, i, p. 94.
35. *Gesta Stephani*, pp. 6–7.
36. Orderic, vi, pp. 454–5.
37. William of Malmesbury, p. 18.
38. *Gesta Stephani*, pp. 14–15.
39. William of Malmesbury, p. 18.
40. S.E. Thorne, 'English feudalism and estates in land', *Cambridge Law Journal*, 1959, pp. 193–209.
41. R.H.C. Davis, 'What happened in Stephen's reign', *History*, xlix, 1964, pp. 1–12.
42. J.C. Holt, 'Politics and property in early medieval England', *PP*, lvii, 1972, pp. 3–52; followed by a series of articles on 'Feudal society and the family' in three parts in *TRHS*, xxxii, 1982; xxxiii, 1983, xxxiv, 1984.
43. E. King, 'The tenurial crisis in the early twelfth century', *PP*, lxv, 1974.
44. The Holt articles in n. 42; S.D. White, 'Succession to fiefs in early medieval England', *PP*, lxv, 1974; J.C. Holt, 'Politics and property in early medieval England: a rejoinder', *PP*, lxv, 1974.
45. Davis, *Stephen*, appendix 4, pp. 150–3. Davis here abandons his point over the date, but still sees it as a cause of conflict, but few agree.
46. *Gesta Stephani*, pp. 22–3, in 1136.
47. D. Crouch, 'Robert Earl of Gloucester and the daughter of Zelophehad', *JMH*, xi, 1985, p. 233.
48. On the attitude of William of Malmesbury, see Bradbury, 'Early Years', p. 17; R.B. Patterson, 'William of Malmesbury's Robert of Gloucester: a re-evaluation of the Historia Novella', *American Historical Review*, lxx, 1964–5, pp. 983–97; J.W. Leedom, 'William of Malmesbury and Robert of Gloucester reconsidered', *Albion*, vi, 1974, pp. 251–62; William of Malmesbury, pp. 18–24.
49. Crouch, 'Zelophehad' disagrees with this view, but his grounds are not strong; *Gesta Stephani*, pp. 14–15.
50. William of Malmesbury, p. 22.
51. Davis, *Stephen*, p. 35.
52. Robert of Torigny, in Howlett, iv, p. 136,

says that an agreement had been made the previous Easter: '*qui circa praeteritum Pascha concordia cum eo fecerat*'; Robert of Torigny, 'The Chronicles of Robert de Monte', in Stevenson, p. 50; Orderic, vi, pp. 514–15 says that Geoffrey brought him over by 'pleas and promises'; William of Malmesbury, p. 23.
53. William of Malmesbury, p. 23.
54. John of Salisbury, p. 85.
55. Chibnall, *Matilda*, p. 71.

2. The Two Sides

1. *Gesta Stephani*, pp. 28–9.
2. J.H. Round, 'Robert of Bampton', *EHR*, v, 1890, p. 746; *Gesta Stephani*, pp. 28–9, n. 1.
3. *Gesta Stephani*, pp. 30–1.
4. Ibid., pp. 40–1 and n. 1.
5. There is an interesting regional parallel with rebellions in the sixteenth century, though it is more difficult to show the causes for twelfth-century discontent.
6. *Gesta Stephani*, pp. 30–1.
7. Ibid., pp. 32–3.
8. Ibid., pp. 38–9.
9. Henry of Huntingdon, ed. Forester, p. 265; Henry of Huntingdon, ed. Arnold, p. 259; *Gesta Stephani*, pp. 40–1.
10. *Gesta Stephani*, pp. 44–5; no source mentions the name of the castle concerned, but it is almost certainly Carisbrooke.
11. John of Worcester, ed. Weaver, p. 40: '*depopulatio et depredatio minime cessat*'; John of Worcester, in Stevenson, p. 350.
12. For the general methods of these raids, see F.C. Suppe, *Military Institutions on the Welsh Marches, Shropshire 1066–1300*, Woodbridge, 1994.
13. Worcester continuator in Stevenson, ii, pt, I, p. 350; Florence of Worcester, *Chronicon ex Chronicis*, ed. B. Thorpe, 2 vols, EHS, 1848–9, ii, p. 97.
14. Richard of Hexham, 'Chronicle', in Stevenson, iv, pt. I, pp. 33–58, p. 57; Richard of Hexam, in Howlett, iii, p. 145.
15. Richard of Hexham, in Howlett, p. 159; John of Hexham, continuation of Symeon of Durham, *Historia Regum*, ed. T. Arnold, RS no. 75, 2 vols, 1882–5, ii, p. 290; Henry of Huntingdon, ed. Arnold, p. 261.
16. Ailred of Rievaulx, 'Relatio de Standardo', in Howlett, iii, pp. 181–99, p. 183.
17. Richard of Hexham, in Howlett, p. 156; Richard of Hexham, in Stevenson, p. 45.

18. Ailred of Rievaulx, p. 182: '*in campo latissimo*'.
19. Orderic, vi, pp. 522–3.
20. J. Bradbury, 'Battles in England and Normandy, 1066–1154', *ANS*, vi, 1983, pp. 1–12.
21. Ailred of Rievaulx, pp. 181–99; Richard of Hexham, in Howlett, p. 163; Henry of Huntingdon, ed. Arnold, p. 263; Richard of Hexham, in Stevenson, p. 45.
22. John of Hexham, in Howlett, p. 294.
23. Ailred of Rievaulx, p. 196.
24. Richard of Hexham, in Howlett, p. 162.
25. Davis, *Stephen*, p. 47.
26. Orderic, vi, pp. 468–9.
27. Orderic, vi, pp. 480–1.
28. R. Helmerichs, 'King Stephen's Norman itinerary, 1137', *HSJ*, v, 1993, pp. 98–97.
29. Orderic, vi, pp. 490–1.
30. Robert of Torigny, in Stevenson, p. 48; Torigny, in Howlett, p. 132: '*facta est discordia magna in exercitu ejus apud Livarrou propter unam hosam vini . . . magna dissension inter Normannos et Flandrenses*'.
31. Orderic, vi, pp. 486–7.
32. Robert of Torigny, in Howlett, p. 132. Orderic, pp. 486–7 makes it two years.
33. Helmerichs, 'King Stephen', p. 96.
34. William of Malmesbury, p. 1.
35. Chibnall, *Matilda*, p. 84.
36. K.S.B. Keats-Rohan, 'The devolution of the honour of Wallingford, 1066–1148', *Oxoniensia*, liv, 1989, pp. 311–18, p. 315 shows that she was the daughter and heiress of Miles Crispin, not his widow.
37. Keats-Rohan, 'Wallingford', p. 317.
38. *Gesta Stephani*, pp. 96–7; Chibnall, *Matilda*, p. 83.
39. John of Worcester, ed. Weaver, pp. 51, n. 1; Worcester, ed. Thorpe, ii, pp. 110–11; Chibnall, *Matilda*, p. 80, n. 66.
40. Davis, *Stephen*, p. 40.
41. On the Beaumonts see D. Crouch, *The Beaumont Twins, the Roots and Branches of Power in the Twelfth Century*, Cambridge, 1986.
42. Davis, *Stephen*, p. 27 is less immoderate, but calls him 'almost unknown'.
43. Orderic, vi, pp. 530–1; R.H.C. Davis suggested that the author was the Bishop of Bath, see below.
44. E.J. Kealey, *Roger of Salisbury, Viceroy of England*, Berkeley California, 1972, p. 4; William of Newburgh, i, pp. 35–6.
45. Kealey, *Roger*, p. 23.
46. Ibid., p. 24.
47. *Gesta Stephani*, pp. 72–3.
48. Orderic, vi, pp. 530–1.
49. William of Malmesbury, p. 26.
50. *Gesta Stephani*, pp. 74–5.
51. Ibid., pp. 76–7; the biblical reference is to Numbers 26 v. 9–11, which is itself rather confusing saying the earth opened up and swallowed them, but they did not die.
52. William of Malmesbury, p. 26: '*facto conuentu magnatum*'.
53. *Gesta Stephani*, pp. 76–7.
54. Orderic, vi, pp. 532–3.
55. William of Malmesbury, p. 27.
56. Orderic, vi, pp. 532–5; Henry of Huntingdon, ed. Forester, p. 271; Henry of Huntingdon, ed. Arnold, p. 265: '*laqueo collum circumnectens ut suspenderetur*'.
57. Henry of Huntingdon, ed. Arnold, p. 266; Henry of Huntingdon, ed. Forester, p. 271.
58. *Gesta Stephani*, pp. 74–7.
59. William of Malmesbury, p. 28.
60. Ibid., p. 29.
61. Ibid., p. 30.
62. Ibid., p. 31.
63. Ibid., p. 33.
64. Ibid.
65. *Gesta Stephani*, pp. 78–9.
66. Ibid., pp. 80–1.
67. Henry of Huntingdon, ed. Forester, p. 267; Henry of Huntingdon, ed. Arnold, p. 261: '*Post Pascha vero exarsit rabies proditorum nefanda*'.
68. *Gesta Stephani*, pp. 58–9.
69. Orderic, vi, pp. 522–3. Orderic says 'about 93' which allowed Ellis Peters some poetic licence, (in 'One Corpse Too Many', 1979).
70. *Gesta Stephani*, pp. 66–7.
71. Ibid., pp. 68–9.
72. Henry of Huntingdon, ed. Forester, p. 270; Henry of Huntingdon, ed. Arnold, p. 265: '*ubi idem Henricus unco ferreo equo abstractus poene captus est, sed ipse rex eum ab hostibus splendide retraxit*'.
73. Henry of Huntingdon, ed. Forester, p. 267; Henry of Huntingdon, ed. Arnold, p. 261.
74. *Gesta Stephani*, pp. 80–1.
75. Ibid., pp. 82–3.
76. Ibid. and n. 4.
77. Davis, *Stephen*, p. 37.

3. *War*

1. J. Bradbury, *The Medieval Siege*, Woodbridge, 1992, pp. 113–14.

2. Orderic, v, pp. 106, 324; Anna Comnena, *The Alexiad*, ed. E.R.A. Sewter, Harmondsworth, 1969, pp. 348–9; *Die Kreuzzugsbriefe aus den Jahren 1088–1100*, ed. H. Hagenmeyer, Innsbruck, 1901, pp. 138–40, 149–52.

3. J. Bradbury, 'Greek Fire'.

4. Bradbury, 'Geoffrey V', pp. 21–38, pp. 34–5; S. and M. Nikitine, *L'Émail Plantagênet*, Nancy, 1981.

5. See F.H. Russell, *The Just War in the Middle Ages*, Cambridge, 1975.

6. *Gesta Stephani*, pp. 86–7.

7. Ibid., pp. 84–5.

8. Davis, *Stephen*, p. 37.

9. *Gesta Stephani*, pp. 84–5.

10. William of Malmesbury, p. 34.

11. *Gesta Stephani*, pp. 86–7; John of Worcester, ed. Weaver, p. 55, says it was in October and the landing at Portsmouth, and n. 4, that the G manuscript gives August, but this seems muddled, and is usually considered to be incorrect; Worcester, in Stevenson, p. 361, following the error of Thorpe has an account with a landing both in August and October! Orderic, vi, pp. 534–5 merely says they arrived in the autumn.

12. Worcester, in Stevenson, p. 361.

13. *Gesta Stephani*, pp. 86–7.

14. Worcester, in Stevenson, p. 361.

15. *Gesta Stephani*, pp. 88–9.

16. Ibid.: '*Datis igitur dextris, et sub iureiurando acceptis induciis*'. This is one of the examples of 'right hands given', probably an actual symbolic handshake to confirm an agreement.

17. Henry of Huntingdon, ed. Forester, p. 272; Henry of Huntingdon, ed. Arnold, p. 266: '*ire permisit ad Bristowe*'.

18. *Gesta Stephani*, pp. 88–91; William of Malmesbury, p. 35.

19. William of Malmesbury, p. 35; Henry of Huntingdon, ed. Forester, p. 272; Henry of Huntingdon, ed. Arnold, p. 266: '*quia castrum videbat inexpugnabile*'; Orderic, vi, pp. 534–5.

20. *Gesta Stephani*, pp. 88–9; and n. 1, where the editor suggests that the bishop may have been Matilda's choice for an escort.

21. William of Malmesbury, p. 35.

22. John of Worcester, ed. Weaver, p. 55, n. 4, from the G manuscript of the Gloucester continuation: Worcester, in Stevenson, p. 361. Since this is in the uncertain account of the Worcester chronicle, the dating remains unclear, but must have been at about the time of the Arundel landing.

23. *Gesta Stephani*, pp. 90–1: '*qui de illorum aduentu eximie laetificatus*'.

24. Tom Hassall, 'Wallingford Castle: life on the bailey', *The Times*, 1976.

25. D. Renn, *Norman Castles in Britain*, 2nd edn, London, 1973, pp. 337–8; R.A. Brown, *Castles from the Air*, Cambridge, 1989, pp. 219–20.

26. *Gesta Stephani*, pp. 90–1: '*firmato inexpugnabili*'.

27. Ibid., pp. 92–3.

28. William of Malmesbury, p. 37; Worcester, in Stevenson, p. 366.

29. John of Worcester, ed. Weaver, pp. 56–8; Worcester, in Stevenson, pp. 362–4.

30. William of Malmesbury, pp. 36, 40–1.

31. Henry of Huntingdon, ed. Forester, p. 273; Henry of Huntingdon, ed. Arnold, p. 267.

32. *Gesta Stephani*, pp. pp. 96–7.

33. W.H. Jones, 'Early Annals of Trowbridge', in *VCH*, Wiltshire, vii, 1953, p. 216.

34. William of Malmesbury, pp. 37, 39.

35. *Gesta Stephani*, pp. 96–9.

36. *Liber Eliensis*, ed. E.O. Blake, Camden Society, 3rd ser., xcii, London, 1962, p. 314.

37. *Gesta Stephani*, pp. 98–9.

38. Ibid., pp. 100–1: '*castellulum*'.

39. Ibid., p. 94.

40. Ibid., pp. 102–3. The castle Reginald retained is not named.

41. William of Malmesbury, p. 42.

42. Worcester, in Stevenson, p. 366; Worcester, ed. Thorpe, ii, pp. 125–6.

43. William of Malmesbury, pp. 43–4.

44. Ibid., p. 44.

45. Ibid., pp. 44–5.

46. Worcester, in Stevenson, p. 365; Worcester, ed. Thorpe, p. 124: '*magnificam domum*'.

47. Worcester, in Stevenson, p. 367; Worcester, ed. Thorpe, p. 128.

48. Worcester, in Stevenson, p. 368; Worcester, ed. Thorpe, p. 128.

4. The Battle of Lincoln

1. Comnena, *The Alexiad*, pp. 163, 416.

2. Bradbury, 'Battles', pp. 1–12.

3. Comnena, *The Alexiad*, p. 165; Bradbury, 'Battles', pp. 1–12, p. 12.

4. Bradbury, 'Battles', pp. 1–12.

5. H.A. Cronne, 'Ranulf de Gernons, Earl of Chester, 1129–1153', *TRHS*, 4th ser., xx, 1937, pp. 103–34, p. 113; J.H. Round, 'King

Stephen and the Earl of Chester', *EHR*, x, 1895, pp. 87–91, p. 87.

6. Davis, *Stephen*, p. 134.

7. F. Hill, *Medieval Lincoln*, Cambridge, 1948; Cronne, 'Ranulf', pp. 103–34.

8. *Gesta Stephani*, pp. 110–11.

9. William of Malmesbury, p. 46: '*pacifice abscesserat*'.

10. Orderic, vi, pp. 540–1.

11. The *Gesta Stephani* says he had gone, but Orderic says he only escaped after the king arrived; *Gesta Stephani*, pp. 110–11; Orderic, vi, pp. 540–1.

12. *Gesta Stephani*, pp. 110–13; Orderic, vi, pp. 544–5; Henry of Huntingdon, ed. Forester, pp. 276–7; Henry of Huntingdon, ed. Arnold, p. 271.

13. *Gesta Stephani*, pp. 112–13; Orderic, vi, pp. 540–3.

14. William of Malmesbury, p. 48, says that they had to swim across, which is possible, but also that the river was the Trent, which seems impossible.

15. C.H. Vellacott, 'Political History', in *VCH*, Lincolnshire, ii, ed. W. Page, p. 252.

16. Orderic, vi, pp. 540–1.

17. *Gesta Stephani*, pp. 112–13.

18. Henry of Huntingdon, ed. Arnold, p. 271: '*quia rex Stephanus festiva carebat voce*'; *BL Arundel MS 48*, f. 168v.

19. Henry of Huntingdon, ed. Arnold, p. 271: '*Loco stans excelso*'.

20. Henry of Huntingdon, ed. Forester, p. 277; Henry of Huntingdon, ed. Arnold, p. 271: '*ubi attentionem eorum modesta taciturnitate stimulavit*'.

21. Henry of Huntingdon, ed. Forester, pp. 275–6; Henry of Huntingdon, ed. Arnold, speeches by Angevins, pp. 268–71, for royalists, pp. 271–3.

22. Henry of Huntingdon, ed. Forester, p. 276; Henry of Huntingdon, ed. Arnold, p. 271: '*terribili clamore*'.

23. Henry of Huntingdon, ed. Forester, p. 277; Henry of Huntingdon, ed. Arnold, p. 272: '*in equitibus non inferior, in peditibus confertior*'; Orderic, vi, pp. 542–43.

24. Henry of Huntingdon, ed. Forester, p. 278; Henry of Huntingdon, ed. Arnold, p. 273; '*inermem bello praeferunt temeritatem, et arte et usu belli carentes*'.

25. Orderic, vi, pp. 542–3.

26. Henry of Huntingdon, ed. Forester, p. 277; Henry of Huntingdon, ed. Arnold, p. 271: '*equis abductis*'; Robert of Torigny, RS, p. 140:

'*Ipse pedes omnem circa se multitudinem loricatorum, equis abductis*'.

27. Henry of Huntingdon, ed. Forester, p. 277; Henry of Huntingdon, ed. Arnold, p. 271; Robert of Torigny, in Stevenson, p. 53, repeats this; Torigny, in Howlett, p. 140.

28. Henry of Huntingdon, ed. Arnold, p. 273; and Robert of Torigny, RS, p. 140: '*et divisio eorum in tria deserit*'.

29. Orderic, pp. 542–3; John of Hexham, p. 134; '*dux et dispositor praelio*'.

30. In *The Medieval Archer*, p. 55, I took the one behind the other formation, but on consideration, have decided that the alternative is just to be preferred. From the chronicles, either could be correct.

31. Orderic, vi, pp. 542–3, and n. 2; Robert of Torigny, in Stevenson, p. 53; Robert of Torigny, RS, p. 146: '*Walenses qui a latere procedebant*'. Henry of Huntingdon, ed. Arnold, p. 268: '*a latere*'; and the Angevin Chronicle, based on Henry of Huntingdon, p. 302: '*a latere vero erat turma Wallensium*'.

32. Henry of Huntingdon, ed. Forester, p. 279, says that William of Ypres' force routed them; Henry of Huntingdon, ed. Arnold, p. 273: '*percussit Walenses . . . et in fugam coegit*'.

33. Henry of Huntingdon, ed. Forester, p. 279; Henry of Huntingdon, ed. Arnold, p. 273; see n. 24 above.

34. *Gesta Stephani*, p. 112: '*antequam manus consererent*'.

35. William of Malmesbury, p. 49.

36. Henry of Huntingdon, ed. Forester, p. 279; Henry of Huntingdon, ed. Arnold, p. 274: '*videns impossibilitatem auxiliandi regi*'.

37. William of Malmesbury, p. 49; Orderic, vi, pp. 542–3.

38. William of Malmesbury, p. 49.

39. Henry of Huntingdon, ed. Forester, p. 279; Henry of Huntingdon, ed. Arnold, p. 274.

40. Orderic, pp. 542–5.

41. Henry of Huntingdon, ed. Forester, p. 279; Henry of Huntingdon, ed. Arnold, p. 274.

42. Orderic, vi, pp. 544–5: '*securi norica*'; and John of Hexham, p. 135: '*securem Danicam*'; Henry of Huntingdon, ed. Forester, p. 279 has the axe broken first and then the sword, which seems a less likely order; Henry of Huntingdon, ed. Arnold, p. 274.

43. Robert of Torigny, RS, pp. 140–1; in Stevenson, p. 53.

44. *Gesta Stephani*, pp. 112–13.

45. Ibid., pp. 112–15; Henry of Huntingdon,

ed. Forester, p. 279, is the only source to say that William of Cahagnes captured Stephen, but may still be correct; Henry of Huntingdon, ed. Arnold, p. 274: '*miles valdissimus*'.

46. William of Malmesbury, p. 49; Orderic, vi, pp. 544–7.
47. William of Malmesbury, p. 49.
48. Ibid., p. 50.
49. Worcester, in Stevenson, p. 368; Worcester, ed. Thorpe, p. 129: '*justo Dei judicio*'.

5. Matilda's Opportunity

1. *Gesta Stephani*, pp. 116–17.
2. *Anglo-Saxon Chronicle*, eds. D. Whitelock, D.C. Douglas, S.I. Tucker, 1961, p. 202.
3. *Gesta Stephani*, pp. 116–17.
4. Ibid., pp. 116–19.
5. Orderic, vi, pp. 546–7.
6. Crouch, *The Beaumont Twins*, p. 51.
7. *Gesta Stephani*, pp. 114–15.
8. Orderic, vi, pp. 550–7. We shall, however, find Orderic useful when we turn back to more detail of Norman affairs.
9. *Gesta Stephani*, pp. 118–19.
10. William of Malmesbury, p. 51.
11. Ibid., pp. 50–1.
12. *Gesta Stephani*, pp. 118–19.
13. Ibid.
14. William of Malmesbury, p. 51.
15. Ibid., pp. 53–4.
16. Worcester, in Stevenson, p. 369; Worcester, ed. Thorpe, ii, p. 130.
17. Henry of Huntingdon, ed. Forester, p. 280; Henry of Huntingdon, ed. Arnold, p. 275: '*Irritata igitur muliebri angore*', this might, however, be taken as 'anguish' rather than bitterness.
18. Henry of Huntingdon, ed. Forester, p. 280; Henry of Huntingdon, ed. Arnold, p. 275: '*ab omni gente Anglorum suscipitur in dominam, exceptis Kentensibus*'; followed by Robert of Torigny, in Stevenson, p. 53; Torigny, in Howlett, iv, p. 141.
19. *Anglo-Saxon Chronicle*, p. 201; Orderic, vi, pp. 546–7.
20. Robert of Torigny, in Stevenson, p. 54; Torigny, in Howlett, p. 141.
21. Henry of Huntingdon, ed. Forester, p. 280; Henry of Huntingdon, ed. Arnold, p. 275.
22. William of Malmesbury, p. 56.
23. J. Gillingham, 'Love, marriage and politics in the twelfth century', *Forum for Modern Language Studies*, xxv, 1989, pp. 292–303, p. 296; Chibnall, *Matilda*, p. 55.
24. William of Malmesbury, p. 56; Henry of Huntingdon, ed. Forester, p. 280; Henry of Huntingdon, ed. Arnold, p. 275: '*superbiam intolerabilem*'.
25. Worcester, in Stevenson, p. 370; Worcester, ed. Thorpe, ii, p. 132, where they ask instead for the laws of Edward the Confessor.
26. *Gesta Stephani*, pp. 120–3.
27. William of Malmesbury, p. 57.
28. Henry of Huntingdon, ed. Forester, p. 280; Henry of Huntingdon, ed. Arnold, p. 275: '*et omnium fere corda a se alienavit*'.
29. N. Pain, *Empress Matilda*, 1978, for example, on p. 100, says she treated David and Earl Robert badly, but gives no reference. Chibnall, *Matilda*, p. 104, sees the Cumin incident as 'one of the errors of judgement that tipped the scales against her'.
30. For example, *Regesta Regum Anglo-Normannorum*, eds. H.A. Cronne and R.H.C. Davis, iii, Oxford, 1968, p. 130, no. 343, p. 258, no. 699: *Anglorum regina*; p. 92, no. 259, p. 99, no. 274, p. 120, no. 316a: *Anglorum domina*; or p. 220, no. 597: '*imperatrix*'.
31. Worcester, in Stevenson, p. 370; Worcester, ed. Thorpe, p. 132: '*sive monachus sive peregrinus*'.
32. *Gesta Stephani*, pp. 122–3.
33. Ibid., pp. 124–5.
34. 'Annales Plymptonienses', in F. Liebermann, *Ungedruckte Anglo-Normannische Geschichtsquellern*, Strasbourg, 1879, p. 29.
35. *Gesta Stephani*, pp. 124–5; William of Malmesbury, p. 57–8.
36. Henry of Huntingdon, ed. Forester, p. 281; Henry of Huntingdon, ed. Arnold, p. 271; Worcester, ed. Thorpe, p. 132; *Gesta Stephani*, pp. 126–7; Symeon of Durham, *Opera*, including the *Historia Regum*, 2 vols, RS no. 75, 1882–5, ii, p. 310.
37. Worcester, in Stevenson, p. 370; Worcester, ed. Thorpe, p. 133; *Gesta Stephani*, pp. 126–7.
38. William of Malmesbury, p. 59.
39. Ibid., blames Henry of Blois for the burning and insists that the citizens were loyal; the Worcester continuator, in Stevenson, p. 370, supports the comment on the role of the bishop; *Gesta Stephani*, pp. 130–1, says the garrison of Wolvesey was responsible.
40. Worcester, in Stevenson, p. 371; Worcester, ed. Thorpe, pp. 133–4.
41. Discussions of the Rout are to be found in

R. Hill, 'The Battle of Stockbridge, 1141', *RAB*, pp. 173–7; S. Painter, 'The Rout of Winchester', *Speculum*, vii, 1932, pp. 70–5; Chibnall, *Matilda*, pp. 113–14; J.H. Round, *Geoffrey de Mandeville*, 1892, pp. 123–35.

42. *L'Histoire de Guillaume le Maréchal*, ed. P. Meyer, 3 vols, *RHF*, Paris, 1891–4, i, pp. 7–11. Worcester, Stevenson, p. 372 places the attack on Wherwell after the other events, but most modern commentators now believe this is incorrect; Worcester, ed. Thorpe, p. 135.

43. William of Malmesbury, p. 60; *Gesta Stephani*, pp. 130–1.

44. Worcester, in Stevenson, p. 371; Worcester, ed. Thorpe, p. 134.

45. *Anglo-Saxon Chronicle*, p. 201; H.W.C. Davis, 'Henry of Blois and Brian fitz Count', *EHR*, xxv, 1910, pp. 297–303, p. 298.

46. *Gesta Stephani*, pp. 134–5: '*immensum per hoc, ipsa et Brienus, nacti praeconii titulum, ut sicut sese anea mutuo et indiuise dilexerant, ita nec in aduersis, plurimo impediente periculo, aliquatenus separarentur*'.

47. Worcester, in Stevenson, p. 371; Worcester, ed. Thorpe, p. 134: '*tristis ac dolens*'.

48. Worcester, in Stevenson, p. 371; Worcester, ed. Thorpe, p. 134.

49. Worcester, in Stevenson, p. 371; Worcester, ed. Thorpe, p. 135: '*pene nudus*'; *Gesta Stephani*, pp. 134–5.

50. William of Malmesbury, p. 62; Worcester, in Stevenson, p. 372; Worcester, ed. Thorpe, p. 136.

51. Henry of Huntingdon, ed. Forester, p. 281; Henry of Huntingdon, ed. Arnold, p. 275.

52. Henry of Huntingdon, ed. Forester, p. 281; Henry of Huntingdon, ed. Arnold, p. 275: '*cum magno susceptus gaudio*'.

53. William of Malmesbury, p. 61–2, details the arrangements for the exchange.

54. *Gesta Stephani*, pp. 136–7.

6. The Castle War

1. P.A. Stamper, *Excavations of a mid-twelfth century siege castle at Bentley, Hampshire*, 1979.

2. Orderic, vi, pp. 186–7: '*Trulla Leporis*'.

3. T.C. Lethbridge, 'Excavations at Burwell Castle', *Cambridge Antiquarian Society Proceedings*, xxxvi, 1934–5, pp. 121–33; *Opera*, RS, ed. Stubbs, i, p. 128: '*Burwelle quod rex construxerat*'.

4. Lethbridge, 'Burwell Castle', p. 121.

5. *RHMC*, Cambridgeshire, Huntingdonshire.

6. Bradbury, *Medieval Siege*, p. 260.

7. William of Malmesbury, pp. 62–3.

8. Ibid., p. 63.

9. Ibid., pp. 63–4.

10. *Gesta Stephani*, pp. 138–9.

11. William of Malmesbury, p. 71.

12. Ibid.

13. D.F. Renn, 'The keep of Wareham Castle', *Medieval Archaeology*, iv, 1960, pp. 56–68.

14. John of Hexham, in Stevenson, iv, pt. I, 1856, p. 23; Surtees Society, xliv, *The Priory of Hexham*, i, Durham, 1864, p. 148.

15. *Gesta Stephani*, pp. 140–1.

16. Ibid., pp. 142–3.

17. William of Malmesbury, p. 74.

18. Ibid.

19. *Anglo-Saxon Chronicle*, p. 202; William of Malmesbury, p. 77. William's is the more prosaic account, but also likely to be the best informed. The chronology of the *Anglo-Saxon Chronicle* for these years is faulty, and one is more inclined to believe William.

20. Henry of Huntingdon, ed. Forester, p. 281; Henry of Huntingdon, ed. Arnold, p. 276; *Gesta Stephani*, pp. 142–3, makes it three knights, though Davis, *Stephen*, p. 69, has four.

21. *Gesta Stephani*, pp. 144–5.

22. Henry of Huntingdon, ed. Forester, p. 281; Henry of Huntingdon, ed. Arnold, p. 276; but the *Gesta Stephani* places Wilton later in the year, after Oxford. However, this latter chronology has a further difficulty, since it places the Wareham incident after Oxford, though William of Malmesbury, well placed to have the facts correct, reports that Robert hoped to draw Stephen from Oxford to Wareham. The positioning chosen here is therefore debatable, but fits better with the general itinerary of the king, while in the west country.

23. *Gesta Stephani*, pp. 150–1.

24. On Geoffrey de Mandeville, see: Round, *Geoffrey de Mandeville*; R.H.C. Davis, 'Geoffrey de Mandeville reconsidered', *EHR*, lxxix, 1964, pp. 299–307; and in Davis, *Stephen*, appendix VI, pp. 157–60, which includes discussion of J.O. Prestwich, *EHR*, ciii, 1988, pp. 288–312, 960–67; J.O. Prestwich and R.H.C. Davis, 'Last words on Geoffrey de Mandeville', *EHR*, cv, 1990; here Davis' argument is preferred. See also

C.W. Hollister, 'The Misfortunes of the Mandevilles', *History*, lviii, 1973, pp. 18–28.

25. Henry of Huntingdon, ed. Forester, p. 282; Henry of Huntingdon, ed. Arnold, p. 276; *Gesta Stephani*, pp. 162–3.

26. William of Newburgh, in Howlett, i, pp. 44–5.

27. *Gesta Stephani*, pp. 162–3.

28. Henry of Huntingdon, ed. Forester, p. 282; Henry of Huntingdon, ed. Arnold, p. 276: '*magis ex necessitate quam ex honestate*'; 'Book of Walden' in W. Dugdale, *Monasticon Anglicanum*, ed. J. Caley and others, 6 vols in 8 parts, 1817–30, iv. H. Collar, 'The Book of the Foundation of Walden Abbey', trans. C.H. Emson, *Essex Review*, xlv, 1936, pp. 73–85, p. 80.

29. *Gesta Stephani*, pp. 160–1.

30. Round, *Geoffrey de Mandeville*, p. 209.

31. Henry of Huntingdon, ed. Forester, pp. 282–3; Henry of Huntingdon, ed. Arnold, pp. 276–7.

32. *Gesta Stephani*, pp. 164–5; Book of Walden, p. 80.

33. *Gesta Stephani*, pp. 162–4; *Monasticon*, iv, p. 142; Round, *Geoffrey de Mandeville*, p. 213.

34. *Gesta Stephani*, pp. 164–5.

35. Most have interpreted Round's idea, in *Geoffrey de Mandeville*, p. 213, of castles to 'hem' the king in to mean this; Davis, *Stephen*, p. 84, uses exactly the same phrase; J. Beeler, pp. 138–9, saw it as a policy of containment.

36. This has not been certainly identified. Wood Walton near Ramsey has been suggested, but this was a castle of the abbot with charter evidence for its existence in 1133–5. It may be that he took over rather than built the castle.

37. Another possible site is Belsar's Camp, near Willingham, but a site at Aldreth itself seems preferable.

38. W. O'Farrell Hughes, 'Burwell, its castle', *Transactions of the Cambridgeshire and Huntingdonshire Archaeological Society*, iii, 1914, pp. 291–3.

39. Book of Walden, p. 82; Gervase of Canterbury, *Chronicle*, i, p. 128.

40. *Chronicon Abbatiae Rameseiensis*, ed. W. D. Macray, RS no. 83, 1886, pp. 329–33; *Monasticon*, p. 142; Book of Walden, p. 82.

41. Henry of Huntingdon, ed. Forester, p. 283; Henry of Huntingdon, ed. Arnold, p. 278:

'*in aeternum absorpta est*'; Robert of Torigny, in Stevenson, p. 57; Torigny, in Howlett, iv, p. 147; William of Newburgh, in Howlett, i, p. 45.

42. *Gesta Stephani*, pp. 166–7.

43. Ibid., pp. 150–1; the writer thought these qualities sullied the good name of a soldier, something they have tended to do down the ages; pp. 154–5 on mercenaries.

44. Ibid., pp. 152–3.

45. Robert of Torigny, in Stevenson, p. 57; Torigny, in Howlett, p. 146.

46. Henry of Huntingdon, ed. Forester, p. 283: Henry of Huntingdon, ed. Arnold, p. 277; William of Newburgh, *The History of English Affairs*, eds. and trans. P.G. Walsh and M.J. Kennedy, i, Warminster, 1988, p. 73.

47. *Gesta Stephani*, pp. 168–9; the chronicler speaks of efforts from sea to sea: '*a mari ex transuerso usque ad mare*'; and order: '*leges et plebiscita ubique iniungebant*'.

48. Ibid., pp. 174–5.

49. Renn, *Norman Castles*, p. 189; I am also grateful to Dr Steve Church for information on this site. A counter castle was built by the king, and there is room for further investigation on the site.

50. *Gesta Stephani*, pp. 180–1.

51. Henry of Huntingdon, ed. Forester, p. 283; Henry of Huntingdon, ed. Arnold, p. 278; *Gesta Stephani*, pp. 180–1.

52. *Gesta Stephani*, pp. 182–3; Robert of Torigny, in Stevenson, p. 59; Torigny, in Howlett, p. 150.

53. Henry of Huntingdon, ed. Forester, p. 284; Henry of Huntingdon, ed. Arnold, p. 278: '*Tunc demum regi fortuna in melius coepit permutari*'.

54. *Gesta Stephani*, pp. 184–5.

55. Ibid., pp. 194–5.

56. R.H.C. Davis, 'King Stephen and the Earl of Chester revised', *EHR*, lxxv, 1960, pp. 654–60, argued for this event occuring in 1146 rather than 1142, an argument which is here accepted.

57. *Gesta Stephani*, pp. 184–5.

58. William of Newburgh, eds. Walsh and Kennedy, p. 74.

59. *Gesta Stephani*, pp. 198–9.

60. Ibid., pp. 186–7; n. 2 suggests that the castle may have been Miserden in Gloucester.

61. *Gesta Stephani*, pp. 190–1.

62. Henry of Huntingdon, ed. Forester, p. 288; Henry of Huntingdon, ed. Arnold, p. 283.

63. William of Newburgh, eds. Walsh and Kennedy, p. 99.
64. Robert of Torigny, in Stevenson, p. 61; Torigny, in Howlett, p. 153.
65. *Gesta Stephani*, pp. 210–11.
66. Chibnall, *Matilda*, p. 152 and n. 52.

7. The Henrician War

1. The new manuscript is known as the Valenciennes or Vicoigne, having been found in the municipal library at Valenciennes, but having formerly belonged to the abbey of Vicoigne, a daughter house of Laon. It seems to be a copy of the Laon ms, made when that was complete to 1154.
2. The lost section begins in *Gesta Stephani*, p. 215, and Henry is the lawful heir in line two of the text, and several times afterwards. The section by the second writer, however, probably begins on p. 205, which Davis suggests as the break point for what in his view was written by the same author in two parts, and the first reference to lawful heir occurs just after this. On King David, pp. 216–17; on Ranulf, pp. 184–5, 236–7 and p. 236 n. 2; on Walter de Pinkeney, pp. 178–9, 212–13.
3. Even the Laon manuscript, which was edited in 1619 by Duchesne but has not been seen since, was probably not the autograph, and had four important gaps due to lost leaves. The Laon ms came to an end in 1147.
4. R.H.C. Davis, 'The authorship of the *Gesta Stephani*', *EHR*, lxxvii, 1962, pp. 209–32.
5. *Gesta Stephani*, pp. 204–07.
6. Ibid., pp. 206–07.
7. Ibid.
8. C.W. Hollister, 'The magnates of Stephen's reign: reluctant anarchists', *HSJ*, v, 1993, p. 79.
9. J.H. Round, 'King Stephen', pp. 87–91.
10. *Gesta Stephani*, pp. 198–9.
11. Ibid., pp. 208–9.
12. Ibid., pp. 216–17.
13. R.H. Cunnington, *Some Annals of the Borough of Devizes*, Devizes, 1925; E.H. Stone, *Devizes Castle*, Devizes, 1920; R.H. Cunnington, 'Devizes Castle: a suggested revision', *Wiltshire Archaeological and Natural History Magazine*, li, 1945–7, pp. 496–9; R.H. Cunnington, 'The Borough of Devizes', *VCH*, Wiltshire, ed. E. Crittall, x, 1975.
14. W.L. Warren, *Henry II*, 1973, p. 33.
15. *Gesta Stephani*, pp. 226–7.
16. Ibid., pp. 228–31.
17. Orderic, vi, pp. 444–5.
18. Robert of Torigny, in Stevenson, p. 46; Torigny, in Howlett, iv, p. 128.
19. Orderic, vi, pp. 482–3.
20. Robert of Torigny, RS, p. 132 says he planned to enter the land of Geoffrey: '*in terram comitis*'.
21. Orderic, vi, pp. 526–9.
22. Robert of Torigny, in Stevenson, p. 52; Torigny, in Howlett, p. 139.
23. Orderic, vi, pp. 546–7.
24. Torigny, in Howlett, p. 142: '*qui omnibus Normanniae primalibus, et firmitatibus et redditibus et affinibus praestabat*'.
25. G.H. White, 'The career of Waleran, Count of Meulan and Earl of Worcester, 1104–1166', *TRHS*, 4th ser., xvii, 1934, pp. 19–48, p. 47.
26. Orderic, vi, pp. 548–51.
27. John of Marmoutier, p. 177.
28. Orderic, vi, pp. 454–62.
29. John of Marmoutier, p. 215.
30. Bradbury, 'Geoffrey V'.
31. John of Marmoutier, pp. 172–5, the prologue.
32. Ibid., pp. 176–7.
33. Ibid., pp. 183–91.
34. Ibid., p. 191.
35. Robert of Torigny, in Howlett, iv, pp. 162–3.
36. Bradbury, 'Geoffrey V' pp. 21–38.
37. C.H. Haskins, 'Normandy under Geoffrey Plantagenet', *EHR*, xvii, 1912, pp. 417–44.
38. Henry of Huntingdon, ed. Forester, p. 291; Henry of Huntingdon, ed. Arnold, p. 285: '*subitis afflata rumoribus infrenduit terra, velut arundinetum Zephyro vibrante collisum*'.
39. *Gesta Stephani*, pp. 226–7.
40. J.W. Leedom, 'The English Settlement of 1153', *History*, lxv, 1980, pp. 347–64, pp. 357, 347.
41. Henry of Huntingdon, ed. Forester, p. 290; Henry of Huntingdon, ed. Arnold, p. 285.
42. *Gesta Stephani*, pp. 230–3.
43. Henry of Huntingdon, ed. Forester, p. 291; Henry of Huntingdon, ed. Arnold, p. 286.
44. Henry of Huntingdon, ed. Forester, p. 292; Henry of Huntingdon, ed. Arnold, p. 286.
45. Henry of Huntingdon, ed. Forester, p. 291; Henry of Huntingdon, ed. Arnold, p. 286: '*ut Deus ipse videretur pro duce rem agere*'; Gervase, *Opera*, i, p. 152, makes the same point 'as if they were contending against God'.
46. *Gesta Stephani*, pp. 232–5, and p. 235, n. 2.
47. Ibid., pp. 234–5; Robert of Torigny, in Stevenson, p. 70; Torigny, in Howlett, p. 172.

48. Ibid., pp. 234–5.
49. *Gesta Stephani*, pp. 226–7.
50. Gervase, *Opera*, i, p. 153.
51. *Gesta Stephani*, pp. 236–9.
52. Ibid., pp. 238–9.
53. Gervase, *Opera*, i, p. 153.
54. Henry of Huntingdon, ed. Forester, p. 293; Henry of Huntingdon, ed. Arnold, p. 288: '*de proditione procerum suorum anxie conquerentes uterque*'.
55. *Gesta Stephani*, pp. 236–7.

8. The Peace

1. *Gesta Stephani*, pp. 234–5.
2. Robert of Torigny, in Stevenson, p. 71; Torigny, in Howlett, iv, pp. 173, 177; Henry of Huntingdon, *EHD*, ii, p. 336; Henry of Huntingdon, ed. Arnold, pp. 287–8.
3. *Gesta Stephani*, pp. 238–9; Henry of Huntingdon, ed. Forester, p. 293; Henry of Huntingdon, ed. Arnold, p. 288.
4. *Gesta Stephani*, pp. 240–1; Henry of Huntingdon, ed. Forester, p. 294; Henry of Huntingdon, ed. Arnold, p. 289.
5. Henry of Huntingdon, ed. Forester, p. 294; in *EHD*, p. 311; Henry of Huntingdon, ed. Arnold, p. 289: '*quam beata dies*'; Gervase, *Opera*, i, p. 154.
6. Leedom, 'The English Settlement', pp. 347–64, p. 347.
7. William of Newburgh, eds. Walsh and Kennedy, p. 126.
8. *Gesta Stephani*, pp. 240–1.
9. Henry of Huntingdon, ed. Forester, p. 294; Henry of Huntingdon, ed. Arnold, p. 289.
10. J.C. Holt, '1153: the Treaty of Winchester', in King, pp. 291–316.
11. Henry of Huntingdon, ed. Forester, p. 294; Henry of Huntingdon, ed. Arnold, p. 289; Robert of Torigny, in Stevenson, p. 73; Torigny, in Howlett, p. 177.
12. *Gesta Stephani*, p. 240: '*castella nova*'; William of Newburgh, p. 444; William of Newburgh, in Howlett, i, p. 101: '*dilapsi sunt*'.
13. *RRAN*, pp. 97–9, no. 272.
14. *The Letters of Osbert of Clare*, ed. and trans. E.W. Williamson, Oxford, 1929, pp. 122, 130.
15. William of Newburgh, eds. Walsh and Kennedy, p. 131: '*munitiones adulterae*'.
16. Robert of Torigny, in Stevenson, p. 73; Robert of Torigny, RS, pp. 177, 183; William of Newburgh, i, pp. 94, 102.
17. C. Coulson, 'The castles of the anarchy', in King, pp. 67–92, pp. 69, 71; William of Newburgh, in Stevenson, p. 444; William of Newburgh, in Howlett, p. 102: '*in locis opportunis sita, quae vel ipse retinere, vel a pacificis ad regni munimen retineri voluit*'; E. Amt, *The Accession of Henry II in England, Royal Government Restored, 1149–1159*, Woodbridge, 1993, pp. 27, 78.
18. Amt, *Henry II*, p. 27.
19. E. King, 'The anarchy of Stephen's reign', *TRHS*, 5th ser., xxxiv, 1984, p. 153; Amt, *Henry II*, p. 52; *Letters of Gilbert Foliot*, pp. 54–5.
20. *RRAN*, p. 64.
21. Amt, *Henry II*, p. 60.
22. Gervase, *Opera*, i, p. 163.
23. E. de Borchgrave, 'Guillaume d'Ypres', *Biographie Nationale*, vol. viii, Brussels, 1884–5, col. 436–9.
24. Robert of Torigny, in Stevenson, p. 74; Torigny, in Howlett, p. 179; '*coepit revocare . . . in jus proprium sua dominica*'.
25. Amt, *Henry II*, p. 113.
26. G. White, 'Continuity in government', in King, pp. 117–43, p. 136.
27. Holt, '1153', in King.
28. King, 'Introduction', p. 35.
29. Amt, *Henry II*, p. 24.
30. *Gesta Stephani*, pp. 210–11.
31. Davis, *Stephen*, p. 90; Warren, *Henry II*, p. 35.
32. *Gesta Stephani*, pp. 210–11.
33. Amt, *Henry II*, p. 36.
34. *Gesta Stephani*, pp. 226–7.
35. D. Crouch, 'The March and the Welsh kings', in King, pp. 255–89, p. 286.
36. Amt, *Henry II*, p. 115.
37. On Ranulf, see P. Dalton, 'In neutro latere: the armed neutrality of Ranulf II Earl of Chester in King Stephen's reign', *ANS*, xiv, 1991, pp. 39–59; Cronne, 'Ranulf' pp. 103–34; Round, 'King Stephen', pp. 87–91.
38. William of Newburgh, eds. Walsh and Kennedy, pp. 74–5.
39. Gervase, *Opera*, i, pp. 154, 159, 63.
40. Amt, *Henry II*, p. 75.
41. Holt, '1153', in King, pp. 301–02.
42. Amt, *Henry II*, p. 60.
43. White, 'The end of Stephen's reign', emphasises the uncertain outcome of events.
44. William of Newburgh, eds. Walsh and Kennedy, p. 126.
45. Ibid., p. 127.
46. John of Hexham, in Stevenson, p. 32.
47. Henry of Huntingdon, ed. Forester, p. 294; Henry of Huntingdon, ed. Arnold, p. 289; '*nunc autem poenitentia motus*'.

48. Robert of Torigny, in Stevenson, p. 66; Torigny, in Howlett, p. 164.

49. See M. Strickland, 'Against the Lord's anointed: aspects of warfare and baronial rebellion in England and Normandy, 1075–1265', *Law and Government in Medieval England and Normandy Essays in Honour of Sir James Holt*, eds. G. Garnett and J. Hudson, Cambridge, 1994, pp. 56–79.

50. Robert of Torigny, RS, pp. 165–6.

51. Robert of Torigny, in Stevenson, p. 68; Torigny, in Howlett, pp. 167–8: '*quod nostra memoria in retroactis temporibus non fuit auditum*'; Walden Chronicle, p. 83.

52. On waste meaning waste, for example E. Amt and C.W. Hollister, 'Magnates'.

53. William of Newburgh, eds. Walsh and Kennedy, p. 99.

54. *Earldom of Gloucester Charters*, ed. R.B. Patterson, Oxford, 1973, p. 95, no. 95, p. 97, no. 96.

55. F.M. Stenton, *The First Century of English Feudalism, 1066–1166*, 2nd edn, Oxford, 1961, pp. 250–3.

56. Davis, *Stephen*, p. 108.

57. Robert of Torigny, in Stevenson, p. 75; Torigny, in Howlett, p. 180.

58. White, 'End', p. 12.

59. Henry of Huntingdon, ed. Forester, p. 295; White, 'End', p. 13.

60. Henry of Huntingdon, ed. Forester, p. 296; Henry of Huntingdon, ed. Arnold, p. 290; *Gesta Stephani*, pp. 240–1.

61. On coinage, see M. Blackburn, 'Coinage and Currency', in King, pp. 145–205.

62. William of Newburgh, *EHD*, p. 323; William of Newburgh, in Howlett, p. 101.

63. William of Newburgh, in Stevenson, p. 444; William of Newburgh, in Howlett, p. 101.

64. Henry of Huntingdon, ed. Forester, p. 294; Henry of Huntingdon, ed. Arnold, pp. 291–2.

65. *Gesta Stephani*, pp. 154–7.

66. William of Malmesbury, pp. 40–1.

67. Henry of Huntingdon, ed. Forester, p. 266.

68. *Anglo-Saxon Chronicle*, p. 199.

69. King, 'Anarchy', pp. 133–53, pp. 135, 142; Round, *Geoffrey de Mandeville*, pp. 414–16, who suggests the idea of blackmail is involved, or protection money.

70. King, 'Anarchy', p. 136–7; *The Letters and Charters of Gilbert Foliot*, eds. A. Morey and C.N. L. Brooke, Cambridge, 1967, no. 3. *Liber Eliensis*, p. 326. Davis, 'King Stephen', p. 80, n. 16.

71. H.W.C. Davis, 'The Anarchy of Stephen's reign', *EHR*, xviii, 1903, pp. 630–41, p. 634.

72. K.J. Stringer, *The Reign of Stephen*, 1993, p. 58.

73. T. Callahan, jr, 'The impact of anarchy on English monasticism, 1135–1154', *Albion*, vi, 1974, pp. 218–32; C.W. Hollister has commented on this with regard to the greater houses.

74. J. le Patourel, 'What did not happen in Stephen's reign', *History*, lviii, 1973, pp. 1–17, points out that Stephen was not hard up, p. 4.

75. Cronne, *Stephen*, p. 224.

76. Bradbury, 'Early Years', p. 25; *RRAN* shows 1,500 charters for Henry I and 900 for Stephen. The average number per annum is William I: 14.7; William II: 15.3; Henry I: 42.5; Stephen: 47.3.

77. E.J. Kealey, 'King Stephen: government and anarchy', *Albion*, vi, 1974, pp. 201–17, p. 207.

78. Cronne, *Stephen*, p. 280.

79. Round, *Geoffrey de Mandeville*, p. 267.

80. White, 'End', pp. 3–22, p. 20.

81. Stringer strongly makes this point, for example on p. 49.

82. M. Chibnall, *Anglo-Norman England, 1066–1166*, Oxford, 1986, p. 98.

83. Davis, 'Anarchy', p. 630.

Bibliography

Place of publication is stated only if outside London

PRIMARY SOURCES

Anglo-Saxon Chronicle, eds. D. Whitelock, D.C. Douglas and S.I. Tucker, 1961
BL Arundel MS 48, Henry of Huntingdon, Historia Anglorum
Charters of the Earldom of Hereford, 1095–1201, ed. D. Walker, Camden Miscellany, xxii, 4th ser., i, 1964
BL Chatteris Cartulary, Cotton MS Julius A i
Canterbury, Gervase of, *Opera*, ed. W. Stubbs, 2 vols, RS no. 73, 1879–80
Chronicle of Battle Abbey, ed. E. Searle, Oxford, 1980
Chronicon Abbatiae Rameseiensis, ed. W. D. Macray, RS no. 83, 1886
Chroniques des Comtes d'Anjou et des Seigneurs d'Amboise, eds. L. Halphen and R. Poupardin, Paris, 1913
Church Historians of England, The, ed. and trans. J. Stevenson, 5 vols, 1853–8 (contains translations of many of the chronicles of the period, a number of which have also been reprinted in a series by Llanerch Enterprises)
Clare, Osbert of, The Letters of, ed. and trans. E.W. Williamson, Oxford, 1929
Comnena, Anna, *The Alexiad*, ed. E.R.A. Sewter, Harmondsworth, 1969
De Expugnatione Lyxbonensis, ed. C.W. David, New York, 1936
Dialogus de Scaccario, ed. and trans. C. Johnson, revised by F.E.L. Carter and D. Greenway, Oxford, 1983
Die Kreuzzugsbriefe aus den Jahren 1088–1100, ed. H. Hagenmeyer, Innsbruck, 1901
Durham, Symeon of, *Opera*, including the *Historia Regum*, and John of Hexham, ed. T. Arnold, 2 vols, RS no. 75, 1882–5
Earldom of Gloucester Charters, ed. R.B. Patterson, Oxford, 1973
English Historical Documents, vol ii, 1042–1189, eds. D.C. Douglas and G.W. Greenaway, 2nd edn, 1981
Foliot, Gilbert, The Letters and Charters of, eds. A. Morey and C.N.L. Brooke, Cambridge, 1967
Foliot, Gilbert, *Epistolae*, ed. J.A. Giles, 2 vols, Oxford, 1845
Gesta Stephani, eds. K.R. Potter and R.H.C. Davis, Oxford, 1976
Howden, Roger of, *Chronica*, ed. W. Stubbs, 5 vols, RS no. 51, 1868–71
Howlett, R., ed. *Chronicles of the Reigns of Stephen, Henry II and Richard I*, 4 vols, RS no. 82, 1884–9 (contains Latin editions of several of the major chronicles of the period)
Huntingdon, Henry of, *Chronicle*, ed. and trans. T. Forester, 1853
Huntingdon, Henry of, *Historia Anglorum*, ed. T. Arnold, RS no. 74, 1965
Huntingdon, Henry of, *Historia Anglorum*, ed. Greenway, Oxford, 1996
Liber Eliensis, ed. E.O. Blake, Camden Society, 3rd ser., xcii, 1962
Malmesbury, William of, *De Gestis Regum Anglorum*, ed. W. Stubbs, 2 vols, RS no. 90, 1887–9
Malmesbury, William of, *Historia Novella*, ed. and trans. K.R. Potter, Edinburgh, 1955
Maréchal, L'Histoire de Guillaume le, ed. P. Meyer, 3 vols, RHF, Paris, 1891–1901
Monasticon Anglicanum, W. Dugdale, ed. J. Caley and others, 6 vols in 8 parts, 1817–30
Newburgh, William of, *The History of English Affairs*, eds. and trans. P.G. Walsh and M.J. Kennedy, i, Warminster, 1988
Peterborough Chronicle, 1070–1154, The, ed. C. Clark, 2nd edn, Oxford, 1970

Pipe Rolls, The Great Rolls of the Pipe, Pipe Roll Society, 31 Henry I, ed. J. Hunter, 1833; 2,3,4 Henry II, ed. J. Hunter, 1844

Regesta Regum Anglo-Normannorum, iii and iv, eds. H.A. Cronne and R.H.C. Davis, Oxford, 1968

Salisbury, John of, *Historia Pontificalis*, ed. and trans. M.C. Chibnall, Edinburgh, 1956

Ungedruckte Anglo-Normannische Geschichtsquellern, ed. F. Liebermann, Strasbourg, 1879

Vitalis, Orderic, *The Ecclesiastical History*, ed. and trans. M. Chibnall, 6 vols, Oxford, 1968–80

'Walden Abbey, The Book of the Foundation of', H. Collar, trans. C.H. Emson, *Essex Review*, xlv, 1936, pp. 73–85

Wales, Gerald of, *Opera*, ed. J.F. Dimock, 8 vols, RS no. 21, 1861–91

Worcester, Florence of, *Chronicon ex Chronicis*, ed. B. Thorpe, 2 vols, EHS, 1848–9

Worcester, John of, *Chronicle*, Anecdota Oxoniensia, ed. J.R.H. Weaver, Oxford, 1908

Worcester, John of, *Chronicle*, eds R.R. Darlington and P. McGurk, ii, Oxford, 1995

SECONDARY SOURCES

Addyman, P.V. 'Excavation at Ludgershall Castle', *CG*, vi, 1972, pp. 7–13

Ailes, A. 'Heraldry in twelfth-century England: the evidence', *England in the Twelfth Century*, Harlaxton Proceedings 1988, pp. 1–16

Amt, E. *The Accession of Henry II in England, Royal Government Restored, 1149–1159*, Woodbridge, 1993

Appleby, J.T. *Henry II*, 1962

——. *The Troubled Reign of King Stephen*, 1969

Archibald, M.M. 'Coins', *English Romanesque Art*, ed. G. Zarnecki and others, 1984, pp. 320–41

——. 'Dating Stephen's first type', *British Numismatic Journal*, lxi, 1991, pp. 9–21

Barber, R. *Henry Plantagenet*, 1964

Barlow, F. *The English Church, 1066–1154*, 1979

——. *The Feudal Kingdom of England, 1042–1216*, 1955

Barrett, C.R.B. *Battles and Battlefields in England*, 1896

Barrow, G.W.S. *David I of Scotland, 1124–53*, Reading, 1985

Beeler, J. *Warfare in England, 1066–1189*, New York, 1966

——. 'The composition of Anglo-Norman armies', *Speculum*, xl, 1965, pp. 389–414

Biddle, M. 'Wolvesey: the *domus quasi palatium* of Henry de Blois in Winchester', *CG*, iii, pp. 28–36

Bishop, T.A.M. *Scriptores Regis*, Oxford, 1961

Blackburn, M. 'Coinage and Currency', in King, pp. 145–205

Boase, T.S.R. *English Art, 1100–1216*, Oxford, 1953

Bolton, B. *The Medieval Reformation*, 1983

de Borchgrave, E. 'Guillaume d'Ypres', *Biographie Nationale*, vol. viii, Brussels, 1884–5

Bradbury, J. 'Battles in England and Normandy, 1066–1154', *ANS*, vi, 1983, pp. 1–12

——. 'The Early Years of the Reign of Stephen, 1135–39', *England in the Twelfth Century*, Harlaxton Proceedings 1988, ed. D. Williams, Woodbridge, 1990

——. 'Winners and losers: the civil war of Stephen's reign', Harlaxton Proceedings 1995 (forthcoming)

——. *The Medieval Archer*, Woodbridge, 1985

——. *The Medieval Siege*, Woodbridge, 1992

——. 'Fulk le Réchin and the origin of the Plantagenets', *RAB*, pp. 27–41

——. 'Geoffrey V of Anjou, count and knight', *IPMK*, iii, 1988, pp. 21–38

Brown, R.A. *English Castles*, 3rd edn, 1976

——. *Castles from the Air*, Cambridge, 1989

——. 'Royal castle-building in England, 1154–1216', *EHR*, lxx, 1955, pp. 353–98

——., (ed). *Castles: a History and Guide*, Poole, 1980

Bur, M. *La Formation du Comté de Champagne, 950–1150*, Nancy, 1977

Callahan, jr., T. 'The impact of anarchy on English monasticism, 1135–1154', *Albion*, vi, 1974, pp. 218–32

Chartrou, J. *L'Anjou de 1109 à 1151*, Paris, 1928

Chibnall, M. *Anglo-Norman England, 1066–1166*, Oxford, 1986

——. *The Empress Matilda*, Oxford, 1991

——. *The World of Orderic Vitalis*, Oxford, 1984

——. 'Normandy', in King, pp. 93–115

Clanchy, M.T. *England and its Rulers, 1066–1272*, 1983

Colvin, H.M., Brown, R.A., Taylor, A.J., (eds.). *The History of the King's Works, The Middle Ages*, 2 vols, HMSO, 1963

Contamine, P. *War in the Middle Ages*, trans. M. Jones, Oxford, 1984

Coulson, C. 'The castles of the anarchy', in King, pp. 67–92

Critchley, J.S. *Military Organization in England, 1154–1254*, unpublished PhD thesis, Nottingham, 1968

Cronne, H.A. *The Reign of Stephen, Anarchy in England, 1135–54*, 1970

——. 'Ranulf de Gernons, Earl of Chester, 1129–1153', *TRHS*, 4th ser., xx, 1937, pp. 103–34

——. 'Charter scholarship in England', *University of Birmingham Historical Journal*, viii, 1962

Crouch, D. 'Earl William of Gloucester and the end of the anarchy', *EHR*, ciii, 1988, pp. 71–2

——. 'Robert Earl of Gloucester and the daughter of Zelophehad', *JMH*, xi, 1985

——. 'The March and the Welsh kings', in King, pp. 255–89

——. *The Beaumont Twins, the Roots and Branches of Power in the Twelfth Century*, Cambridge, 1986

Cunnington, R.H. *Some Annals of the Borough of Devizes*, Devizes, 1925

——. 'The Borough of Devizes', *VCH*, Wiltshire, ed. E. Crittall, x, 1975

——. 'Devizes Castle: a suggested revision', *Wiltshire Archaeological and Natural History Magazine*, li, 1945–7, pp. 496–9

Dalton, P. 'In neutro latere: the armed neutrality of Ranulf II Earl of Chester in King Stephen's reign', *ANS*, xiv, 1991, pp. 39–59

——. 'William Earl of York and royal authority in Yorkshire in the reign of Stephen', *HSJ*, ii, 1990, pp. 155–65

Davis, C.L. 'The Norman castle of South Mymms', *Transactions of the London and Middlesex Archaeological Society*, new ser., vii, 1937, pp. 464–71

Davis, H.W.C. *England Under the Normans and Angevins*, 13th edn, 1949

——. 'The anarchy of Stephen's reign', *EHR*, xviii, 1903, pp. 630–41

——. 'Henry of Blois and Brian fitz Count', *EHR*, xxv, 1910, pp. 297–303

——, (ed.). *Essays in History Presented to R.L. Poole*, Oxford, 1927

Davis, K.R. *The Story of Potters Bar and South Mimms*, Potters Bar, 1966

Davis, R.H.C. 'The treaty between William Earl of Gloucester and Roger Earl of Hereford', *A Medieval Miscellany for D.M. Stenton*, eds. P.M. Barnes and C.F. Slade, Pipe Roll Society, new ser., xxxvi, 1962, pp. 139–46

——. 'King Stephen and the Earl of Chester revised', *EHR*, lxxv, 1960, pp. 654–60

——. 'The authorship of the *Gesta Stephani*', *EHR*, lxxvii, 1962, pp. 209–32

——. 'Geoffrey de Mandeville reconsidered', *EHR*, lxxix, 1964, pp. 299–307

——. 'What happened in Stephen's reign', *History*, xlix, 1964, pp. 1–12

——. *King Stephen*, 3rd edn, Harlow, 1990

Douglas, D.C. *The Norman Fate*, 1976

Eales, R. 'Local loyalties in Stephen's reign: Kent', *ANS*, 1985

——. 'Royal power and castles in Norman England', *IPMK*, iii, 1988, pp. 49–78

Falkus, M., and Gillingham, J., (eds.). *Historical Atlas of Britain*, 1981

Gillingham J. 'Love, marriage and politics in the twelfth century', *Forum for Modern Language Studies*, xxv, 1989, pp. 292–303

——. *The Angevin Empire*, 1984

Gransden, A. *Historical Writing in England*, i, *c.* 550–*c.* 1307, 1974

Green, J. *The Government of England under Henry I*, Cambridge, 1986

——. 'Financing Stephen's war', *ANS*, xiv, 1992, pp. 106–14

——. 'The last century of Danegeld', *EHR*, xcvi, 1981, pp. 241–58

——. 'Lords of the Norman Vexin', *War and Government in the Middle Ages*, eds. J. Gillingham and J.C. Holt, Woodbridge, 1984, pp. 47–63

Hallam, E.M. *Capetian France, 987–1328*, 1980

Halphen, L. *Étude sur les Chroniques des Comtes d'Anjou et des Seigneurs d'Amboise*, Paris, 1906

Haskins, C.H. *Norman Institutions*, Harvard, 1918
——. 'Normandy under Geoffrey Plantagenet', *EHR*, xvii, 1912, pp. 417–44
Hassall, T. 'Wallingford Castle: life on the bailey', *The Times*, 1976
Helmerichs, R. 'King Stephen's Norman itinerary, 1137', *HSJ*, v, 1993, pp. 89–97
Hope-Taylor, B. 'The excavations of a motte at Abinger', *Archaeological Journal*, cvii, 1950, pp. 15–43
O'Farrell Hughes, W. 'Burwell, its castle', *Transactions of the Cambridgeshire and Huntingdonshire Archaeological Society*, iii, 1914, pp. 291–3
Hill, F. *Medieval Lincoln*, Cambridge, 1948
Hill, R. 'The Battle of Stockbridge, 1141', *RAB*, pp. 173–7
Hodge, B. *A History of Malmesbury*, Malmesbury, 1969
Holdsworth, C. 'The Church', in King, pp. 207–29
——. 'War and peace in the twelfth century, the reign of Stephen reconsidered', *War and Peace in the Middle Ages*, ed. B.P. McGuire, Copenhagen, 1987
Hollister, C.W. 'Stephen's anarchy', *Albion*, vi, 1974, pp. 233–7
——. *The Military Organization of Norman England*, Oxford, 1962
——. *The Twelfth-Century Renaissance*, New York, 1969
——. 'The magnates of Stephen's reign: reluctant anarchists', *HSJ*, v, 1993, pp. 77–87
——. 'The Misfortunes of the Mandevilles', *History*, lviii, 1973, pp. 18–28
——. 'The Anglo-Norman succession debate of 1126: prelude to Stephen's anarchy' *JMH*, i, 1975, pp. 19–41
——. 'The Aristocracy', in King, pp. 37–66
Hollister, C.W., and Keefe, T.K. 'The Making of the Angevin Empire', *Journal of British Studies*, xii, 1973, pp. 1–25
Holt, J.C. '1153: the Treaty of Winchester', in King, pp. 291–316
——. 'Politics and property in early medieval England', *PP*, lvii, 1972, pp. 3–52
——. 'Politics and property in early medieval England: a rejoinder', *PP*, lxv, 1974
——. 'Feudal society and the family', *TRHS*, xxxii, 1982; xxxiii, 1983; xxxiv, 1984
Hucher, E. *L'Émail de Geoffroi Plantagenêt*, Paris, 1860
Johnson, G.C. *The Military and Naval Terms in the Norman and Anglo-Norman Chronicles of the Twelfth Century*, unpublished PhD thesis, Leeds, 1949
Jones, W.H. 'Early Annals of Trowbridge', *VCH*, Wiltshire, vii, 1953
Kealey, E.J. 'King Stephen: government and anarchy', *Albion*, vi, 1974, pp. 201–17
——. *Roger of Salisbury, Viceroy of England*, Berkeley California, 1972
Keats-Rohan, K.S.B. 'The devolution of the honour of Wallingford, 1066–1148', *Oxoniensia*, liv, 1989, pp. 311–18
Kent, J.P.C. 'Excavations at the motte and bailey castle of South Mimms, Hertfordshire, 1960–67', *Transactions of the London and Middlesex Archaeological Society*, new ser., vii, 1937, pp. 464–71
King, E. 'John Horace Round and the "Calendar of Documents Preserved in France"', *ANS*, iv, 1981
——. 'King Stephen and the Anglo-Norman aristocracy', *History*, lix, 1974
——. 'The tenurial crisis in the early twelfth century', *PP*, lxv, 1974
——. 'The anarchy of Stephen's reign', *TRHS*, 5th ser., xxxiv, 1984, pp. 133–53
——. 'Waleran, Count of Meulan and Worcester, 1104–1166', *Tradition and Change, Essays in Honour of M. Chibnall*, eds. D. Greenway, C. Holdsworth, J. Sayers, Cambridge, 1985, pp. 165–76
——. (ed.). *The Anarchy of Stephen's Reign*, Oxford, 1994, including the Introduction
Knowles, D. *Saints and Scholars*, Cambridge, 1962
Leedom, J.W. 'William of Malmesbury and Robert of Gloucester reconsidered', *Albion*, vi, 1974, pp. 251–62
——. 'The English Settlement of 1153', *History*, lxv, 1980, pp. 347–64
Lethbridge, T.C. 'Excavations at Burwell Castle', *Cambridge Antiquarian Society Proceedings*, xxxvi, 1934–5, pp. 121–33
Leyser, C.K. 'England and the Empire in the early twelfth century', *TRHS*, 5th ser., x, 1960
Leyser, H. *Hermits and the New Monasticism*, 1984
Lyon, B.D. *From Fief to Indenture*, Cam. Mass, 1957

——. 'The money fief under English kings, 1066–1485', *EHR*, lxvi, 1951, pp. 161–93

Megaw, I. 'The ecclesiastical policy of Stephen, 1135–39', *Essays in British and Irish History in Honour of J.E. Todd*, ed. H.A. Cronne and others, 1949, pp. 24–45

Miller, E. *The Abbey and Bishopric of Ely*, Cambridge, 1951

Milsom, S.F.C. *The Legal Framework of English Feudalism*, Cambridge, 1976

Nelson, L.H. *The Normans in South Wales, 1070–1171*, Austin Texas, 1966

Nicholl, D. *Thurstan Archbishop of York, 1114–40*, York, 1964

Nikitine, S. and M. *L'Émail Plantagenêt*, Nancy, 1981

Norgate. K. *England under the Angevin Kings*, 2 vols, 1887

Oakeshott, W. *The Artists of the Winchester Bible*, 1945

Oman, C. *A History of the Art of War in the Middle Ages*, 2 vols, 1924

Onslow, Earl of. *The Empress Maud*, 1939

Pächt, O. *The Rise of Pictorial Narrative in Twelfth-Century England*, Oxford, 1962

Pain, N. *Empress Matilda*, 1978

Painter, S. 'The Rout of Winchester', *Speculum*, vii, 1932, pp. 70–5

——. 'The family and the feudal system in twelfth-century England', *Speculum*, xxxv, 1960, pp. 1–16

Partner, N.F. *Serious Entertainments*, Chicago, 1977

le Patourel, J. 'The Norman succession, 996–1135', *EHR*, lxxxvi, 1971

——. 'What did not happen in Stephen's reign, *History*, lviii, 1973, pp. 18–28

——. *Normandy and England, 1066–1144*, Reading, 1971

——. *The Norman Empire*, Oxford, 1976

Patterson, R.B. 'Anarchy in England, 1135–54', *Albion*, vi, 1974, pp. 189–99

——. 'William of Malmesbury's Robert of Gloucester: a re-evaluation of the *Historia Novella*', *American Historical Review*, lxx, 1964–5, pp. 983–97

Peirce, I. 'The knight, his arms and armour in the eleventh and twelfth centuries', *IPMK*, i, 1986, pp. 152–64

Poole, A.L. *Domesday Book to Magna Carta*, 2nd edn, Oxford, 1955

——. *Obligations of Society in the Twelfth and Thirteenth Centuries*, Oxford, 1946

Pounds, N.J.G. *An Economic History of Medieval Europe*, 1974

Power, D. 'What did the frontier of Angevin Normandy comprise?', *ANS*, xvii, 1994, pp. 181–201

Prestwich, J.O. 'The military household of the Norman kings', *EHR*, xcvi, 1981, pp. 1–35

——. 'War and finance in the Anglo-Norman state', *TRHS*, 5th ser., iv, 1954, pp. 19–43

Prestwich, J.O., and Davis, R.H.C. 'Last words on Geoffrey de Mandeville', *EHR*, cv, 1990

Renn, D. 'The keep of Wareham Castle', *Medieval Archaeology*, iv, 1960, pp. 56–68

——. *Norman Castles in Britain*, 2nd edn, 1973

——. 'South Mymms Castle', *Barnet and District Record Society Bulletin*, x, 1957

Renna, T. 'The idea of peace in the West, 500–1150', *JMH*, viii, 1982

Reynolds, S. 'The rulers of London in the twelfth century', *History*, lvii, 1972, pp. 337–53

Richardson, H.G., and Sayles, G.O. *The Governance of Mediaeval England*, Edinburgh, 1963

Rössler, O. *Kaiserin Mathilde*, Berlin, 1897

Round, J.H. *Geoffrey de Mandeville, a Study of the Anarchy*, 1892

——. *Feudal England*, London, 1895

——. 'Robert of Bampton', *EHR*, v, 1890, p. 746–7

——. 'King Stephen and the Earl of Chester', *EHR*, x, 1895, pp. 87–91

Rowley, T. *The Norman Heritage, 1066–1200*, 1983

Russell, F.H. *The Just War in the Middle Ages*, Cambridge, 1975

Saltman, A. *Theobald Archbishop of Canterbury*, 1956

Sands, H., and Denoon, D.G. 'South Mymms Castle excavations', *Transactions of the London and Middlesex Archaeological Society*, new ser., vii, 1937, pp. 175–9

Schlight, J. *Monarchs and Mercenaries*, Connecticut, 1968

Schnith, K. 'Regni et pacis inquietatrix: zur Rolle der Kaiserin Mathilde in der "anarchie"', *JMH*, ii, 1976

——. 'Kaiserin Mathilde', *Grossbritannien und Deutschland Festschrift für J.W.P. Bourke*, Munich, 1975

Seaby, P.J. 'King Stephen and the interdict of 1148', *British Numismatic Journal*, 1, 1980, pp. 50–60

Seaman, R.J. 'King Stephen's first coinage, 1135–41', *Seaby Coin and Medal Bulletin*, London, 1968, pp. 60–2

Southern, R.W. 'The place of Henry I in English history', *Proceedings of the British Academy*, xlviii, 1962

Stamper, P.A. *Excavations of a mid-twelfth century siege castle at Bentley, Hampshire*, 1979

Stenton, F.M. *The First Century of English Feudalism, 1066–1166*, 2nd edn, Oxford, 1961

Stiefel, T. *The Intellectual Revolution in Twelfth-Century Europe*, Beckenham, 1985

Stone, E.H. *Devizes Castle*, Devizes, 1920

Strickland, M. 'Against the Lord's anointed: aspects of warfare and baronial rebellion in England and Normandy, 1075–1265', *Law and Government in Medieval England and Normandy, Essays in Honour of Sir James Holt*, eds. G. Garnett and J. Hudson, Cambridge, 1994, pp. 56–79

Stringer, K.J. *The Reign of Stephen*, 1993

Suppe, F.C. *Military Institutions on the Welsh Marches, Shropshire 1066–1300*, Woodbridge, 1994

Taylor, C. *The Cambridgeshire Landscape*, 1973

Thomson, M.W. 'Excavations in Farnham Castle keep, Surrey, England', *CG*, ii, pp. 100–05

Thomson, R.M. 'England and the twelfth-century renaissance', *PP*, ci, 1983

Thorne, S.E. 'English Feudalism and estates in land', *Cambridge Law Journal*, 1959, pp. 193–209

Van Caenegem, R.C. *Royal Writs in England from the Conquest to Glanvill*, Selden Society, lxxvii, 1959

Vellacott, C.H. 'Political History' *VCH*, Lincolnshire, ii, ed. W. Page

Verbruggen, J.F. *The Art of Warfare in Western Europe during the Middle Ages*, trans. S. Willard and S.C.M. Southern, Amsterdam, 1977

Voss, L. *Heinrich von Blois, Bischof von Winchester, 1129–71*, Berlin, 1932

Walker, D. 'Crown and episcopacy under the Normans and Angevins', *ANS*, v, 1982

——. 'Miles of Gloucester, Earl of Hereford', *Transactions of the Bristol and Gloucester Archaeological Society*, lxxvii, 1958, pp. 66–84

——. 'The "honors" of the Earls of Hereford in the twelfth century', *Transactions of the Bristol and Gloucester Archaeological Society*, lxxix, 1960, pp. 174–211

Walne, P. 'A "double charter" of the Empress Matilda and Henry Duke of Normandy, *c*. 1152', *EHR*, lxxvi, 1961, pp. 649–53

Warren, W.L. *Henry II*, 1973

——. *The Governance of Norman and Angevin England, 1086–1272*, 1987

White, G. 'King Stephen, Duke Henry and Ranulf de Gernons Earl of Chester', *EHR*, xci, 1976, pp. 555–65

——. 'Continuity in government', in King, pp. 117–43

——. 'The end of Stephen's reign', *History*, lxxv, 1990, pp. 3–22

——. 'Were the midlands "wasted" during Stephen's reign?' *Midland History*, x, 1985, pp. 26–46

White, G.H. 'The career of Waleran, Count of Meulan and Earl of Worcester, 1104–1166', *TRHS*, 4th ser., xvii, 1934, pp. 19–48

——. 'King Stephen's earldoms', *TRHS*, 4th ser., xiii, 1930, pp. 56–72

White, S.D. 'Succession to fiefs in early medieval England', *PP*, lxv, 1974

Wightman, W.E. *The Lacy Family in England and Normandy, 1066–1194*, Oxford, 1966

Yoshitake, K. 'The Exchequer in the reign of Stephen', *EHR*, ciii, 1988, pp. 950–9

——. 'The arrest of the bishops in 1139 and its consequences', *JMH*, xiv, 1988, pp. 97–114

Zarnecki, G., Holt, J., Holland, T., (eds.). *English Romanesque Art, 1066–1200*, 1984

Index

Page numbers given in italic refer to illustrations